THE CRANE BAG
and other
disputed subjects

THE CRANE BAG
and other
disputed subjects

ROBERT GRAVES

CASSELL · LONDON

CASSELL & COMPANY LTD
35 Red Lion Square, London WC1
Melbourne, Sydney, Toronto
Johannesburg, Auckland

First published, April 1969
First edition, second impression May 1970

ISBN 0 304 93291 4

Made and printed in Great Britain by
The Camelot Press Ltd, London and Southampton
470

CONTENTS

FOREWORD

Typescripts of lectures, essays, reviews and press articles on a great variety of subjects had been accumulating in a sea-chest next to my work-table ever since 1958 when Messrs. Cassell published a similar collection called *Steps*. One lecture, 'Five Score and Six Years Ago', had been given to six thousand American school-teachers in the Jesse Jones Auditorium at Houston, Texas, on Thanksgiving Day, 1966; another, 'The Uses of Superstition', at the Massachusetts Institute of Technology in 1963; a third, 'The Phenomenon of Mass-tourism', I gave the next year in Spanish to the Ateneo Club, Madrid, at the request of my friend, H. E. Don Manuel Fraga Iribarne, the Spanish Minister of Information and Tourism. The reviews had appeared in the *New York Times Magazine*, the London *Sunday Times* and elsewhere; the essays and articles in numerous journals including *Life*, *Encounter*, *Horizon*, *Homes and Gardens*, *Harper's Magazine*, the *Weekend Telegraph*, *Playboy* and the *Family Gazette*. I omit most of the dates.

Messrs. Cassell have now invited me to bind up the less ephemeral of these pieces in a new miscellany, to which I am adding six pieces written too late for publication in *Steps* but included in *Food for Centaurs* (Doubleday, 1960).

'The Crane Bag' is the oddest of the twenty-eight pieces. Last year I happened to stumble on a curiously detailed proof of the blind intuitions which I had followed while writing *The White Goddess* as to exactly what the famous mythological Crane Bag contained. It belonged, the Irish poets agreed, to their Sea-God Manannan, who named the Isle of Man, and I had already discussed the subject at length in a chapter called 'Palamedes and the Cranes'. This Crane Bag stood for a complex and secret system of poetic discipline based on the ancient Pelasgian Greek alphabet imported from Spain to Ireland in the late second millennium. By its use Marvan the Swineherd was, according to the eighth century Irish classic, *The Proceedings of the Grand Bardic Academy*, enabled to humble the pretentious academic bard Sanchan Torpest—the very same Sanchan whose fame for rhyming rats to death eventually reached Shakespeare's ears. By answering all Sanchan's difficult questions and asking him others which he could not answer, Marvan was privileged to make Sanchan and his colleagues perform the bass *cronan* for him until their eyes gushed out on their cheeks.

The crane, a bird everywhere sacred to the moon, whose colours red, white and black it displays, makes annual pilgrimages from the Tropic of Cancer to its breeding-places in the Arctic. It is associated with the moon's willow-magic, and has been from time immemorial sacred to poets and scholars—from China to Persia, from Persia to Greece, and from Greece to Ireland. Our last wild crane was shot in the Isle of Anglesey when I was eleven years old, since when poets of this ancient tradition have grown fewer and fewer. In Hungary, which I first visited in 1968, cranes still survive, but are credited only with bringing news, not with alphabetic and poetic secrets.

My approach to all other random problems discussed in this collection is always a practical, poetic one, eventually based on the Crane Bag. I use it, for instance, when asked who or what are poltergeists, where did the lost continent of Atlantis lie, why did Plato disparage Xanthippe, how should the Bible be translated into English without a loss of holiness, why does Blake's *Tyger, Tyger* not make good prose sense, what is the nature of absolute crime, and when will the glory of Albuhera fade. The answer nearly always causes offence in the Great Bardic Academy, but I cannot force them to a Command performance of the bass *cronan*. As a rule they stifle their embarrassment by suggesting that I write tongue in cheek; but the other day a whole school of them accused me and my fellow poet Omar Ali-Shah of resorting to literary forgery in Classical Persian—which we both found, in the circumstances, most diverting.

Deyá, Mallorca, Spain   R. G.

ACKNOWLEDGEMENTS

Thanks are due for permission to quote passages from the following:

Why I am Not a Christian by Bertrand Russell (George Allen & Unwin Ltd)

Menander's *Dyskolos* translated by Professor Arnott (The Athlone Press)

The Young Caesar by Rex Warner (William Collins Sons & Co. Ltd)

Witchcraft Today by Gerald Gardner (Hutchinson & Co. Ltd)

Reviews of Robert Graves's translation of the *Rubaiyyat* of Omar Khayaam (reproduced from *The Times*, the *Listener* and the *Glasgow Herald* by permission)

New English Bible © 1961 Oxford and Cambridge University Presses

Religion without Revelation by Julian Huxley (Max Parrish) (reprinted by permission of A. D. Peters & Co.)

1

The Crane Bag

I was sent for review a beautifully produced book by Dr. Anne Ross with splendid photographs of what archaeologists call 'cult objects' but published under the misleading title: *Pagan Celtic Britain*. 'Pagan' properly refers to the superstitious survival of pre-Christian beliefs in country villages remote from a Christian city; yet most of Dr. Ross's exhibits date from before the arrival of Christianity. And 'Celtic' is properly applied only to the well-armed Danubian tribes of the Iron Age who, under the Greek name of 'Celti' or 'Galates', and the Latin name of 'Galli', over-spread wide regions of Europe and Asia Minor, and eventually sacked both Rome and Delphi. They are said to have reached the British Isles in two waves: Goidels, or Q-celts, in the seventh century B.C.; Brythons, or P-celts, in the fifth. There they imposed their language and customs on the even more gifted non-Aryan Bronze-Age agriculturists who, over a thousand years before, had come to the British Isles from North Africa, one horde by way of Central Europe and Norway, another by way of Spain.

Since Dr. Ross's chief interest lies in Roman Britain she includes among her photographic subjects not only pre-Celtic pieces which she styles 'proto-Celtic', but such later non-Celtic work as a Roman statue of Mars with the usual woodpecker crest. About a third of them come from France, Germany, Switzerland and elsewhere on the Continent. Yet the legendary material that she relies on is almost wholly Irish, not British—if only because the Romans never reached Ireland and so destroyed its Druidic culture, as in Gaul and Britain, and because Irish poets of the Early Middle Ages who inherited this culture were therefore better educated and held in far greater esteem than their abased Welsh or Scottish contemporaries.

As a girl of seventeen Dr. Ross had done what anthropologists call 'field-work' by learning Gaelic for six months in a West Highland peasant's hut. Then after graduating at Edinburgh, she took an educational job in the same Goidelic region, but later returned to Edinburgh for a degree in Celtic studies and a Ph.D, in Celtic archaeology. At Edinburgh University, a most academic ambience, she forgot, it seems, how to think in Gaelic crofter style, which means poetically, and grew afraid of having her newly acquired scientific intelligence warped by any magic material she might handle in the course of excavation. I hope Dr. Ross will forgive me if I reject the established view that an ichthyologist knows more about the nature of the fish he studies than the fish themselves do. One can prove that by putting an ichthyologist naked in a sealed water tank and telling him, or her, to behave like a fish for just three minutes. . . . The truth is that no dedicated scientist can afford to think in religio-poetic terms, and Dr. Ross had to make her choice. She is now a titled and polished Celtologist and can lecture on primitive magic without even giving it *de facto* recognition for its effectiveness.

I can best make my point by quoting her three-page treatment of an important Celtic myth, that of the Sea-God's Crane Bag; and her general view of cranes in Celtic tradition. The Crane Bag, she informs us correctly, belonged in Irish legend to Manannan God of the Sea and had been made from the skin of Aoife ('pleasing'), a woman magically transformed into a crane. In this context Dr. Ross quotes an early mediaeval Irish text* which she calls 'full of interest from a mythological point of view'. It certainly startled me:

'This crane-bag held every precious thing that Manannan possessed. The shirt of Manannan himself and his knife, and the shoulder-strap of Goibne, the fierce smith, together with his smith's hook; also the King of Scotland's shears; and the King of Lochlainn's helmet; and the bones of Asil's (Assail's) swine. A strip of the great whale's back was also in that shapely crane-bag. When the sea was full, all the treasures were visible in it; when the fierce sea ebbed, the crane-bag was empty.'

* MacNeill, 1904, VII, 21

As a Celtologist Dr. Ross can make nothing of such fairy-tale material; so is content to point out with a sweet smile that though Aoife had been transformed into a crane by a jealous rival, she was 'a treasure of powers with many virtues', and that her skin was therefore a fit receptacle for the Sea-God's treasures. Also that in another Irish legend, one Midir who lived in the Isle of Man (named after Manannan) kept three cranes which cried out inhospitably to all would-be visitors: 'Do not enter—keep away— pass on!' She suggests that this is the reason why in Ireland mean and disagreeable women were called 'cranes', which gave cranes a bad name, so that eating crane's flesh was held disgusting in the Gaelic Western Highlands. She explains that St. Columba was called a 'crane-cleric' because he was disagreeable—rather than because he was so well-instructed in Christian mysteries. Finally, and irrelevantly, she refers us to a Gaulish carving found under the choir of Notre Dame at Paris in 1711. It consists of three cranes perched on a bull's back, beside a bearded god who is shown cutting branches from a willow; the inscription is *Tarvotrigaranos* ('The Bull with three Cranes').

Specialistic concern with Romanized Gaul and Britain has distracted Dr. Ross's attention from Julius Caesar's explicit statement that the Celtic Druids never committed their religious secrets to writing, and in all secular matters used Greek, not Roman, letters. This should have reminded her of the Asiatic-Greek colonies in Southern France; also of the close trade relations between pre-Classical Greece and the pre-Celtic British Isles, proved by the *lunulae*, new-moon-shaped collars, of Wicklow gold found in mainland Greece and by the imprint of a Mycenaean dagger lately noticed on one of the pre-Celtic Stonehenge pillars. Why should this trade connection not have implied common religious ties, as the Greek (not Latin) name *Tarvotrigaranos* suggests—and as the word 'Druid' itself suggests? In Greek 'Druid' means a priest of the *drus*, an oak tree with edible acorns, like those of the oracular grove at Dodona in Northern Greece. Indeed, close religious ties seem to have bound Greece and the British Isles down to Classical times, and the first British coinage was modelled on the Greek, not the Latin. The Land of the Hyperboreans ('Back-of-the-North-wind-men') was, as the historian Hesychius makes clear, Apollo's other island, Britain. And from there certain secret straw-wrapped gifts were annually passed, from tribe to tribe, all the way across the Continent until they reached Apollo's shrine at Delphi. My view, for what it may be worth, is that these were the scarlet white-spotted hallucinogenic mushrooms, *amanita muscaria*, which the Greeks had used in Central Asia but which grew only under birches and in a more northerly latitude than Greece. These mushrooms are now known to have provided the famous *soma* of the Vedic hymns.

I can find no reference in Dr. Ross's book to the religious importance of the crane in Greece, where it was sacred both to the ancient Pelasgian Goddess of Wisdom, Athene, and to Apollo the Hellenic God of Poetry and Music. In fact, at the period of panic when, according to a well-known myth, most of the Olympian Gods disguised themselves as animals or birds and fled to Egypt from the monster Typheus—apparently the violent eruption of the Santorin volcano back in the fifteenth century B.C.—Apollo chose to appear as a crane. Moreover in Greece, as in Ireland, cranes were always sacred to poets; a belief commemorated in the story of the Pelasgian poet Ibycus of Samos whose death was avenged by a flock of cranes which revealed his murderer to a crowded theatre at Corinth.

Well, to be brief, what this fabulous Crane Bag contained was alphabetical secrets known only to oracular priests and poets. The Greek mythographers credited a poet of the Trojan war, Palamedes son of Nauplius ('Ancient Intelligence, Son of Navigator'), with having invented such of the letters as had not already been invented by the Triple Goddess. His inspiration came, it is said, from observing a flock of cranes, 'which make letters as they fly'. And Hermes, messenger to the Gods, afterwards reduced these to written characters. Cranes were, in fact, totem birds of the poetically educated priests who gave counsel to Queens and Kings and ranked above mere warriors. Hence on Gallic coins dating from before the Roman occupation cranes are often shown perched on horses' backs or standing beside them. On the Notre Dame carving, a Gaulish king is pictured as a bull, as Kings had been in Mycenaean Greece and Minoan Crete; his druids, who drew their wisdom from the Triple Goddess, appear as three cranes. In Ireland the Triple Goddess Brigid—among the Pelasgian Greeks the same goddess was called 'Brizo'—protected poets, physicians and smiths, and was popular enough to become eventually canonized as a Christian saint—St. Brigid of Kildare. All this rigmarole explains why the eating of crane-meat was tabooed in Ireland and Scotland; just as the hazel, the tree sacred to poets, was tabooed fuel on any hearth. And why Midir, the Irish Hermes who lived in Manannan's island and guarded the secrets of the Crane Bag, kept three cranes to discourage curious visitors. This druidic alphabet needed to be kept secret because it was not a mere traders' convenience like the one openly used by the Phoenicians, but a religious calendar, a fortune-telling device, a mathematical system based on the use of π, a means of signalling in deaf-and-dumb language, and the base of a hundred and fifty Ogham speech-ciphers.

The arrangement of the alphabet was Pelasgian in origin—'Pelasgian' meant People of the Sea, hence Manannan's possession of it—but its druidic nicks were invented (according to the Irish myth) by one 'Ogma Sun-Face'—who is authenticated by the second century A.D. Greek historian Lucian. Lucian writes of Ogmius, a white-haired Celtic Hercules, who drew men by golden chains. The original twenty-letter Pelasgian alphabet, beginning with the signs for B, L and N, was regulated by a stem-line and consisted of four parts. These were one, two, three, four or five upright nicks cut above the stem-line—one stood for B, two for L, three for N, etc; next, the same number of upright nicks cut below it; then the same number of diagonal nicks crossing it—all these fifteen letters being consonants; and finally the same number of upright nicks crossing the stem line, namely the five vowels.

One may read about Ogham in R. A. S. Macalister's *Secret Languages of Ireland*, and in George Calder's *The Scholar's Primer*: how the poets used it as a secret signal code, by treating the shinbone or nose as a stem-line and laying their fingers across or against it according to the letter required. For example, one finger laid diagonally across the stem-line stood for the letter M; two fingers laid diagonally across it stood for the letter G; and five fingers placed squarely on the lower or right-hand side of the stem-line, but not crossing it, stood for the letter S.

That the Crane Bag filled when the sea was in flood, but emptied when it ebbed, means that these Ogham signs made complete sense for poetic Sons of Manannan, but none for uninitiated outsiders. The Crane Bag, in fact, was not a tangible object, but, like Athene's Goatskin Bag, the Aegis, which contained the Gorgon's head, existed only as a metaphor. No more than two of the regular twenty letters which it contained are described in pictographic form by the poets quoted by Dr. Ross: namely M and G, the initials of Manannan and Goibne the Smith. These consist, respectively, of one, and two nicks of the diagonal letter-group crossing the stem-line. They are here disguised in riddling pictorial terms as 'Manannan's knife' (stuck in his belt) and 'Goibne's shoulder strap' (which crossed his belt to his sword) and are offered merely as samples of the more ancient letters. As for the other miscellaneous objects found in the Crane Bag: if one thinks poetically, not scientifically, their meaning leaps to the eye. They stand for a group of five extra characters borrowed (as Macalister shows) from the fourth century B.C. Formello-Corvetri Western-Greek alphabet, to supply consonants not used in Goidelic Celtic but needed for Brythonic, Gallic, Norse and other languages. You will notice that these characters have not kept their original Greek shape, but are adapted for use in deaf-and-dumb language so as to indicate particular positions of the signallers' hands. Thus:

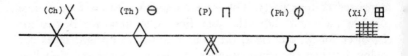

They are described from left to right. 'The King of Scotland's Shears', made by crossing the forefingers; 'The King of Lochlainn's helmet' (with his face underneath), made by opening the thumbs and forefingers of both hands and making the tips touch; 'the bones of Assail's swine', made by crossing one's thumbs; 'Goibne's smith-hook', made by crooking the thumb and forefinger of the left hand; and 'Manannan's own shirt', which is a map of the sea showing lines of longitude and latitude, made by crossing the four slightly open fingers of one hand over the four fingers of the other.

But why, you may ask, were the shears ascribed to the King of Scotland? Because, I suppose, Scotland was famous for its wool and because the King had a name beginning with Ch, pronounced K as in Christopher. And why was the helmet ascribed to the King of Lochlainn (Norway or the Norse Settlement of Dublin)? I suppose because of its Norse shape, and because the King's name began with a Th—maybe he was the Thunder God Thor. As for the bones of Assail's swine, they seem to be the crossed stalks of sacred mushrooms, because according to Rahilly's *Early Irish*

Myth and History, Assail was a lightning god and because mushrooms, called 'little pigs' in Latin and Italian, were believed to be
created by lightning and because hallucinogenic varieties of mushroom (see page 4, first paragraph) were used in Greek and several
Eastern religions for oracular purposes. Why 'bones'? Because
wherever mushrooms are ritually eaten (always in pairs) the stems
are discarded, as bones are from meat. Yes, the argument is
complicated, but the druids and later Irish poets delighted in
reducing a difficult concept to a single phrase such as 'the bones
of Assail's swine', and this again to an even simpler sign of
crossed thumbs—which no ignorant men-at-arms could understand. Nor any irreligious philosophers either, for that matter, such
as Socrates and his pupil Plato who had turned their backs on
poetic myths.

I am tempted to go on about cranes in Celtic and Greek myth:
for instance to identify *Tarvotrigaranos* with the three-bodied
Geryon whom Hercules killed and robbed of his cows during the
long Tenth Labour which took him through Spain and France by
way of the Pyrenees. The Irish poetic tradition holds that the
Ogham alphabet was brought from Spain by Ogma Sun-Face.
Then there was the spirally-performed Crane Dance celebrated on
the island of Delos in honour of Apollo and his sister Artemis—
Delos being the centre of the sacrosanct poetic guild called the
'Sons of Homer'. But I hear some conscientious reader complaining, 'Hi, wait a bit! What about the strip of whale's back in
the Crane Bag?'

That was so easy that I left the explanation out. Ogham nicks
make no certain sense without a stem line; and for a Sea-God the
only possible stem line was the horizon—dark and slightly arched
like the back of a whale.

Let me express my great gratitude to Dr. Ross for all she has dug
up, even if she seldom recognizes the importance of her finds. She
stands solidly by her academic conditioning which can accept no
poetic or religious magic other than that of the Bible, if only
because the University Chair of Theology is traditionally held by a
Christian Professor. All else is branded as mythical—*mythical*
being, like *pagan*, a word that denies truth to any ancient non-
Christian emblem, metaphor or poetic anecdote.

But an archaeologist's job is to quarry, date and compare rather
than to understand. And how blind some archaeologists can be!
Recently I came across some photographs of Etruscan antiquities

which included a carved steatite stone, vaguely labelled 'cult object—use unknown'; yet any properly brought up Jewish child could have recognized it at once as representing rolls of dough plaited and baked into a ritual loaf of the same immemorial shape.

2

The language of monsters

What is a monster? In modern English the word can be used in very different senses. As a rule it either means something of remarkable size, such as a monster pumpkin or a monster wedding cake, or else a creature of remarkable savagery: as most husbands, if not worms, tend to be monsters, and most children, if not little angels, tend to be little monsters. Millions of years ago of course huge natural monsters roved the Earth, among them the harmless vegetarian Diplodocus, whose skeleton dominates an immense hall in the Natural History Museum in London, also the flying pterodactyl, the ichthyosaurus, the brontosaurus, the fearsome sabre-toothed tiger and mammoth—some of these coeval with man.

Whether or not we inherit dream-memories of these beasts is arguable, but they can at any rate be distinguished from the equally zoological but grossly enhanced monsters of legend. Legendary cats, for example, such as the Irish Irusan who lived on the banks of the river Boyne: he could carry off a plough-ox in his claws, and is said to have once kidnapped Sanchan Torpest, the celebrated Irish poet (see p. viii). Yet a monster cat remains more or less a cat; so also a hundred-foot giant is no more than a man blown up by unrestrained fancy. Such enhanced, though otherwise normal monsters seem to have been born from psychotic visions, or under the influence of hallucinogenic drugs. The predicament of Alice who, in Wonderland, nibbled a piece of mushroom and found herself shooting up to monstrous height, and then diminishing to so small a size that a mouse became a monster for her, has recently been explained. Lewis Carroll had been reading M. C. Cooke's

A Plain and Easy Account of British Fungi, 1862, which tells how when the Korjaks of Siberia eat fly-agaric (*amanita muscaria*, a red toadstool with white spots, growing under birch trees and associated with dwarfs and Santa Claus) 'erroneous impressions of size and distance are of common occurrence. A straw lying in the road becomes a formidable object, to overcome which a leap is taken sufficient to clear a barrel of ale or the prostrate trunk of a British oak.'

Some years ago I ate the Mexican mushroom *psilocybe* and at one point in the resultant trance felt myself fourteen feet high. These strong natural hallucinogenes, which account for many divine visions, include the fungus found on manna (a honey-dew excreted by aphids on tamarisk leaves), the taste of which seems to have confused Moses's Israelites into enlarging its quantity by a hundred thousand times. But gods are made in man's image, rather than contrariwise. Ancient story-tellers have invented still more grossly exaggerated monsters to pretend that they were speaking oracularly; each outdid the other in hyperbole. The prize can be awarded to certain early mediaeval Jewish embroiderers on the *Book of Genesis*. Not only was Leviathan, an enhanced crocodile, said by them to grip his tail between his teeth and form a ring around the entire ocean but:

> 'Once the Rabbi Saphre, sailing in a ship saw a two horned beast lift its head from the waters. He read engraved on its horns: "This small sea-creature, measuring barely three hundred leagues, is on its way to serve as Leviathan's dinner." '

Their Behemoth, likewise, was an enhanced hippopotamus, with a tail bigger than the trunk of a cedar and bones like brass conduit-pipes, which could crop the Thousand Mountains bare in a single day; and 'all the water that flows down the Jordan in a whole year barely serves for Behemoth's single gulp'. The Ziz, an enhanced crane, was King of the birds. Rabbi Bar-Hana on a voyage once saw a Ziz standing in mid-ocean, yet the waters wetted only its ankles. 'We judged that the sea must be shallow and were about to disembark and cool ourselves, but a voice from Heaven warned us: "Seven years ago a ship's carpenter dropped his axe in this spot and it has not yet touched bottom!" '

Enhanced legendary monsters are often confused with fabulous or mythological monsters, which are pictorial devices explaining

man's relations with nature. Plato either misunderstood, or pretended to misunderstand, the language of myth; and his view was
adopted by the practical Romans. The poet Horace, for example,
satirized such 'unnatural' forms as Centaurs and Satyrs; though
these simply represented totemic Pelasgian-Greek tribesmen
disguised in their ritual dances as horses and goats. Similarly, the
bull-headed Cretan Minotaur, which Theseus the Greek killed in
the middle of a Sacred Labyrinth, will have stood for the King of
Cnossos while he was impersonating the Semitic Bull-God, El;
Bible readers will recall how once the prophet Zedekiah, son of
Chenaanah, speaking with the mouth of El, bound iron horns on
his forehead and told King Ahab: 'Thus shalt thou push the
Assyrians.' Greek mythographers accounted for the monstrous
Minotaur by saying that Queen Pasiphaë of Crete indulged her
monstrous sexual yearning for a bull, and was punished by bearing
it a bull-headed child; but they were saying no more than that the
original matrilineal nobles of Crete, immigrants from Libya, had
worshipped the Moon-Goddess Neith—'Pasiphaë' was a royal
moon-title meaning 'She who shines for all'—and that their
Queen, Neith's High Priestess, was unhappily forced to acquiesce
in the Semitic conquest of Crete and to accept patriarchal rule and
patrilineal marriage with the invading chieftain. The Queen's
union with this Bull-God's representative will have disgusted and
horrified all true Cretans as much as the act of bestiality with
which they compared it. There was also, by the way, a Cretan
Minotragos, meaning a King who impersonated a Semitic Goat-
God, as well as a Minotaur.

More complicated mythological animals, such as the Chimaera
and the Unicorn, began as simple pictographs of astronomical
concepts. Though Plato and his followers treated the 'Chimaera' as
a ridiculous or insane fancy, yet Homer, who recorded that this
monster with a lion's head, a serpent's tail and a goat's body was
killed in Asia Minor by the Corinthian hero Bellerophon, suffered
from no Chimerical delusions. He knew that the Lion (*Leo*), the
Goat (*Capricornus* in Latin, but *Chimaera* in Greek) and the
Serpent (*Draco*) were constellations; and will therefore have understood that Bellerophon had dethroned a Sun-king, whose emblem
was a combination of *Leo*, *Capricorn* and *Draco* in a single pictograph. The pictograph probably represented the Sun's widest
annual orbit, at an epoch when the Lion, not the Crab, was the
midsummer Sign. The Sun, when rising among the north-easterly

stars of the constellation Draco (which encircles the Great and
Little Bear) and setting in the north-west, could be said to overlap
at both ends his far shorter midwinter course when he rose in
Capricorn.

The original Unicorn was described by the mythographers as
having the horn of a rhinoceros, the head of a deer, the body of a
horse, the feet of an elephant, the tail of a lion; and began, it seems,
as a calendar-pictograph of the five 72-day seasons in the Pharaonic
calendar. The Phoenix was another calendar pictograph. Since the
ancient Egyptians had no leap-year, their calendar of exactly 365
days grew yearly more and more out of touch with the solstices and
equinoxes, because of the troublesome extra few hours occurring
annually which after each spell of 1,460 years added up to an extra
year. The Phoenix was portrayed as an Eagle, the royal Sun
symbol, and said to have been born in the form of a small worm, on
the palm-tree (*phoenix* in Greek) sacred to the Great Goddess Isis.
The worm symbolized these extra hours, which after about four
years amounted to a whole extra day: the Phoenix chick thereafter
gradually maturing into a full-grown eagle. At the end of the
1,460-year Phoenix cycle, the bird returned to its palm-tree nest
for the inauguration of a fresh cycle, and was burned alive in a nest
of aromatic twigs. From the ashes, it was said, a new worm hatched
which grew to a chick again, and so a new Phoenix cycle or
'Sothic Year' began. The Jews and early Christians, however,
continued to believe in a literal, zoological Phoenix even after 30
B.C.: the year in which the Emperor Augustus killed it when, after
abolishing the long line of Pharaohs, he reformed the Egyptian
calendar by intercalation. In late Jewish legend the Phoenix
figures in the Noah's Ark story not only as the sole beast without a
mate, but as the one that gave the least trouble to Noah and his
sons when they were perpetually busied with the task of feeding
and watering their comprehensive menagerie.

The Sphinx, another mythological beast, had a woman's head, a
lioness's body and an eagle's wings. She stood for the Great
Goddess who claimed domination of the air as an Eagle, Queen of
Birds, and of the earth as a Lioness, Queen of Beasts. Sphinx means
'the throttler'—a throttler of men. Ritual murder was executed
without bloodshed, by throttling, as in Spain today. When
Oedipus overcame the Sphinx at Boeotian Thebes, his victory
represented the same patriarchal triumph over matriarchy as the
Minotaur had gained at Cnossos.

Mythological birds and beasts often change their semantic associations as society changes. Thus the Sphinx eventually turned male, and the Unicorn became confused, in the Vulgate translation of the Bible, with the solitary wild-ass of the desert. Thus the poet Darley writes of the Unicorn:

> Lo, in the mute mid-wilderness
> What monstrous creature of no kind
> His burning lair doth largely press,
> Gaze-fixed and feeding on the wind!
> His coat is of the desert dye
> With tissue adust, dun-yellow and dry. . . .

In mediaeval times this Unicorn was associated with the male pride that can be chastened only by a woman's love. A unicorn would lay his horn in a pure virgin's lap and allow her to lead him tamely away with a halter about his neck. Until the Reformation the Unicorn's actual existence was everywhere accepted, and unicorn's horn—either that of a desert oryx or of a narwhal ('sea-unicorn')—fetched immense prices because, when dipped in a drinking cup, it was held capable of detecting poison. Still more confusion was caused when James VI of Scotland became James I of England and used the royal Unicorn of Scotland and the royal Lion of England in his coat-of-arms as opposite supporters of the Crown. The famous nursery-rhyme occasion when the Unicorn fought the Lion for the Crown took place in 1651. The Scottish Army had invaded England under James's grandson Charles II, recently crowned at Scone, but the lion-hearted English Commonwealth forces drummed the Unicorn out of Worcester town.

The Dragon represents sometimes a huge legendary red-coloured serpent—the Greek word *dracon* means 'serpent'—sometimes a lizard. St. George, who killed the Dragon, is a Christianized version of the Babylonian god Marduk who similarly killed a sea-serpent, the Goddess Tiamat. The worship of St. George came to England quite late, imported by a group of Lombardy bankers; his bones are shown at Porto Fino, near Genoa. Pope John XXIII, aware perhaps that the killing of the sea-serpent had been attributed by the prophet Isaiah to Jehovah Himself, removed St. George from the canon of genuine historical saints, but allowed his worship to continue in places where he was still honoured.

The lizard-type of dragon comes from China: the Chinese, doubtless impressed by the gigantic lizards found on the East Indian island of Komodo, had told travellers' tales about them. Thus the *Dra Goch*, the lizard-like Red Dragon of Wales, has a very different origin from St. George's Dragon. The *Dra Goch* was brought to Britain from China by way of Constantinople, over a thousand years before St. George's arrival, because a red silk dragon, shaped like a wind-sock, had long been used as a banner by Byzantine generals. The archers watched the dragon to see from which quarter the wind was blowing, and with what force; and were thus able to correct their aim. By the time of King Arthur, a fifth century A.D. Romano-British cavalry leader, the Red Dragon had come to be the banner used by successive Commanders-in-Chief of Rome's British allies. King Arthur's father, King Uther, held the title *Pen-Dragon* or 'Chief Dragon'; thus Arthur inherited the banner and fought behind it, against the invading Saxons. When after his death Saxon hordes drove the British back into the hills of Wales, the Red Dragon remained the British emblem. Since the Saxons also had a dragon banner, but a white one, the battle between these two dragons was recorded in Welsh legend.

The only new mythological monsters, so far as I know, that have been invented in Europe since Christianity displaced the old Graeco-Roman religion, are the products of heraldry. Most of them are based on the mediaeval bestiaries—fanciful zoological compendiums that drew morals from the natural, or unnatural, histories of animals. The Lion as King of Beasts was, for instance, credited with kingliness, courage, honour, generosity and the other royal virtues; the Fox was a shrewd, sly politician or bandit; the Bear was a fierce, stupid, blustering soldier with a sweet tooth and a sore head. A proud prince might choose his crest by combining the Eagle as King of Birds—with its sharp eye, remorseless swoop, and inaccessible eyrie—with the Lion as King of Beasts; naming the combined animal a 'Gryphon'. The same Alice, it will be recalled, met an unusually somnolent gryphon in Wonderland. Uneducated men-at-arms believed in the actual existence of *gryphons*, also of *allerions* which were beakless, clawless, heraldic eagles—symbols of pacific royalty; and of warlike *wyverns*, which were winged dragons with eagles' legs and barbed tails.

The Romans, who invented the word *monstrum*, classified monsters as in the same class as portents and prodigies: being, according to Cicero, signs *pointing out* that something sinister was afoot; just as a portent *portended*, and a prodigy *foretold*, any usually evil event. The birth of a two-headed calf, a typical monster, demanded from its owner a ritual sacrifice to avert disaster; so did a cock with hen's plumage, or Siamese twins. The colt foaled on Julius Caesar's farm with each of its hooves divided into five toes was a monster; but Caesar determined to make it an evil sign for the enemies of Rome, rather than for himself, by breaking it in and riding it to victory after victory. Yet in fact its monstruosity portended fresh civil war and the Roman Republic's eventual extinction. The Old English word for any monster of this sort, particularly a hermaphrodite, was *baeddel*, something that *boded* ill; from which the word *bad* comes.

Thalidomide-babies are typical *baeddels*, or monstrous births. The particular warning that they convey is one against rash scientific experiment and against putting drugs on the market before all possible side-effects have been investigated. The thalidomide-baby warning has been unfortunately disregarded. Though the Swiss firm of Hofmann which first sold L.S.D. to psychiatrists no longer manufactures the drug, its formula has been widely published and thus become available to junior assistants in every college chemical laboratory. There is now little hope of stopping its secret manufacture, though L.S.D. has much the same chemical structure as thalidomide and may result in equally significant monsters. It may, however, be soon superseded by still more disastrous compounds of the same sinister drug. And the eventual result will be monsters of the mind that dim the horror of any monster, portent or prodigy hitherto known to even the most luckless of mankind. Meanwhile cannabis, or 'pot', has also fallen under suspicion as a genocide.

3

Two studies in scientific atheism[*]

Professor Bertrand Russell spent the first thirty years of his life as a subject of Queen Victoria, in an era of profuse material prosperity, political toughness, social inequality and assiduous church-going. He was born a member of the over-privileged class which then controlled all departments of government, including the Established Church; and is indeed, though he dislikes being reminded of it, a belted Earl. What I miss from this collection of talks and essays (edited by his friend, Professor Paul Edwards of New York University) is a short biographical statement about Russell's childhood and adolescence that would justify so provocative a title as *Why I am Not a Christian*: the sort of statement provided by the late Dr. Ernest Jones in his account of the younger Freud to explain certain intemperate obsessions which vitiate the elder Freud's psychological researches. The resentful hatred implicit in all Russell's discussions of early religious and moral training suggests that he lived as a child under constant threats of hellfire, and as an adolescent under frantic obsessions of sexual guilt.

Warm human affection being apparently denied him, and success at games eluding him because of myopia, he began to cultivate his intellect (which will have left him even lonelier in a sternly anti-intellectual Public School society), and by the turn of the century had become one of Britain's foremost mathematicians. Then, though mathematic genius is as short-lived a flower as athletic prowess—it slowly wilts after the middle twenties—he

[*] *Why I am Not a Christian*, by Bertrand Russell. *Religion without Revelation*, by Julian Huxley.

presently achieved equal eminence in logic and metaphysics. His main obsession seems to have been the desire to free himself from the terrors of his youth, and to free others exposed to the same cruel conditioning. A courageous free-thinker in the line of John Wilkes, Tom Paine and Charles Bradlaugh, he has long played the part of fugleman to the 'Stage Army of the Good'—as we British call the small band of earnest liberal thinkers who come marching up with banners, slogans, protests and placarded manifestoes wherever personal freedom is threatened, justice burked or sabres rattled. Generous emotion often beguiles Russell into unsupportable statements. Thus he asserts that 'millions of unfortunate women' were burned as witches by mediaeval Christians, when any historian could have warned him to strike three zeros off this estimate; even so, many of these victims were real witches, members of a mystical cult, who died as martyrs to their faith. Again, as an example of senseless superstition, he cites the Deuteronomic ban on seething a kid in its mother's milk. Brief enquiry would have shown him that this was a practical rule, directed by the Temple authorities against participation in a heathen rite. The Orphic formula 'like a kid I have fallen into milk', refers to this sacrifice.

Russell's single-minded pursuit of intellectual and moral freedom tempts him to censure Jesus of Nazareth himself, his principal charges being that Jesus believed in hellfire, threatened his hearers with it if they refused to obey him, and decried family affection. On the contrary, however, Jesus (like his saintly predecessor Hillel) preached God's mercy as extended to the full wherever a man showed the least spark of repentance for sins of greed, faithlessness, cruelty or the like. Hell, in Hillel's and Jesus's view, was reserved for those who deliberately and maliciously chose the path of evil. Jesus also insisted on perfect family affection, except in the rare case of one member choosing the path of evil: after all attempts to restrain him had failed, he might be regarded as dead.

Often Russell, though hedging himself with an unresolved doubt as to Jesus's historical existence, uses the Gospels as a stick to beat Christians with:

'Christ taught that you should not fight, that you should not go to Church, that you should not punish adultery.'

True, Jesus was orthodox enough to discourage armed rebellion against the Romans, arguing that in the approaching Battle of Armageddon the legionaries would be more effectively engaged by hosts of avenging angels than by undisciplined Galilean peasants armed only with daggers. But to forbid warfare on moral grounds would have been to condemn Moses and his fellow-Israelites for defending themselves against their enemies in the Wilderness, and Joshua for seizing the Promised Land. Nor did he forbid his disciples to attend synagogue services—'Church' did not yet exist—but himself expounded Scripture in the synagogues of Nazareth and Capernaum. He certainly never forbade the punishment of adultery. This would have been to gainsay the Mosaic Law, not one jot or tittle of which, he declared, should ever pass away; but once, it seems, when a woman was charged with using witchcraft for adulterous purposes in some Samarian village— Jerusalem is historically ruled out as the scene of the incident, and so is plain adultery as the charge—Jesus counselled a scrupulous observation of *Deuteronomy* xvii. 2 –7: the first stones must be flung at the witch, not by the crowd at large, but by the eyewitnesses of her crime. He then courageously reminded these that, to avoid Divine wrath, they must be free from sin themselves before they let fly. Thus he saved the woman's life and gave her an opportunity for repentance.

As a master of metaphysics, Russell has little difficulty in demolishing the stock Catholic philosophical arguments held to prove the existence of God: the First Cause Argument, the Natural Law Argument, the Moral Argument, the Argument from Design, the Remedying of Injustice Argument. But he cannot avoid granting *de facto* recognition to the idea of God, since trustworthy statistics show a constant increase of religious worship in the United States throughout the present century. At the worst, God persists as a solemn metaphor for the Ultimate: even agnostics will say 'God only knows'. What is more, Professor Edwards includes in this collection a lyrical early essay (1903), *A Free Man's Worship*, which grants God a favourable mention. Russell does not altogether disavow this piece, but excuses it as 'the outcome of an experience not unlike what religious people call conversion . . . I became suddenly and vividly aware of the loneliness in which most people live, and passionately desirous of finding ways of diminishing this tragic isolation.' His view there is that mankind has been condemned to live in a hostile universe, but that:

'. . . In this lies man's true freedom: in determination to worship only the God created by our own love of the good, to respect only the heaven which inspires the insight of our best moments. In action, in desire, we must submit perpetually to the tyranny of outside forces; but in thought, in aspiration, we are free, free from our fellow men, free from the petty planet on which our bodies impotently crawl, free even, while we live, from the tyranny of death. Let us learn, then, that energy of faith which enables us to live constantly in the vision of the good; and let us descend, in action, into the world of fact, with that vision always before us.'

Organized religion is to him an infection of the hostile world, 'a disease born of fear and a source of untold misery to the human race.' He himself has not entirely escaped the infection: 'the petty planet on which our bodies impotently crawl' is a slavish phrase borrowed from the Evangelical pulpit. Nevertheless:

'Science can help us to get over this craven fear in which mankind has lived for so many generations. Science can teach us, and I think our own hearts can teach us, no longer to look around for imaginary supports, no longer to invent allies in the sky, but rather to look to our own efforts here below to make this world a fit place to live in, instead of the sort of place that the churches in all these centuries have made it.'

In his attack (1925) on Church leaders who oppose contraceptive devices, cheerfully letting poor women exhaust themselves by bearing enormous, unwanted families to drunken or syphilitic husbands, he claims that free-thinkers have been the most powerful advocates of this merciful innovation. From his list of six such advocates he disingenuously omits the two most distinguished, and most persuasive of all: Dr. Marie Stopes, and her husband, Sir A. V. Roe, the aeronautical pioneer, joint-founders of the Constructive Birth Control Society. For the past four years this very religious couple had been busily converting the Church leaders of Britain and America to their views, and setting up clinics in working-class districts at their own expense: with such success that, by 1930, Russell began to worry about the decline of the birthrate. In the same essay he had taunted the Church leaders with condoning the expensive road improvement in residential districts undertaken at a time when supplies of milk to nursing mothers were being cut for economy's sake. He accused them of deliberate murder, and threw in their teeth Jesus's advice to the rich young man: 'Sell all that thou hast and give to the poor!' The Church leaders would, of course, have been foolish had they urged the government to better the situation of working-class wives, in a time of acute unemployment, by discouraging municipal relief work and keeping their husbands on the dole; nor did Russell himself sell all that he had and buy milk for nursing mothers.

His further contention, that free-thinking had won mankind more benefits than had the exercise of so-called Christian charity, by forcing on the Church successive mitigations of its cruel and heartless reign, was later challenged by the rise of Stalinism and Hitlerism, movements clearly derived from Godless free-thinking. Russell side-stepped the issue by noting that Stalin had been trained for the Orthodox priesthood; and that Hitler was using the methods of the Spanish Inquisition to secure executive power.

By the way of an appendix, Professor Edwards records an unfortunate occurrence in 1940, when Russell was appointed Professor of Philosophy at New York City College, a State-supported institution. His duties were to lecture on the relation of logic to science, mathematics, and philosophy; also on the reciprocal influence of metaphysics and scientific theory. A bishop of the Protestant Episcopalian Church protested against the appointment. Despite Russell's philosophical eminence, could he be trusted not to infect the students with his militant atheism, his advocacy of pre-marital sexual commerce, his recommendation of nudism, and his condonation of marital unfaithfulness? The Faculty stood fast, but Tammany Hall and the Catholics supported the Episcopalians, and a convenient tax-payer was found to file a suit in the New York Supreme Court for voiding Russell's appointment on moral grounds. As a result, Judge McGeehan revoked it as an 'insult to the American people'. However, Russell was soon lecturing with acclaim at Harvard, an endowed university not subject to veto from the tax-paying populace, and his much-publicized championship of intellectual freedom later won him the Nobel Prize for Literature—an award that caused some surprise, since he had made no notable contributions to literature as such. Still, Professor Edwards notes, it could be applauded as a nasty smack in the eye for the Episcopalian Church, Judge McGeehan and Tammany Hall.

At the age of eighty-six, Russell still boldly declares that, in his opinion, 'all the great religions of the world, Buddhism, Hinduism, Christianity, Islam and Communism are both untrue and harmful'. He includes Communism (though plainly no religion, but an avowedly materialistic faith) to scotch the charge passionately flung at him by the American press, that he is a dangerous Red. But must Jews regard the omission of Judaism from his list as a denial of its greatness, or does he hesitate (for anti-anti-Semitic reasons) to make out a case for its harmfulness? We may never know.

* * * * *

Another collection of essays on the same general subject, *Religion without Revelation*, has been republished by a distinguished colleague of Russell's—Professor Julian Huxley, sometime Director-General of UNESCO. It first appeared thirty years ago, but is now brought up to date. Huxley (born 1887) was somewhat luckier in his early life than Russell. He recalls that, as children, he and his brother Aldous 'escaped invocation of the fear of Hell and the wrath of God in relation to the ordinary delinquencies of boyhood'. Their father being a son of the celebrated biologist Thomas Huxley, and their mother a granddaughter of the equally celebrated pedagogue, Dr. Arnold of Rugby, 'the home atmosphere combined puritan morality with religious unorthodoxy, and intellectual freedom with a sense of the ultimateness and supreme value of truth and goodness'. The brothers, it appears, were given no formal religious education at home, apart from certain simple prayers introducing the word 'God', and some brief account of Jesus's life; a regimen that kept them uncomfortably out of touch with their orthodox school-fellows. Polite visits to church at Christmas, Easter and Harvest Thanksgiving, but no regular church-going, made the young Julian Huxley feel cheated of religious communion, his native birthright. A passionate devotion to wild-flowers and poetry could not supply this lack, nor could the intellectual exercises which he imposed on himself in a resolve to serve the world by patient scientific research. Yet he had this in common with the young Bertrand Russell: that his family's awesome reticence on all sexual matters confused and disturbed him, as also did his guilty sense of belonging to the governing class.

Huxley's education at Eton, a school for tough, wealthy Empire-builders, culminated in a nervous break-down; but he never felt the urge to become an aggressive free-thinker and, though now holding that 'God is one of several hypotheses and an inadequate one', admits that a religious devotee is happier than a sceptic, and that it is necessary to believe in *something*. Alas, in what can a conditioned sceptic believe? Christian dogma, when he came to examine it, left him cold and, like Russell, he decided that science alone could provide a satisfactory basis for belief—by ruling out all faiths dependent on revelation or magic. He writes that 'myths are irrational, being founded on incomplete knowledge and false premises' and, disagreeing with Russell's view that all religions are necessarily evil, longs for a single sensible one which will some day unify all spiritual aspirations and all knowledge.

A short essay in this collection deals with the defeat of the old magical gods by the new improved philosophical gods; but he concludes that the Christian God, who eventually triumphed over his unimproved rivals, is now in rapid decline:

> 'Today he can no longer be considered as the controller of the universe in any but a Pickwickian sense. Operationally he is beginning to resemble not a ruler, but the last fading smile of a cosmic Cheshire Cat. . . .'

(Although Huxley was not subjected to severe religious pressure at his preparatory school or at Eton, so gentle a man must have felt pretty strongly about religion to choose so jaunty a metaphor.)

'. . . Today, gods are no longer spearheads of history, as they were in early Islam or in the Spanish conquest of the New World; they no longer operate in international politics as the Christian god did in the mediaeval days of the Holy Roman Empire; they no longer enforce opinion and doctrine by war or punishment, torture or death as in the Albigensian Crusade, or in the early days of the Inquisition, or in Calvin's theocracy; nor are they effective in inciting large-scale persecutions, as against witches; they no longer have much to say in laying down the curriculum of universities, or in dictating how citizens shall spend their time on Sundays; they no longer dictate economic behaviour, as for instance by prohibiting the lending of money at interest in mediaeval Christendom.

'. . . Their functions are now confined to providing individual salvation and assurance, and awareness of a reality transcending customary limitations of time and space. . . . The time is ripe for the dethronement of gods from their dominant position in an interpretation of destiny, in favour of a naturalistic type of belief-system. It will soon be as impossible for an intelligent, educated man or woman to believe in a god, as it is now to believe that the earth is flat. Belief in a personal god is in no way indispensable to religious experience.'

He then quotes various definitions of religion:

MATTHEW ARNOLD: 'Morality tinged with emotion.'

SALOMON REINACH: 'A body of scruples which impede the free exercise of our faculties.'

MAX MULLER: 'The perception of the infinite under such manifestations as are able to influence the moral character of man.'

SIR JAMES FRAZER: 'A propitiation of powers superior to man which are believed to control the course of nature and human life.'

PROFESSOR A. N. WHITEHEAD: 'A force of belief cleansing the inward parts: a system of general truths which transform character.'

G. M. STRATTON: 'The appreciation of an unseen world and an unseen company.'

PROFESSOR WILLIAM WALLACE: 'Belief in an ultimate meaning of the universe.'

Huxley himself, basing his view on the writings of Drs. R. R. Marett and Rudolf Otto, defines religion as *'awe of what is sacred'*.

It is strange that he did not take the simple scientific precaution of finding the etymology and therefore the original meaning of 'religion'. The Roman Catholics preach that the Latin *religio* represents *re-ligio*, 'the sense of being bound back to God'. But that cannot be, since *re*, the first syllable, is long, not short, and Lucretius, an early writer, spells the word *relligio*. The *ll* denotes an elision; and the only consonant that could have been elided before the second *l* is an *m*. Thus *relligio* must be formed from *rem legere*: 'to choose the very thing'; which confirms Frazer's view (based on a lifelong study of European folk customs) that religion is the exact art of propitiating the external powers.

Huxley, as a small boy, turned religious in this original sense when he spontaneously initiated a private rite one Easter: every year he would visit a neighbouring copse before breakfast to pick great armfuls of white cherry blossom for the saining of his puritanical home—the sacredness of the day and the sense of pilgrimage, he writes, drew out his suppressed feelings of holiness. Though unaware that Easter had once been a pagan festival of the Love-goddess Eostre, to whom white fruit-blossom was offered, he chose the very thing in her honour, and further confirmed the religious peculiarity of his rite by never picking flowers before breakfast on any other day of the year.

This religious custom fell into desuetude after four Easters, as his inspired sense of holiness was gradually stifled by formal education; a change which he does not, however, connect with the intellectual pursuits to which he was devoting himself; though he quotes as a parallel Wordsworth's similar experiences in the *Intimations of Immortality*. The fact is that 'philosophy' not only (as stated by Lucretius) rids man of religious terrors, but also banishes that sense of illumination which from time to time lightens the heart. A graceful volume of verse, *The Captive Shrew and Other Poems* (1932), marks the triumph of Huxley's reason over his poetic inspiration.

He rests great hopes on the scientific spirit, which

'is making its influence felt by its uncompromising hostility to all the magical, semi-magical or superstitious elements in religion; its insistence upon natural law; its achievements in controlling nature; its narrowing down the field of the supernatural towards a vanishing point. If the process continues—and in spite of conflict there is every appearance of its so doing—religious thought is due to enter on a new phase of relative stability, based upon the naturalistic and humanistic outlook brought in by the scientific spirit.

'The great achievement to be hoped for from this would be the achievement of unity. At present we are the slaves of a dualistic system of thought which continually produces false antitheses, as between soul and body, or between natural and super-natural . . . Science is now providing the basis for a single-minded naturalism. Its twin goals would be the development of the individual soul and the greater good of the human community.'

Ought not a philosopher to include the emotionally moralistic antonyms 'good' and 'evil' among the false dualisms that enslave mankind? Huxley believes that 'nothing can make religious human sacrifice anything but evil.' By this he may mean no more than that the spectacle of an innocent man being put to death by priests against his will is repugnant to the English moral tradition. Yet, as a rule, only when religions have lost their sacred force—this happened at Carthage during the struggle with Rome—is the chosen victim a prisoner of war, a slave, or some other expendable person, rather than a volunteer. The royal *okrafu* priests of Ghana who, three or four centuries ago, periodically died for their queen or their king, did so in loving free will. The Aztecs' sacred victims, at the barbarousness of whose deaths both Huxley and Russell shudder, were always volunteers; and are moreover said (I do not know how truly) to have died under complete anaesthesia, enjoying blissful hallucinatory visions. At all events, such self-sacrifices, performed for the good of others, are humanly no less deserving of praise than is the action of a driver whose brakes fail and who deliberately crashes his car against a tree to avoid running into a group of children.

'Evil' is a magical term, not a scientific one; and science claims to be eliminating magic. A true scientist observes, compares, and classifies fact, deduces effect from cause, computes probable results. He cannot, *qua* scientist, describe the voluntary death of, say, a sixteenth century *okrafu* priest as evil. Even if he were to pronounce it unnecessary, on the ground that kings and queens of England during the same period managed well enough without human sacrifice, his verdict would be questionable. Voluntary human sacrifice was held to strengthen the royal government of the Akan States, and confirm the people in courage, industry, and loyalty. Again, the mystique of the Crown, the greatest single steadying factor in British political life, has always been enhanced by the theory that soldiers who die fighting heroically, do so for their Queen—Sir Richard Grenville, commander of the *Revenge* under Elizabeth I, is a famous example—or for their King; and only as an afterthought for their Country. This theory (distasteful

to pacifists) has, of course, been endangered by forcible conscription; so that British volunteers of the First World War (King
George V's willing *okrafu* priests) suffered immensely heavier
casualties without losing their fighting morale than did the conscripts of the Second.

Huxley, unlike Russell, is in favour of Jesus (another willing
sacrificial victim): to the degree of ascribing to him the 'great
discovery' that perfect love of God casts out fear—which happens
to have been orthodox Pharisaic doctrine preached long before the
Christian era. He also cheerfully ascribes to St. Paul the pre-
Christian Jewish doctrine that God is a Universal Deity who offers
salvation to all who obey His Law—irrespective of race, rank, or
sex. And he flatly contradicts Russell by glorifying Christianity for
its 'dethronement of false primitive values based on cruelty and
pride, and their replacement by love, mercy, sacrifice and humility'.

True religion implies awe, ecstasy, possession, the hair rising on
the worshipper's nape, tears of joy breaking from his eyes: in this
condition he soon learns to choose the very thing. Huxley's talk of a
universal religion based on science, 'that shall unite man in
brotherhood', is as woolly as such talk must always be. Religion
needs *bite*, and science can never supply the necessary teeth. The
pursuit of science (to borrow its own jargon) produces no abnormal
psychosomatic effect in its devotees. At its best, it furnishes
fascinating intellectual problems for a few bright research-fellows
to solve, and makes possible the manufacture of numerous labour-
saving amenities. But it also destroys numerous ancient amenities;
dulls the minds of its countless mechanical servitors; separates man
more and more from his natural context in wild nature; and so far
enthrones intellect as the greatest of all human attributes as to
remove all checks on its irresponsible functioning.

It is a pity that these two philosophers cannot overcome their
complacency at having somehow kept sane, throughout the
emotional hazards of childhood, by the exercise of stern intellectual
self-discipline: will not pause to consider dispassionately, in
practical terms, whether myth and magic should be extinguished
by science. Had they been born into some as yet un-missionized
African tribe, they would not have suffered from the torturing
sexual inhibitions of their Victorian childhood, or from any
aggrieved sense of having been given the wrong sort of religious
training. Soul-shaking magical initiation rites at puberty would
have taken care of that: for one great mistake of the Christian

Church has been a failure to combine the ceremony of First Communion with a dramatic religious disclosure of sexual mysteries. They might also have learned to respect myth as the practical authorization of social change by priestly fable and drama.* Someone—I have forgotten who, forgive me!—called man a religious animal, and religious he must continue to be, because of the uncontrollable imaginative processes which take over the human mind when its critical function is in abeyance.

Another great mistake of the Church has been to freeze its myths beyond the point where they can be unfrozen. If the Christian God finally abdicates and is succeeded by some more immediately potent deity or deities, the reason will be that his myth no longer corresponds with recent developments in the Western social system. He is still presented as an absolute Oriental male monarch, too holy ever to reveal himself in public, whose existence is apprehended only by a symbolic male dove, his spiritual emanation; and whom mortals cannot approach unless they have first secured the good offices of his sole son. This son, formerly a mortal, is said to have been parthenogenously born from a mother who, though now assumed to Heaven, does not participate in his godhead. The Father-god's royal court consists of winged, sexless angels having no other functions but to offer him perpetual adulation, and to stand ready with swords and spears for battle against those hosts of darkness whose evil machinations he strangely permits.

In modern republics and in constitutional monarchies (often ruled by queens) this myth makes little sense. If the system— refined by the ancient Greeks, Libyans, Palestinians and Irish, and perpetuated by present-day Africans, of keeping divine myths abreast of the times—had been maintained in the Western world for the last two millennia, all the major social and political changes that have meanwhile occurred would be wholesomely incorporated in Christian dogma. For the United States, God would now appear as a sage, democratic, always accessible, President; assisted by his son, an industrious Vice-President; by archangels, acting as his Secretaries of State; and by angels, as representatives of various sectional interests. How long any such myth continued viable would depend, of course, on the survival of the present wholly masculine idea-system; for one can credibly postulate the system's

* In 1944, Huxley was appointed a member of the Royal Commission for Higher Education in West Africa; but that came too late.

eventual collapse, even without atomic wars, and recourse thereupon taken to the underdeveloped riches of the female mind. Such
a change would restore to myth either goddesses or such bi-sexual
deities (importations from West Africa) as figure powerfully in
Haitian Voodoo. I mention this possibility because, apart from
Russell's concern for the harassed working mother of pre-Welfare
State Britain, and his advocacy of frequent pre-marital, and occasional extra-marital, sexual adventures; and apart from Huxley's
scorn for the mawkish sentimentality of certain female churchgoers, there is hardly a mention in either book—and none in Aldous
Huxley's more ambitious *Perennial Philosophy*—of a most crucial
religious question, namely the proper spiritual relation of the
sexes. Priestesses were banished from all civilized countries with
the downfall of the Olympians, because the Church would not
trust women to direct even the religious affairs of women. Does
their continued exclusion from religious life, except as deaconesses,
Sunday-school teachers, and the like, make for social stability?
Would the triumph of science—most women are distinctly short on
science—improve their position?

As a scientist, Huxley advocates naturalistic religion. Anthro-
pology is, of course, a department of science, and scientists are
concerned with recording and classifying primitive customs before
they die out. The primitive habit of objectifying human aspirations,
fears and obsessions by calling them 'gods' is as logically tenable as
the scientific habit of coining abstractions and formulating laws.
Moreover, gods, though courteously named 'immortal', can at
least be challenged and superseded by deities corresponding more
closely with natural passionate human demands: demands never
satisfied by immutable scientific laws and abstractions. But
primitive religion is entailed in magic, which scientists consider
based on false premises.

Dr. Arnold defined religion as 'morality tinged with emotion'.
'Tinged', forsooth! Religious morals, in a healthy society, are best
enforced by drums, moonlight, fasting, dancing, masks, flowers,
divine possession; though Professors Russell and Huxley are unlikely to accept this thesis. As a boy, Russell invoked Apollo, the
cold God of Science, to rescue him from the Infernal demons that
oppressed his childhood; Huxley, in his turn, invoked Apollo to
smother the social embarrassment caused by having privately felt
awe for Our Lady of the Wild Things. Both now believe Apollo
capable not only of superseding the senile Christian God, but of

initiating a new Golden Age of perfect naturalistic freedom. Will even their fellow-scientists agree with them?

One odd emotional phenomenon, common to both books, is an inveterate hatred of Roman Catholicism. I am reminded of Nell Gwyn: when her sedan-chair was mobbed by an angry London crowd, who mistook her for the extravagant Duchess of Kendall, King Charles II's Catholic mistress, she looked out through the curtains and cried with spirit: 'Let me be, good people! I am the King's *Protestant* whore.' English ruling-class conditioning has made both Huxley (now knighted) and Russell (now decorated with the Order of Merit) Queen Elizabeth II's *Protestant* atheists.

4

The Dour Man

The discovery of *Dyscolos* (*The Dour Man*), a complete prize-winning play by Menander (of whose work only fragments had hitherto been extant) has roused little excitement, considering that the Greeks once regarded him as their greatest poet—Homer alone excepted. Born in 342 B.C., an admiral's son, a well-known dramatist's nephew, and a boyhood friend of the philosopher Epicurus, Menander was sophisticated, handsome, ambitious. An epigram tells how he visited Demetrius Phalereus, a fellow-Epicurean and for ten years head of the Athenian government: 'entering his presence with languid tread and a powerful whiff of perfume.' Menander, Philemon, Diphilus, Philippides, and Apollodorus ranked as the five leading 'New Comedy' playwrights.

It was Philemon, Menander's senior by twenty years, who broke the last ties with Aristophanes' 'Old Comedy'. Aristophanes had caricatured all the most distinguished men of his day, mercilessly mocking at Pericles the warmonger, Cleon the demagogue, the irreligious Sophists (including Euripides), the corrupt city magistrates; yet he escaped punishment, Pericles being shrewd enough to keep this vent of public opinion unstopped. About 405 B.C., however, Pericles' successors imposed severe censorship on the theatre, and indiscreet political references meant gaol. What safe object of comedy could playwrights thereafter find? They might take off some semi-barbarous foreign potentate who was not sufficiently powerful to make effective diplomatic protest—as in the English nineteenth century the Mikado and the Akhond of Swat were considered fair game. Or they might burlesque established classics and popular myths. Or exploit common character types,

hoping that voices from the audience would cry delightedly:
'There's my mother-in-law and my old pedagogue to the life!' But
they resented the cramping of their style. Seventy years went by
before the censorship laws were cheerfully accepted as stage
conventions.

Philemon first formalized these character types. Apuleius wrote
approvingly:

> 'You find in Philemon's works the perjured pimp, the impas-
> sioned lover, the cunning slave, the wheedling mistress, the
> domineering wife, the indulgent mother, the explosive uncle, the
> helpful friend, the boastful soldier; also greedy parasites, close-
> fisted parents, and shameless harlots.'

Ninety-seven plays by Philemon are recorded, a high percentage of
which won the annual City wreath. None survive. Menander
staged a hundred and four, but to his disgust won no more than
eight wreaths. He once asked Philemon—a Cilician adventurer,
and suspected of bribing the judges—whether he did not blush to
be crowned at the expense of a genius like himself. The famous
courtesan Glyphera amused herself by embittering their rivalry.

Meanwhile one Theophrastus had written a compendium of
'Ethical Characters', described in richly circumstantial detail; and
Menander needed only to provide comic plots for their interaction.
Yet however emancipated a playwright's life, he might stage
nothing in the nature of bedroom farce that would offend a chaste
Athenian matron with marriageable daughters. Also, problem
plays, or fantasies of the sort invented by Aristophanes, would be
far above the heads of his audience. There remained straightfor-
ward, light modern comedy, centring on the deathless themes of
love and money; into which smut or personal satire could not
infiltrate unless through *hyponoea* (innuendo and *double entendre*)
or unauthorized silent 'business' on the part of some privileged
buffoon.

Menander thought Philemon too literary a dramatist. Since the
Athenians queued up whenever he read a new play aloud, he
seems to have been a prototype of Dickens, whose stage-plays did
not provide such good theatre as his dramatic recitations. Menander aimed at verbal slickness, and put effective slapstick before
rhetoric. In the course of the next hundred years, stock companies
took his plays to every city where Greek was spoken. Also, the

Romans Plautus and Terence adopted or plagiarized him. Through
them he ended as the father of the English Morality Play, of the
Punch and Judy show, and of Classical French comedy.

Yet mere laughter at his jokes dissatisfied Menander. He wished
to earn a household name for proverbial wisdom. Aristophanes, in
his *Frogs*, had satirized a similar ambition in Euripides. 'I suppose,'
the god Dionysus scornfully asks him, 'that you want to be quoted
on all questions of domestic economy—such as what happened to
that left-over sprat head and the garlic clove, or who's been
nibbling at this plate of olives?' But some school-master eventually
collected 'Menander's Moral Monostiches' in a text-book, from
which many of them entered the *Dictionary of Familiar Quotations*:
such as 'Friendship implies common property,' and 'Evil communications corrupt good manners' (quoted by St. Paul from Menander's *Thais*). He specialized in phrases of condolence for deserted
lovers or bereaved parents: among them 'Whom the gods love die
young'—but Menander himself, at the age of fifty-two, ventured
out of his depth while bathing in Peiraeus Harbour, and the
appropriate monitory maxim went down with him.

*　　*　　*　　*　　*

The text of *Dyscolos* has been published by *La Bibliothèque
Bodmer* of Geneva, with Professor Victor Martin's scholarly notes,
a facsimile of the entire papyrus (*P. Bodmer IV*), and competent
French and German renderings. Also an English version from
which (as a dreadful warning against the academic colloquial
style) let me quote the following dialogue between Getas the
Slave, Sicon the Cook and Cnemon the Dour Man:

GETAS (*banging on the door*): Hallo there, hey, fellows! I am
    calling, come on, hi! (*Aside*) Gosh, I'm fagged out! Come on
    out, lackeys!
CNEMON: I can't bear any more. . . . What do you want?
SICON: I ask you for cooking pots and a bowl. You have some,
    you have some in very truth! (*Redoubles his knocks.*)
CNEMON: Hapless man that I am, how have I been brought out
    here? You caitiff, may all the gods make you perish mis-
    erably!
SICON: I should like a bronze mixing bowl. You've got one, I
    know you've got one, little father!
CNEMON: That Simike, I'll kill her!

Dyscolos is recorded to have won the wreath in 317 B.C., Menander then being twenty-five years old. Professor Martin writes:

> 'The place and the circumstances on which this early 3rd-century papyrus was found are unfortunately unknown, as is nearly always the case when pieces of this kind are acquired in the market of antiquities. . . .'

In other words, workers probably stole it from an Egyptian dig. The scribe's carelessness has demanded a deal of skilful emendation; so have various lacunae due to damaged margins.

By way of Prologue, Pan emerges from a grotto which lies between two houses, and tells the audience about the main characters:

> 'Consider this place to be Phyle in Attica. . . . The domain on my right is where Cnemon dwells. . . . He has always detested a crowd—did I say a crowd?—and in the course of his already long life he has never pronounced a single kind word, nor has he been the first to speak to anybody except by sheer necessity, or when he passes before me, Pan. And even that he promptly regrets, as I well know. And yet, with such a character, he married a young widow, whose husband had left her with an infant boy. Bickering with her under the yoke of marriage . . . he lived miserably. A baby girl was born to him. The conflict became unbearable, and the wife returned to the home of her son, issue of the first marriage. The latter owns a small property here where he poorly maintains himself, his mother, and a faithful slave inherited from his father. The son is now grown to a youth who has discernment beyond his age; for the experience of hardship matures us. The old man lives alone with his daughter and an aged woman servant, carrying wood, for ever digging, toiling, hating everybody all around. . . . The maiden has always been left to her own innocent devices: she knows no evil. . . . A young man, son of a very rich father who cultivates prosperous lands in the district, but he himself a man of the town, came here hunting with a friend and saw the girl. I sent him madly in love with her. That is the main point.'

A bad start. Pan says nothing that could not have been developed by later dialogue between the various persons mentioned, whom the audience has difficulty in identifying when they appear. Also, he is a 'throw-away' character; though his worshippers, the chorus, choose the Phyle grotto as a scene for their outing, we never see him again.

Dyscolos recalls all the home-made plays ever performed in church halls and made amusing only by the incompetence and heroism of their amateur casts. Change the sacrifice at Pan's grotto to a vicarage picnic and, there you are! Cnemon, a small farmer, keeps himself to himself. A rich squire's son falls chastely in love with Myrrhine, the innocent daughter, to whom he has never been introduced, and sends Cnemon, whom he has never met, a message offering marriage. The messenger having been rightly chased away with a shower of clods and a stake, the squire's son seeks help from Myrrhine's half-brother. To deceive Cnemon into thinking that he is no city idler but an honest labourer, the squire's son agrees to handle a hoe for the half-brother. 'If the girl has indeed not been subject to lessons from an aunt or nurse, knows nothing of the ugly side of life, but has grown up without too much supervision under a rustic father who hates evil, how could it be other than a blessing to win her? But this hoe weights two hundredweight! It will be the death of me!' Since the half-brother and his step-father Cnemon never even bid each other good morning, the stratagem of course fails.

After antagonizing all the picnickers by refusing to lend their cook a stew-pot, Cnemon accidentally falls down his own well. Myrrhine is dazed with grief—a voice from inside: 'Oh, how terrible! He will drown! Save my darling father'—but the unkind picnickers suggest that a large stone should be mercifully dropped on Cnemon's head. The noble step-son, however, leaps in and rescues him—rather hindered than helped by the squire's son, at the well-head, who is so busy embracing Myrrhine that he lets go the rope three times. Cnemon thereupon undergoes a change of heart, re-calls his wife—'Fetch your mother, my boy; it seems that one learns most from adversity!'—adopts his rescuer, marries Myrrhine to the squire's son, and even dances in Pan's honour. (Cries of 'Author! Author!')

*   *   *   *   *

Moral platitudes load the air: 'Enrich the needy and lay up an imperishable treasure for your days of need!'—'Self-praise is no recommendation!'—'A true friend is better than buried treasure!' But all decent people will have sympathized with the unreformed

Dour Man. If he did not like being tricked by squires' sons and mocked by rowdy slaves, if he preferred Diogenes to Epicurus, if he worked his farm alone except for his affectionate daughter, whose earthly business was that?

One strange dramatic defect: Myrrhine never exchanges a single word with the squire's son; nor does he even confide her feelings for him to the audience. Even the well-head incident is described instead of acted. And why? Because under Athenian law all women characters were played by boys or men; and handsome boys could not star in romantic parts, laying bare their love-lorn hearts, lest they provoked improper homosexual interest. The Elizabethan dramatists were hampered by a similar political censorship; but fortunately by a less repressive moral one—otherwise Romeo would have had no Juliet, and Antony no Cleopatra. In fact, though neither this play, nor the large fragments, found in 1905, of *The Arbitrants*, *The Girl from Samos*, or *The Short-haired Lass*, stir much regret for the loss of Menander's other works, we should blame his age, not himself; and be satisfied at least that ten complete comedies of Aristophanes survive. Their humour may demand copious annotation, but they are still alive and real: *Lysistrata* can even play to packed houses.

5

Praise me,
and I will whistle to you!

It is surprising how much excitement has been caused by, and how much ignorance shown in, the poltergeist case reported last March (1958) from the six-roomed, ranch-style Long Island home of James Herrmann and his family of three (1638 Redwood Avenue, Seaford, is the address). Bottles containing such varied liquids as peroxide, nail-polish remover, bleach, and holy water blew their screwed tops; a plate was snatched from the table at dinner; a plaster statuette of the Virgin flew off a dresser, knocking down a wedding picture and alighting on a table; a large terrestrial globe was carried some fifteen feet; a heavy book-case containing a twenty-five volume encyclopaedia was found up-ended and tightly wedged between a radiator and the corner of a bed.

Joseph Tozzi, a Nassau County police detective, came to investigate. While acquitting the children, a twelve-year-old boy and a thirteen-year-old girl, of complicity, since neither of them had been present during some of the manifestations, he remained nonplussed. Next, Dr. J. Gaither Pratt, Assistant Director of the Parapsychology Laboratory at Duke University, arrived to assist Detective Tozzi; but what new light could parapsychology shed on this ancient and well-known phenomenon—unless perhaps an infra-red camera might see more than the limited human eye? (Dogs' eyes, by the way, are said to register infra-red rays; and also at times to follow, terror-stricken, the passage of otherwise invisible presences.) The manifestations temporarily ceased, but started up again as soon as Dr. Pratt had left the house. The

Herrmanns then called in Father William Mcleod, a Roman Catholic priest, who blessed all six rooms but failed to lay the poltergeist. He said he would apply to his Bishop for permission to exorcize it.

The *poltergeist* (German for 'noisy ghost') occasionally satisfies itself with mere knocks, raps and groans but, as a rule, also tosses furniture and crockery about: not throwing such things in a straight arc but carrying them, with a swerve or wobble, often around corners, at a moderate speed.

A useful rule for investigators is *'Cherchez l'enfant!'*, since in nearly every case an adolescent has become the poltergeist's unwitting agent; and the charming innocence of his (or her) own activities tends to disarm suspicion. Yet the phenomena are always such as would please a naughty child. Most poltergeists show a dislike of religious objects, priests and parents, and do a great deal of haphazard destruction; nevertheless, serious injury to human beings or animals seldom occurs, the missiles having only a slight impact.

The precise means by which a possessed child—more rarely an adult woman—conveys a large object through the air without handling it or even being present in the room, cannot be discovered; and some of the objects seem beyond the child's physical strength to lift. This does not, however, worry me as an intellectual problem; we know so little about the human brain and body, anyhow. When I once saw a poltergeist knock the shade off a table-lamp within a few feet of where I stood, it certainly gave me quite a turn; yet other equally startling phenomena—levitation, second sight and ghostly visitations of the unpleasant sort called *taradh* by the Scots—happen often enough to carry statistical conviction. The appearance of a real poem is among the strangest of all such happenings and, of course, real poems do get written. But real poems are different and unique; whereas all poltergeists everywhere show an appalling sameness of behaviour: humourless, pointless, unco-ordinated.

The apparent rarity of American poltergeists surprises me. Can the climate be responsible? Throughout Europe, where poltergeists have so often played havoc both in famous or well-to-do homes and obscure or poor ones, they are accepted casually enough as well-known nuisances of no great duration. It would never occur to anyone this side of the Atlantic that the hauntings could possibly be caused by radio waves—a theory which led R.C.A.

Communications to operate high-frequency receivers at Seaford 'lest any unusual or phenomenal signals might be passing through the area'. Or that the explanation might be found in a freak magnetic field caused when jet planes flew over a deposit of water deep under the Herrmann house; as Robert E. Zider of the Brookhaven National Laboratory surmised. Not that all poltergeists are genuine: a good many are certainly fraudulent, and some genuine cases are muddied by fraudulent interference, as seems to have happened at Ringcroft in 1695—the earliest British poltergeist authenticated by signed evidence from a number of reputable witnesses.

The printed account is headed:

'A True Relation of an Apparition, Expressions and Actings of a Spirit which infested the House of Andrew Mackie in Ringcroft of Stocking in the Parish of Rerwick, in the Stewardship of Kirkcudbright in Scotland, 1695, by Mr. Alexander Telfair, Minister of that Parish and attested by many other persons, who were also eye and ear witnesses.'

The Revd. Alexander Telfair, formerly chaplain to Sir Thomas Kirkpatrick of Closeburn, came to live at Rerwick by accident, though he had distant kin settled in the neighbourhood. Contrary winds detaining him while he awaited a sea-passage across to Northumberland, he borrowed a lime-kiln for use as a conventicle and there preached God's word to the inhabitants. They so enjoyed his ministrations that one day a huge crowd gathered at the Manse and ordered the resident curate, whom they disliked, to vacate it in Telfair's favour at twenty-four hours' notice. The curate fled, and apparently lodged no protest nor made any effort to return. When the Synod of Galloway later inquired into Telfair's fitness to act as minister, they confirmed him in his cure; he died in 1731, after a useful and respected life. Though some Rerwickers regarded him as an interloper and spread a rumour that he had never been ordained, this hostility appears irrelevant to the Ringcroft hauntings.

As a good Christian, the Revd. Alexander Telfair never doubted that the poltergeist was an evil spirit, and in a foreword to the *Relation*, he rails against atheists who, denying the existence of spirits or devils, dare 'impute their actions to the melancholic disturbance of the brains in those who pretend to hear, see or feel them'. The *Relation* unfortunately omits some particulars of importance, which inquisitive atheists might have gone into, but on the whole the minister has done pretty well. He starts by recording that Andrew Mackie, a stone-mason by trade, had allegedly dedicated his first child to the Devil when he took the oath as a free-mason; but that Mackie denied taking any such oath, and that nothing was known to his moral discredit. Mackie kept good company, behaved honestly, spoke civilly and, when the hauntings began, joined devoutly in the prayers offered to abate them. Nor had any charge been raised against his wife or children as somehow implicated in the sorry business. Also, when charged to declare whether it were true that a woman of evil reputation, since dead, had once left a sack of clothes at his house, and that her friends later accused him of withholding some of these, Mackie and his wife both denied any knowledge of the sack's contents: they had handed it over to the woman's friends without examining it. This seemed to be the truth.

There was also a story told about an earlier tenant of Ringcroft, one Macnaught, the victim of constant ill-luck. He sent his son to a witch-woman who lived by Routing Bridge at Irongray, asking whether a spell had been cast on the house, but the son joined a party of soldiers on their way to Marlborough's army in Flanders, and never came back with the answer. Some years later, a Rerwick man named John Redick met young Macnaught overseas. They fell into conversation, and when Redick announced that he was soon sailing for home, young Macnaught begged him to visit his father, or whoever might be living in Ringcroft, with a message: namely, that unless a tooth buried underneath the threshold were removed and burned, none who lived in the house would ever thrive. Redick, on his return, learned that old Macnaught was dead and the widow gone away. So he said nothing to anyone about the tooth until the hauntings began during Mackie's tenancy. He then confided the story to the minister alone. The intermediate tenant had been Thomas Telfair who, somehow hearing of the spell, raised the threshold stone one day and discovered underneath something resembling a tooth. When burned, it blazed up like tallow. Telfair, examined by the minister, said that even after comparing the tooth with those of a man, a horse, a cow and a sheep, he could not identify it; but that his action had, at all events, freed the house of ill-luck.

The new hauntings started in February 1695. Andrew Mackie

D

kept some calves tied to stakes in a stable; and every morning found their halters snapped. At first he thought that the calves had grown restive, and tied them up more securely with withies; but they always broke free again. Suspecting malice on the part of a neighbour, he removed the calves elsewhere, yet the next morning he came upon one of them so tightly bound with a hair-tether to the back-wall of the house that its feet only just reached the ground. Soon afterwards a huge basketful of peat was piled at night on his living-room floor, and set ablaze. The smoke woke the family. Nothing was seen or heard which might have explained the incident.

On March 7th, stones began mysteriously flying about the house, and continued to do so for the next four days and nights; especially the nights.

On the evening of Saturday, March 9th, when the family came home from the fields, the children were startled by what looked like a figure sitting at the fireside, clothed in a blanket. The younger child, a boy of nine or ten, reproved the other two with: 'Why are you afeared? Let us sain [bless] ourselves, and then there is no ground to fear it.' Suddenly he recognized the blanket as his own, crossed himself, and crying that whatever the apparition might be, it must not borrow his property, ran forward and pulled the blanket away. All was well: someone had merely placed a four-legged stool upside-down on the settle and draped the blanket over.

On Sunday, March 10th, the hook and chain from which the Mackies' cooking pot hung were stolen from the chimney, and discovered, four days later, hidden in a loft—though this had already been searched several times. (*Witnesses:* Charles Maclellan of Colline and John Cairns.)

Mackie reported his troubles to the minister that same day at the Church door, after the sermon; and on March 14th, the minister visited Ringcroft, where he stayed for a considerable time and prayed twice. Nothing disturbed him. However, as he stood talking to some men by the barn-end of the house, two pebbles dropped on the roof. Someone then shouted from inside that matters were as bad as ever, so he re-entered and went on with his prayers. Several small stones hit him, but did no damage.

Little of importance happened until Sunday, March 17th. Trouble then began in earnest, with larger stones more frequently thrown. This continued for three days. Witnesses agreed that the stones had not half their natural weight when they struck, and that more were flung on Sundays than on week-days, but oftenest at the prayer-leader.

On March 21st, the minister went to Ringcroft again and stayed most of the night. He was pelted with stones and other objects, and whacked loudly several times on the shoulders with a heavy stick. The side of the bed flew off, and knocks sounded from the chests and tables as if someone were demanding entrance. (*Witnesses:* Charles Maclellan, William Mackminn and John Tait.) That same night, as the minister leaned praying at a bedside, he felt a pressure on his arm and, looking around, observed a little white hand and arm from the elbow down. It soon vanished. This was the sole occasion on which anyone saw the spirit in human shape; except that a friend of Andrew Mackie's claimed to have once seen it as a boy about fourteen years old, dressed in grey, and wearing a bonnet—who soon likewise vanished.

Matters grew still worse on March 22nd. Not only the family but curious neighbours were pelted with stones and beaten with sticks, so that a few of them had to retire in disappointment. (*Witnesses:* Charles Maclellan and Andrew Tait.) Among those attacked as they approached through the yard, and again as they left, was Thomas Telfair, the former tenant. Andrew Mackie sustained a slight cut on his forehead, and had his shoulder thrust at with a stick. When he paid no attention, something gripped him by the hair, and he could feel fingernails scratching his scalp. Several visitors were dragged around the living-room by their clothes. (*Witness:* Andrew Tait.) A miller from Auchencairn named Keige was seized so violently that he begged his neighbours for assistance, yelling that the spirit would tear his side out. When night came, the bed-clothes floated off the sleeping children, and they were beaten on the hips by an invisible hand; everyone in the house heard the slaps. A door-bar and other objects would now sail through the doorway as though an invisible person went out carrying them in his hand. (*Witnesses:* John Telfair in Auchenlech, and others.) A stick rattled loudly on the chests and bed-sides. These manifestations continued for eleven days; so did the former stone-throwing and beating with sticks.

On April 3rd, whistling was heard, and a voice that said '*Whisht, whisht!*' (*Witness:* Andrew Tait.)

On April 4th, Charles Maclellan of Colline, the landlord, accompanied by Andrew Mackie, took a report of the hauntings to a meeting of several ministers at Buittle. The ministers thereupon offered public prayers for the Mackie family; and two of them, the Revd. Andrew Ewart, of Kells, and the Revd. John Murdo, of Crossmichael, visited Ringcroft and spent the night there in prayer and fasting. They were, however, pelted with stones, some of them weighing seven pounds. The Revd. Andrew Ewart lost a good deal of blood from two head wounds, and had his wig snatched off while praying; on another occasion he happened to be holding out a napkin between his two hands, when a stone dropped into the napkin and flew off with it. The Revd. John Murdo was struck several times, as was everyone else present. That night, during prayers, a flaming peat fell among the gathering, but did no damage. When the company rose from their knees at dawn, stones came pouring down. (*Witnesses:* Revds. Andrew Ewart and John Murdo; Charles Maclellan and John Tait.)

On April 5th, some thatching straw caught alight in the barn-yard, and at night the gathering of neighbours was constantly pelted. Mackie and his wife went out into the yard to fetch peat, but as she returned the broad threshold stone moved under her. Since it had never been loose before, she decided to examine it next morning.

On April 6th, while the house was quiet for a while, she lifted the stone, and beneath it found a soiled paper package containing seven small, bloody bones with flesh adhering to them: the blood was new and bright. This scared her: she put back the package, and ran for help to Charles Maclellan's house, a quarter of a mile off. The children reported, on her return, that the spirit had mean-while thrown a red-hot stone into the bed between two of them, burning a hole through the clothes. The eldest boy removed it, but more than an hour and a half later it was still too hot for Charles Maclellan to handle; or so he said. 'Fire-balls' had also flown in and around the house, yet set nothing alight; and a stick, thrust through the lath-and-plaster wall above the bed, had been shaken at them to the sound of groans. When Charles Maclellan came to Ringcroft and knelt down to pray, stones were flung at him most cruelly. However, as soon as he lifted the package from the hole everything grew quiet. He sent the package to the minister, who at once visited the house and prayed again. Large stones hit him, though harmlessly; no further trouble occurred that night.

On Sunday, April 7th, William Macminn, the blacksmith, was wounded on the head by a flying plough-share, and a stone trough of about three hundred pounds' weight struck his back, but did no damage. (*Witness:* William Macminn.) The house caught fire twice; neighbours fetched water and extinguished the blaze. At twilight, John Mackie, coming home from the fields, reported an extraordinary light which had suddenly appeared and illumined his path. That night the usual hauntings went on.

On the morning of April 8th, Andrew Mackie found a letter in the farmyard, written and sealed with blood. The back carried this message:

'3 years thou shalt have to repent a nett [and know] it well!'

Inside he read:

'Woe be to thee Scotland Repent and tak warning for the doors of haven ar all Redy bart [Heaven are already barred] against thee, I am sent for a Warning to thee to flee to God yet troublt shall this man be for twenty days repent repent repent Scotland or else thou shall . . .'

Here the warning broke off. A secret murder being now suspected, the civil magistrate ordered all persons who had lived at Ringcroft since it was built, twenty-eight years previously, to appear before Charles Maclellan and the minister; they had to touch the bones in proof of their innocence. All passed the ordeal without flinching.

On April 9th, the letter and the package went to another meeting of ministers, at Kirkcudbright. These chose five representatives to accompany the Revd. Alexander Telfair to Ringcroft, and there spend as much time as they could spare in prayer and fasting. The Revd. Andrew Ewart did not come forward again, but the Revd. John Murdo went, together with the Revds. James Monteith of Borgue, Samuel Spalding of Parton, William Falconer of Kelton, and James Macmillan (parish not named).

On April 10th, a solemn prayer meeting took place at the house. Stones at once flew, but most menacingly at whatever minister was leading the prayer. The house shook with the concussions, and stones kept coming down through a hole broken in the thatched roof. A thirty-pounder fell on the Revd. James Monteith's back; another of about two pounds hit him smartly but ineffectually on the breast as he preached. Shifts were therefore sent out, consisting of a minister and a lay assistant, to watch the hole. Thereupon the stone-throwing ended, but the barn door was violently broken down, and the wall between the barn and the house breached; further stones came flying through. Moreover, those kneeling at prayer felt an invisible hand touching and gripping their legs; sometimes they were hoisted up from the ground. The trouble ceased at 10 p.m. (*Witnesses:* the six ministers named, and John Tait.)

Between April 11th and April 25th, the hauntings grew even worse. While young Andrew Tait, who had offered to stay in the house all one night, was walking over from the hamlet of Torr, his dog caught and killed a 'thulmart', or pole-cat, which he displayed on arrival and then flung down on the floor. Three other young men called but, as soon as they started praying together, were all beaten about the heads with the dead pole-cat. These new-comers, unaware that Andrew Tait had brought along the pole-cat, grew terrified; they thought it was alive. One of them, a pedlar named Samuel Thompson, collapsed with fright when he felt himself invisibly clutched by the side and back, while something like a hand searched his clothes and pockets. (*Witness:* Andrew Tait.)

On Sunday, April 14th, a pile of straw in the barnyard caught fire, and stones flew until 10 p.m. A ditching spade struck Andrew Mackie, blade foremost, without hurting him. As a flour-sieve went leaping around the house, he caught it by the rim and struggled to hold on. The whole inside of the sieve was torn out and later tossed at Thomas Robertson of Airds, rolled in a ball. (*Witness:* Thomas Robertson.)

On the evening of April 15th, a drover named William Anderson and his son-in-law James Paterson came to Ringcroft with Charles Maclellan. When Maclellan went home for a while, Mackie told the three children to accompany him; stones struck them as they all returned together, and boulders rolled dangerously at their legs. Soon afterwards, William Anderson got a cut on the head, which bled profusely. Prayers that night were interrupted by whistles, groans and cries of '*Whisht, whisht!*' (*Witness:* John Cairns.)

On April 16th, stones flew about during prayer and the same noises continued, with the addition of '*Bo, bo!*' and '*Kick cuck!*' The men found themselves pushed backwards and forwards on their knees, and attempts were made to hoist them up in the air. (*Witness:* Andrew Tait.) That night, the entire Mackie family moved out of the house to stay with neighbours, leaving five reliable friends on guard. The trouble at once ceased, and none occurred at the neighbour's place either. The only mischief at Ringcroft was reported from the stable, where the calves were 'cast over one another to the hazard of killing them as they were bound to stakes; and some of them loosed.' (*Witness:* John Cairns.)

On April 18th, the Mackies came home again. The house remained quiet, but someone or something took a bale of straw from the stable loft and plaited ropes with it. These straw ropes were then used in a sheepcote, which stood three or four bow shots away from the house, to couple pairs of sheep together by the neck; too much rope having, however, been prepared, the rest of it lay unused on the sheepcote floor. (*Witness:* Andrew Tait.)

On April 19th, a fire started in the barn, where Andrew Mackie was threshing, but he put it out. Sticks came shooting at him through the lath-and-plaster walls, without doing any harm.

On April 20th, the stone-throwing began again, and so did cries of '*Whisht, whisht!*', '*Bo-bo!*', '*Kick-cuck!*', also groans and whistling. Yet the ghost now spoke articulately with 'Take you that!' when a stone hit anyone, or 'Take you that till you git more!' if a second shot were on the way. (*Witness:* John Tait.)

Between April 21st and April 23rd, stones flew, sticks struck, and peat dust peppered everyone's eyes, especially during prayer.

On April 24th, which the minister had appointed a day of humiliation for the parish, stones flew 'without intermission from morning till night, with such cruelty and force that all in the house feared they should be killed.'

On April 25th, the hauntings continued all night.

On the evening of April 26th, stones flew as usual, and several knocks sounded from a chest, as though someone were asking for admittance. Then a voice was heard saying: 'You are all witches and rooks [ruffians], whom I shall take to Hell!'

The company decided that if the ghost had any message to give, now was the time: so they awakened the sleeping Andrew Mackie, who heard a voice saying: 'Thou shalt be troubled till Tuesday.'

He asked boldly: 'Who gave thee this commission?'

The reply came: 'God gave me a commission, and I am sent to warn the land to repent; for a judgement is to come, if the land do not quickly repent!'

The voice further ordered Mackie to spread this message, or it would be the worse for him, adding: 'And if the land do not repent, I will arise and go to my father, from whom I shall get a commission to return with an hundred worse than myself. Then will we trouble every particular family in the land!'

Mackie turned to his companions saying: 'If I should tell this, I would not be believed!'

The voice answered: 'Bring betters: fetch the minister of the parish and two honest men upon Tuesday's night, and I shall declare before them what I have to say.' Then, changing its tone, it continued: 'Praise me, and I will whistle to you; worship me, and I will trouble you no more!'

Mackie cried: 'The Lord who delivered the three children out of the fiery furnace, deliver me and mine this night from the temptations of Satan!'

The voice sneered: 'You might as well have said "Shadrach, Meshach, Abednego." '

Another member of the Telfair clan, James Telfair in Buittle, interrupted Mackie when he was justifying his scriptural use of the word 'children,' but the voice reproved him: 'You are basely bred, meddling in other men's discourse wherein you are not concerned!'

Then it warned Mackie: 'Remove your goods, for I will burn the house!'

Mackie prayed: 'The Lord stop Satan's fury and hinder him of his designs!'

But the voice had the last word: 'I will do it or [unless] you shall guide [manage the affair] well!'

(*Witnesses:* John Tait; and others unnamed.)

On April 27th, the house caught fire several times.

On Sunday, April 28th, fresh attempts at arson were made from dawn to dusk; as soon as the flames had been extinguished in one part of the house, another part caught. The end wall then collapsed; so the family moved to the stable, where they cooked their meal. That night, one of the children felt himself seized by the neck and shoulders and hauled out of bed. A tree trunk as big as a ploughbeam rose in the air above the three of them, and a voice cried: 'If I had a commission I would brain them!' (*Witnesses:* William Macminn and John Crosby.)

On April 29th, fire broke out in the house so often that Andrew Mackie grew weary of quenching it, and poured water on the hearth; so that the nearest source of fire was Colline, a quarter of a mile off. Yet flames continued to spring up. (*Witnesses:* Charles Maclellan and John Cairns.)

About noon, as Mackie was threshing in the barn, he heard a whisper from the wall: 'Andrew, Andrew!'

Mackie made no answer.

The voice, now austere and angry, cried: 'Speak!'

Mackie remained silent.

The voice then said mildly: 'Be not troubled! Thou shalt have no more trouble except some casting of stones upon Tuesday, to fulfil the promise. . . . Take away your straw!'

At 11 p.m., the minister visited the house, and, as he sat down by the hearth, two pebbles dropped beside him; but the spirit did not keep its promised appointment. Though a last attempt was made to fire the house, nothing else happened. He went home again at about three o'clock the next morning. Stones started flying once more after he left. (*Witnesses:* Charles Maclellan and John Tait.)

On the night of Tuesday, April 30th, while Charles Maclellan and several neighbours knelt at prayer in the barn, barley chaff, with other refuse, was thrown in their faces and some of them were gripped so tightly by the arms and other parts of the body that they still felt sore five days later. Charles Maclellan claims to have seen a black, formless, cloudlike apparition in a corner, which grew and grew until it threatened to fill the entire barn; everyone was terrified. (*Witnesses:* Charles Maclellan, Thomas Macminn, Andrew Paline, John Cairns and John Tait.)

The trouble died down before midnight; and that was the end of it for ever—except that on the following night, Wednesday, May 1st, the sheepcote caught fire and burned down. The sheep were saved.

Since Scotland was riddled with witchcraft in the sixteenth and seventeenth centuries, we need hardly question the possibility of that tooth having been buried under the threshold by old Macnaught's ill-wishers; and it looks as if his soldier son knew of the plot. Why else did he not return to Ringcroft after consulting the witch-wife, or at least write home to report her alleged warning? Thomas Telfair, the next tenant, lived there without being haunted, and though we are not told in what circumstances he relinquished it, there is no evidence that he bore Andrew Mackie any grudge. The incident of a sackful of clothes left in Mackie's custody by a woman of evil reputation—a witch?—but how, or why?—and her friends' later accusation that he had robbed them, was brought up to account for the malice of the hauntings, which might have been caused by her aggrieved spirit. The minister, however, did not think that there was anything in this theory.

Though the Ringcroft poltergeist's normal horseplay has a good deal in common with the Seaford poltergeist's, it must be distinguished from such uncharacteristic features as the package of bones and flesh which Mrs. Mackie found (and was perhaps intended to find) under the loose threshold stone; also from the tricks played on the farm animals; and from the religious warning written in blood; and from the eloquent voices said to have been heard in the house and barn.

Cherchez l'enfant! Yet so little suspicion attached to Mackie's three children that two of their names remain unrecorded, and we are not told even the sex of the middle one; though he is likely to have been a boy, since he shared a bed with two brothers. (By the way, the newspaper accounts of the Seaford case contain a great deal about young Jimmy Herrmann's habits at home and at school, but hardly mention his elder sister Lucille. Did her parents, or the nuns of her convent school, impose a ban?) Mackie was, however, popularly accused of being a free-mason and of having devoted John, his first-born son, to the Devil when he took the Masonic oath; which suggests that Rerwickers found something sinister in John Mackie's behaviour. It should be remembered, here, that all this took place a generation before the reform of Masonry, at a time when the craft was still confined to practising masons and so violently anti-ecclesiastical that Kirke, in his *Secret Republic*, identified it with the witch cult. Mackie's denial of having taken the Masonic oath means nothing, either one way or another. He may not have joined the craft; but if he had, would hardly have ventured to reveal his membership, even on the gallows. And though we may confidently assume that one of the children acted as the unconscious agent of the poltergeist, which of them was it? I should guess the second one, if only because nothing particular is told about him.

Witnesses to the mysterious flight of stones—from pebbles to sixty-pound boulders, a stone trough weighing three hundred pounds, a plough-share, a spade, and other heavy objects—include the five local ministers who sign the report. All agree that the missiles landed with so little impetus that they seemed only half their true weight, and did no harm worth mentioning: even when a seven-pound stone struck one of the ministers on the breast as he preached, and a thirty-pound one fell on his back. The source of the stones appears to have been the end wall of the house, to

which the barn was attached; because this wall eventually collapsed. A not unparalleled phenomenon was that many people
were gripped around the waist, caught by the hair, or hoisted from
the floor. Raps, groans, and the inarticulate noises here transcribed
as '*whisht, whisht!*', '*bo-bo!*', and '*kick-cuck!*' are characteristic of
poltergeists.

As for the uncharacteristic spoken threats: the main witnesses to
these were John Tait in Torr and Charles Maclellan of Colline—
sometimes called simply 'Colline,' because he was the local laird.
They even attest words which apparently Mackie alone heard; and
which Mackie has refrained from confirming. The only other
witnesses to the poltergeist's articulate speech are William
Macminn and John Crosby: when once, on a Sunday night, it pulled
one child out of bed and threatened them all with a log as big as a
plough-beam, Macminn and Crosby report it as saying: 'If I had a
commission I would brain them.' The poltergeist did not, however,
address this remark directly to the children; and perhaps one of the
men, seeing a heavy log poised above them, cried out in alarm:
'Nay, the spirit has no commission to harm an innocent child!'
Because the poltergeist had already been credited with discussing
commissions in a human voice, and was probably making its usual
whistling, *bo-bo*, and *kick-cuck* noises, the frightened men may well
have put their own comments into its mouth.

Charles Maclellan being, it seems, Mackie's landlord, the task of
removing the packet of bones and flesh and presiding at the ordeal
ceremony devolved on him. On the ground that the remains might
prove to be human, all who had ever lived at Ringcroft were
obliged to touch the packet and swear that they were innocent of
murder. Nobody else, apparently, was required to swear; so
Thomas Telfair must have been the particular person on trial.
Since Redick had not told him about the buried tooth, and since
nobody else knew of it, he will have incurred the suspicion of
having himself cast the spell on Macnaught; and therefore of
having cast this new one on Mackie. But he passed the ordeal
successfully: and when the removal of the bones did not end the
trouble, he went free.

If one classifies the manifestations, they fall into three distinct
kinds: practical jokes; poltergeist hauntings; and threats, combined with exhortations to repentance. The sequence began with
practical jokes. First the halters of Mackie's young cattle were
broken at night; next, a calf was tied to the wall of the house so that

its feet only just touched the ground; then a basket of smouldering peats was placed in the middle of the kitchen. The arrangement of a blanketed stool on the fireside settle, to make it look like a shrouded figure, seems the work of the same hand; so does the hiding of the pot-hook. Neither Mackie, nor his wife (who would have been as annoyed by the loss of her pot-hook as he by the treatment of his animals) falls under suspicion; yet only a member of the family could have played these tricks without attracting notice, or being barked at by the house dog. John Mackie, the eldest son, a likely culprit.

Andrew Lang, who wrote the long and well-documented article on poltergeists in the *Encyclopaedia Britannica*, notes that the phenomena are often brought on by a severe emotional shock: for instance, in a case reported from Bargarran, only two years after the Ringcroft hauntings, a girl named Christian Shaw had been three times cursed by a witch-woman who 'prayed that her soul might be hurled through Hell'. Christian's symptoms included levitation. At Great Grimsby in East Anglia, as late as 1901, a poltergeist developed from a similar threat, but confined itself mainly to stone-throwing. Whether one of the Mackie children had been threatened by a witch, perhaps in revenge for his parents' theft of the dead woman's belongings, or whether the first three practical jokes were enough to unsettle him emotionally, does not matter much. Certainly the jokes preceded the poltergeist, though they continued to be played from time to time throughout the haunting. The same trickster may have buried the bones beneath the threshold. If John Mackie, he knew of the tooth found there by Thomas Telfair. The remains were probably those of a dead lamb.

Charles Maclellan and John Tait came on the scene early, and experienced the stone-throwing and rapping. If asked to guess the authors of the 'Repent, repent!' messages fathered on the poltergeist, I should point confidently at Maclellan. Like the minister, he believed the poltergeist to be an evil spirit, and seems to have taken advantage of its only too evident activities for setting on foot a nation-wide evangelical campaign. We need not speculate whether he projected the message by ventriloquism, used a disguised voice in the darkness, or spoke through a chink in the wall. Everyone was so scared that deception would have been easy enough. The poltergeist's petulant remark, that James Telfair was 'basely bred' for butting into a conversation, could hardly have come from any other member of the company but the laird of Colline. At all events, the letter reads like the composition of a single-minded, semi-educated religious man, incapable of burying bones under the threshold or playing witch-tricks on the cattle.

Since the poltergeist itself could not have written the letter, nor buried the bones, nor woven those straw ropes, three separate people were, I think, involved but uncollusively. Ministers, strangers, and Mackie himself bore the brunt of the attacks; the children, except for the doubtful case of a loud spanking on the hips one night, escaped. The hot stone that burned through the bed-clothes between the two youngest could have been John Mackie's practical joke; we are told that he removed the stone afterwards. It seems established that the poltergeist played about with burning peats; but probably John also indulged in arson, armed with a tinder-box, since on April 29th his father put out every fire in the house, but to no avail. The stones pitched through a hole in the thatch were perhaps John's further contribution to the fun: because when the ministers posted two watchers outside the house, stone-throwing ceased. An unnamed friend of Mackie's claims to have glimpsed the poltergeist in the form of a fourteen-year-old boy wearing grey clothes and a bonnet; but does not say where. Perhaps this was the occasion.

There remains the mystery of the small white hand and arm which the minister saw early in March. Poltergeists do not thus reveal themselves; so maybe he had prayed himself to sleep, and the nine-year-old boy, feeling frightened, wrapped himself in a blanket for warmth, stole up through the darkness, and touched his shoulder; but fled when the minister awoke with a yell of alarm.

Why did the hauntings cease? Perhaps Charles Maclellan, as soon as the message of repentance had gained wide enough currency, chose to end his campaign by promising Mackie, in the spirit's name, only twenty more days of trouble, and allowing Scotland three years to repent of her sins. This being accepted by the neighbours as a genuine undertaking, the boy who was the poltergeist's agent will have been unconsciously influenced to desist when the twenty days ended. And John, reckoning that he could not hope to escape discovery, if he continued his jokes once the spirit had vanished, indulged himself once more, just after the promised date, by burning down a sheepcote. The sheep were saved; for John would inherit the stock on his father's death, whereas the sheepcote belonged to Maclellan. I do not know whether it is relevant to the story that this final Tuesday of the haunting was May Eve, a feast celebrated by witches all over the British Isles.

Cases are known in which a poltergeist's agent, not realizing his own occult power, secretly throws things about by hand, to increase the confusion; so a single boy may have caused all the mischief at Ringcroft. However, that two of them were independently at work seems a more acceptable solution of the problem.

It is not known what happened to the Mackies; but Scotland had certainly failed to repent by 1699. Will Seaford have repented by 1961, I wonder?

6

What was that war like, sir?

(November 11th, 1958)

As a young subaltern in World War I (not yet known by that ominous name) I sometimes asked senior officers wearing antique medal ribbons, mostly South African, Peking, Burma and North-West Frontier: 'What was that war like, sir?' They usually choked me off with the gruff answer: 'Not a bad affair, young fellow-me-lad, when the supply of arrows didn't give out.'

World War I ended forty years ago today, in a sudden eerie hush, since commemorated by the annual two minutes' silence of Armistice Day. As a lucky survivor—two-thirds of my age group were killed or maimed—I am now asked the same question, and feel tempted to give the same answer. But, though our primitive trench armoury included coshes, knuckle-dusters, home-made bombs extemporized from jam tins, and bayonets secured to broom-sticks with surgical tape, I must admit that we never, in fact, used bows and arrows. One ingenious Welshman, an amateur archer, did once talk of sending home for his equipment. He argued that arrows fitted with war-heads could carry farther than the stick-bombs we lobbed by hand into the enemy front-line, and be more accurately aimed than rifle-grenades. However, the Germans got him, before he could try.

The two lines were absurdly close together at certain points; not the length of a cricket pitch separated them in one frontage, near Givenchy, which my company held on several occasions in 1915. We chalked up about ten casualties a day there. Why neither side pulled out and retired to a decent distance may seem puzzling.

But it should be explained that though the battlefront had been stabilized late in 1914, all the way from Ostend to Switzerland, we were taught, as the Germans also were, to regard this clinch as temporary; soon there would be a breakaway, and the cavalry arm would come into its own once more. Our Givenchy salient would serve as a useful springboard for the coming offensive—if it wasn't first flattened by German shells, of course, or blown up by a mine. . . . No: the clinch never got broken, not even with the use of massed artillery, poison gas and tanks. Defence always proved stronger than attack; we lost four hundred thousand men at Passchendaele alone, despite our formidable rolling barrages, and that was only one bad show of a series. In November 1918, when the Germans shortened their line and let us reoccupy a huge devastated area, they were still making us pay for every square yard of it.

The British Army of World War II was incomparably better trained, better fed, better led than ours. As junior officers in World War I, its generals had doubtless resolved never to become brasshats of the sort they suffered under. Some of these, as Desmond Young wrote in 1916:

> Had lived retired from public scrutiny
> Since just before the Indian Mutiny . . .

and were capable of mounting a full-scale attack, intended to raise the flagging November morale, across a stretch of no-man's-land marked on the map: '*Marsh: sometimes dry in the summer.*' One I knew ordered gas to be discharged from our trenches 'at all costs', though the wind was blowing in our faces. Most of them seemed capable of limitless folly. None ever tried a short spell of trench life himself, to discover in what conditions his troops lived; but how they all swore if our cap-badges weren't brightly enough polished to attract enemy fire!

World War I was monolithic, compared to World War II. Our War Cabinet, encouraged by the Gallipoli failure, had put all their eggs into one basket: the Western Front. Commanders of 'sideshows' in Mesopotamia, Greece, Palestine, German East Africa, and elsewhere were starved of troops and guns. Allenby's decisive break-through at Gaza was achieved only by surprise and the flank support of Colonel Lawrence's Arab irregulars. Thus four out of every five of us soldiers had much the same overseas service: in what we called 'the sausage machine', because it was fed with live men, churned out corpses, and remained firmly screwed in position.

From the winter of 1914, to the winter of 1918, the French and
Flemish trenches were our homes, our prisons, our graveyards.
And what were they like? Like air-raid shelters hastily dug in a
muddy field, fenced by a tangle of rusty barbed wire, surrounded
by enormous craters; subjected not only to an incessant air-raid of
varying intensity, but to constant surprise attacks by professional
killers, and without any protection against flooding in times of
heavy rain. No trees; no birds; no crops; no flowers, except an
occasional rash of wild poppies; no wild animals, except rats.

We soon learned to disregard whatever noise did not immediately concern us: for instance, the howitzer shells from some miles
away, which went high over our heads with the roar of an express-
train, towards a distant rail-head, lorry park, or rival heavy battery.
When German field guns opened close-range 'whizz-bang' fire, we
had a second or two to drop on our faces. Heavier stuff allowed us
more time for evasive action—some dugouts were supposedly
shell-proof. Casual bullets whipped unnoticed over the trench
with a sharp crack, or pinged against the barbed wire entangle-
ments but a sharp-shooting sniper was another matter; he had to
be located and killed, as a machine-gun had to be located and
knocked out. Sentries watched the German lines through box-
periscopes, but rarely saw any sign of Fritz's presence, except
wood-smoke around dinner time. Our ears were alert, even during
shell-fire, for the muffled 'pop' of a German rifle-grenade being
fired. We would look up, spot it in the air, calculate its trajectory,
then skip behind the appropriate traverse. The same with *minen-
werfer* shells. I will not try to describe an intense bombardment
by guns of all calibres. We staggered about drunkenly in the
heaving wreckage of our lines, unable to communicate except by
signs and grimaces.

Other familiar trench noises were the hammer, scrape and
clatter of working-parties, squeak of rats, rattle of dixie lids,
mouth-organ music, curses, groans, laughter, ribald talk, the shrill
cry of 'Stretcher-bearers!' often followed by 'Old Bill got it all
right, the poor bastard!' and the sunset and sunrise alarm: 'Stand
to! Stand to!' Our songs were music-hall hits, such as 'If you were
the only girl in the world, and I were the only boy' and 'Johnny
O'Morgan with his little mouth-organ, playing Home, Sweet
Home'. Or our own trench ballads: 'Whiter than the whitewash on
the wall'; 'If the Sergeant drinks your rum, never mind!'; 'I've
lost my rifle and bayonet'; and 'Do you want to find the General?

I know where he is . . . Pinning another ribbon on his chest . . .'
This last, bitter ballad, contained a number of verses in descending
order of rank. The Colonel was 'home again on seven days' leave';
and the 'Quarter' (i.e. the C.Q.M.S.) was 'drunk upon the dug-out
floor'. Praise was reserved for the Corporal, 'watching for the
sniper's flash'; and the 'Lance-jack', 'crouching at the listening-
post'. Finally, the private soldier:

> Do you want to find your sweetheart?
>   I know where he is,
>   I know where he is,
>   I know where he is—
> Do you want to find your sweetheart?
>   I know where he is:
> Hanging on the front-line wire!
>   I saw him, I saw him,
> Hanging on the front-line wire I saw him,
> Hanging on the front-line wire!

We had a certain respectful sympathy for the Fritzes—later we
called them 'Jerries,' in envy of their capacious steel-helmets—
and the 1914 precedent of a Christmas truce had to be ruthlessly
quashed in 1915. On the whole, they fought fairly and courageously; and I felt most grateful, after Loos, when they held their
fire and allowed us to get our wounded in from no-man's-land.
'Kaiser Bill' might deserve hanging as Lloyd George claimed, but
he was no Hitler. The need to regard Hitler's Nazis as a horde of
criminal lunatics robbed war of its few remaining decencies,
and the idea of fraternizing with them would have been ridiculous
from the very start. The Desert Rats were fortunate to have a
somewhat old-fashioned enemy in Rommel; but his men left
abominable booby-traps behind in their retreat, a custom begun by
their predecessors in the Hindenburg Line.

The familiar trench smell of 1915–17 still haunts my nostrils:
compounded mainly of stagnant mud, latrine buckets, chloride of
lime, unburied or half-buried corpses, rotting sandbags, stale
human sweat, fumes of cordite and lyddite. Sometimes it was
sweetened by cigarette smoke and the scent of bacon frying over
wood-fires (broken ammunition boxes); sometimes made sinister
by the lingering odour of poison gas. For rations we got bullybeef,
large, thick, square, tasteless ration-biscuits (often used for fuel),

also plum-and-apple jam ('When the hell will it be strawberry?'),
tinned butter, strong tea with condensed milk. Sometimes, for a
treat, fresh bread, a loaf to four men, hauled up in muddy sandbags.
At morning stand-to, a tot of rum for each man went into the tea-
dixie. When we trudged back for an occasional spell to reserve
billets—barns or cellars in some village two or three miles behind
the line, where civilians still hung on—the men would buy *ving
blong*, *oomlets*, and 'Bombadier Fritz' (*pommes de terre frites*). On
weekly pay-days, a private received a pale blue five-franc note,
then worth four shillings; but his needs were modest, and he saved
the rest of his pay—which varied from three shillings to six
shillings and sixpence, less stoppages—for when he went on leave
or, with luck, 'got a blighty one'. 'Blighty' came from the Hindustani word *bilayeti*, 'foreign'—hence 'English'; and a 'blighty' or
'cushy' one was a wound that would take a man home but not
permanently disable him. 'Blighty', like most other Army borrow-
ings from the Hindustani—such as *cushy*, for 'pleasant' or 'easy';
bobbajer, for the regimental tailor; *pozzy*, for 'jam'; *cooch nay*, for
'nothing at all'; and *bundook*, for 'rifle'—has now faded out of
general circulation. Only *char* remains.

I was attached to three different regular battalions in my fifteen
months with the B.E.F. By Armistice Day, over five thousand men
had passed through each of them (average strength, around six
hundred), a great many of these several times, after a sequence of
blighty ones. Only one rifle-and-bayonet man had served without
a break from Mons and Le Cateau, 1914, to Mons and Le Cateau,
1918; though occasional cooks, headquarter clerks, and members
of the Transport could make the same claim. This lone unwounded
survivor, Private Frank Richards, D.C.M., M.M., 'A' Company,
2nd Royal Welch Fusiliers, later wrote *Old Soldiers Never Die*,
which gives the most down-to-earth account of our war that I have
come across.

The expected trench-service of a private soldier in a good (and
therefore readily expendable) division, was reckoned at four or
five months; of a junior officer or sergeant, at half that. Then the
chance of being killed was about one in four: as against two chances
of blighty wounds, good for a few weeks or months, and the chance
of one serious wound which might incapacitate a man for a year,
two years, or a lifetime. Another difference between the two wars
was the immensely higher proportion of fatal wounds and am-
putations in World War I: our surgeons being overworked, forced

to operate under appalling difficulties, and still innocent of anti-biotics. Yet life in the open was healthy; I can remember very few bronchial cases, and we took careful precautions against lice, which carried 'trench-fever'. And though, in winter, we were as a rule soaked at least to the ankles, we would stamp about on duck-boards or the fire-step to restore our circulation, before dossing down, and then use sandbags as foot-muffs. This staved off 'trench-feet'. Mental health was another matter: with a few obstinate exceptions, we became jittery after six months, morose and unreliable after a year, a dead loss after eighteen months. In World War II, the deterioration would have been early diagnosed as 'combat fatigue', and the sufferer rushed to a base hospital for treatment. In World War I, nothing like this happened; a nervous break-down in face of the enemy made a man liable to be shot—unofficially by his comrades, or officially by a firing-squad. Before being diagnosed as a 'shell-shock' case, he would have to be either paralysed or maniacal.

A World War II colonel asked me the other day: 'How was it that, in your war, a battalion could lose up to eighty per cent of its effectives, and be ready for a counter-attack the next day? In Normandy, ten per cent losses were considered enough to destroy a battalion's offensive spirit.'

Perhaps it was because we were most of us serving for private, patriotic reasons. Morale began to fray only when the Coalition Government ended the voluntary system and swelled our ranks with unwilling conscripts. As volunteers, our sense of personal contract had fostered a suicidal pride in being front-line soldiers. We belonged to the trenches, we and our friends, come what might; the only honourable release was either death or a blighty one. Yet the noise, the lack of sleep and the physical discomfort often made us long for release. To attack seemed a good gamble, because in ordinary trench warfare, especially before tin hats came in, most wounds were head wounds. A rush across the open, where bullets hissed instead of cracking, offered a better chance of getting shot neatly through a leg or arm. Nevertheless, when the fortunate 'Blighty boy' had finished with hospital and been posted to a reserve battalion, he found himself at odds with peacetime soldiering. He resented spit-and-polish, he resented being marched up and down the barrack-square; he saw no point in the unrealistic tactical exercises staged by stay-at-home colonels. Hospital life could be even more soul-destroying; and medical boards were always being begged by browned-off invalids to pass them fit for active service. ('Browned-off', though, was a World War II phrase: we called it 'being fed up and far from home'.)

In World War I, a great gulf of heroism and uncommunicable horror separated the trench soldier from the civilian. In World War II, no such gulf existed: conscription had placed everyone on an equal footing. Little virtue could be attached to the wearing of uniform, especially in the long pause between Dunkirk and the invasion of France, when civilians worked harder than most soldiers, faced more responsibilities and worries, ate worse, slept worse, and in heavily blitzed industrial towns or sea-ports, suffered hideous casualties. Besides, a majority of the elder men were World War I veterans, who tended to draw most unflattering comparisons between the pampered present-day soldier and themselves.

Six wound-scars, and the usual three campaigning medals (called 'Pip, Squeak and Wilfred,' after characters in a children's comic strip) are my mementoes of the earlier war; also a light-weight trench-pack, still useful for picnics. The trenches themselves have, travellers tell me, disappeared so completely that I would not recognize the terrain now, even with the help of a large-scale trench-map. Traffic runs between Béthune and La Bassée, between Lille and Armentières. The shattered villages, long ago rebuilt, are now looking shabby again; the flattened poplars have had forty years to re-establish themselves. But I still sometimes revisit the original trenches in nightmare; we all do. They gave us an absolute zero of discomfort against which to measure all subsequent experiences, and made us all well conscious of our own mortality. Death lurked around every traverse, killing our best friends with monotonous spite. We had been spared, but why? Certainly not because of our virtues.

Though confirmed cynics, we are still grateful for this new lease of life, and live it to the full: above all, I think, we rejoice in the company of women. The real sordidness of trench-warfare lay in its being a sort of prolonged stag-party, without table-cloths, napkins, finger-bowls, floral decorations, home cooking or careless laughter. We fed like pigs, we stank like pigs, and we shared our hard, narrow beds only with loaded rifles.

7

The case for Xanthippe

Though I rely on intuition for the writing of poems and for the general management of my life, intuition must obviously be checked by reason whenever possible. Poets are (or ought to be) reasonable people; poems, though born of intuition, are (or ought to be) reasonable entities, and make perfect sense in their unique way. I should not, however, describe either poems or poets as 'rational'. 'Reasonable' has warm human connotations; 'rational' has coldly inhuman ones. Examine the abstract nouns that both adjectives yield. The stock epithet for 'reasonableness', first used by Matthew Arnold, is 'sweet'. The usual epithets for 'rationality' are not at all affectionate; and those for 'rationalization' are often positively crude.

Dear, useful Reason! The technique of isolating hard facts from a sea of guess, or hearsay, or legend; and of building them, when checked and counter-checked, into an orderly system of cause and effect! But too much power and glory can be claimed for this technique. Though helpful in a number of routine tasks, Reason has its limitations. It fails, for example, to prompt the writing of original poems, or the painting of original pictures, or the composing of original music; and shows no spark of humour or religious feeling.

Reason was still warmly reasonable three thousand years ago. Even geometry ('the measurement of land') began as a practical means of redistributing the cornlands of Egypt, which were left without landmarks after each annual Nile flood. But Greek philosophers could not keep their fingers off geometry. To convince doubters that the lands had been justly divided, they took it upon themselves to prove the measurements rational as well as reasonable, by abstract argument. Hence the theorems of Pythagoras and Euclid. Reason gets out of hand once it deals with abstractions.

Abstract reasoning under the name of 'philosophy' became a new sport for the leisured classes of Greece, and was applied not only to mathematics and physics, but to metaphysics. Abstract reason soon ranked higher than practical reason, as seeming more remote and godlike, and as further distinguishing mankind from the beasts. Indeed, philosophers belittled poetic myth; and their habit of substituting rational abstractions for gods and goddesses conceived in the human image caused a religious malaise from which Greece never recovered. When old gods lost their hold, the sanctity of oaths and treaties dimmed. The infection spread through neighbouring countries. Jesus' warning 'Do not put new wine into old bottles!' seems to have been directed against the Grecians—Jewish-Egyptian followers of the philosopher Philo, who had given Jehovah's practical laws of 'thou shalt!' and 'thou shalt not!', promulgated by Moses, an exciting new Platonic interpretation.

Philosophy is antipoetic. Philosophize about mankind and you brush aside individual uniqueness, which a poet cannot do without self-damage. Unless, for a start, he has a strong personal rhythm to vary his metrics, he is nothing. Poets mistrust philosophy. They know that once heads are counted, each owner of a head loses his personal identity and becomes a number in some government scheme: if not as a slave or serf, at least as a party to the device of majority voting, which smothers personal views. In either case, to use an old-fashioned phrase, he will be a 'mere cipher'. An ominous count of man-power always precedes its translation into sword- or cannon-fodder. Shortly before our Christian era began, the Romans took to philosophy and rationalized their politics by killing more than three million people in a few years of civil and foreign warfare. Politics were further rationalized when Julius Caesar, after gaining supreme power, established a semblance of order by making godhead the superman's privilege.

Women and poets are natural allies. Greek women had opposed the philosophers' free exercise of abstract reasoning—which was then, as now, a predominantly male field of thought. They considered it a threat to themselves; and they were right. Many important discoveries had been made in bygone centuries: such as plough-agriculture, the potter's wheel, the alphabet, weights and measures, navigation by the stars. But each of these had been reasonably absorbed into the corpus of poetic myth, by attributing its discovery to some god, goddess or hero, and hallowing its use with religious rites. Poetic myths gave city-states their charters and kept society on an even keel—until the metaphysicians proved myth irrational and chose Socrates as their revolutionary hero and master. Sweet reasonableness was wanting in Socrates: 'So long as I breathe,' he declared, 'I will never stop philosophizing!' His homosexual leanings, his absent-minded behaviour, his idleness, and his love of proving everyone wrong, would have endeared him to no wife of mettle. Yet Xanthippe is still pilloried as a shrew who could not understand her husband's spiritual greatness; and Socrates is still regarded as a saint because he patiently bore with her reproaches.

Let me break a lance for Xanthippe. Her intuitions were sound. She foresaw that his metaphysical theories would bring the family into public disgrace and endanger the equipoise of the world she knew. Whenever the rational male intellect asserts itself at the expense of simple faith, natural feeling and sweet reasonableness, there follows a decline in the status of women—who then figure in statistics merely as child-bearers and sexual conveniences to men; and a decline in the status of poets—who cannot be given any effective social recognition; also an immediate increase in wars, crime, mental ill-health and physical excess.

With Christianity, the pendulum at first swung back towards personal religion. But fourth century Roman bishops, by offering a simple faith to every class in the Empire and winning over a large part of the Army, rose to be the Emperor Constantius's State priests. They soon closed the pagan universities and took control of education. All reputable branches of learning and the arts were brought into the Christian fold, poets ceased to exist, and all schools became Church schools. Yet the Church, while basing her doctrines on primitive Jewish beliefs, and the hope of salvation, had not dared to ban philosophy and thus admit herself irrational. Theologians married personal faith with abstract reason, taking immense pains to make Christian doctrine logically unassailable. And though Jesus had warned his disciples not to prepare their arguments beforehand, but to extemporize them intuitively, missionaries and apologists were trained as rhetoricians. Nor did rhetoric any longer mean the practical art of reasoning from evidence: it had been rationalized as the science of dazzling with irrelevances, and of misleading by ingenious twists of argument. Worse: abstract theological speculations about the Otherworld, which now engrossed intellectuals, bred an unreasonable disregard for the practical problems of living. Gregory Nazianzenus' fourth century metrical homilies were considered enough for the Greek-speaking world: the works of famous pagan poets went to light fires—which accounts for our loss of Sappho's poems, except in quotation. Rome decayed, fresh barbarian hordes descended from the North, the Dark Ages ensued.

*   *   *   *   *

The Church's close monopoly of all mental exercises did not weaken until the Crusaders, coming into contact with the Orient, tapped new sources of knowledge; and until vernacular poetry sprang up again in the ruins of the Empire. This monopoly weakened still more after the Reformation, when the pursuit of experimental science was revived in territory outside the Pope's control. The Church, having frozen her dogma a thousand years before, failed to check, or even keep track of, new scientific heresies. Nevertheless, she still applied a severe censorship within her own realm. As late as 1632, Galileo was imprisoned by Papal authority for endorsing a heretical German view that the Earth goes round the Sun, and not contrariwise: as though it made a pennyworth of difference to agriculture, navigation, medicine, industry or morals which went round which! Galileo's misfortune set religious dogma and anti-religious science at loggerheads: a struggle culminating in the bloody French Revolution, when the Paris mob disavowed its Catholicism by enthroning Reason as a goddess.

Since those unhappy days, tacit agreements of co-existence have been reached between rival systems of abstract thought. Scientists abstain from attacks on theology; theologians tolerate the free pursuit of science. But co-existence is not integration. The belief in miracles, when first preached by the Church, was reconcilable with contemporary Greek thought—parthenogenesis, resurrections from the dead, and ascensions to Heaven having been widely accepted as rare yet authenticated occurrences. If, some centuries later, miracles seemed anti-scientific, the Church's belief could be framed in more cautious terms: 'From time to time, during the Biblical epoch, certain Laws of Nature which had hitherto always held good, and still hold good, were briefly suspended by God within a chosen geographical area.' This doctrine is logically defensible, given All-Powerful God as an axiom, and still prevails among the elder Churches. Even Catholic priests now give scientific technology their blessing, though aware that scientists pursue knowledge for the sake of knowledge alone; remain officially divorced from religion; and, as scientists, have a very limited moral code. The code prevents them from faking the results of their experiments, from withholding due credit to fellow-scientists, and from suppressing newly discovered knowledge; but that is all.

Abstract reason, formerly the servant of practical human reason, has everywhere become its master, and denies poetry any excuse for existence. What were the Nazi surgeons who conducted 'devilish' experiments on 'non-Aryan' prisoners—if not dedicated scientists taking full advantage of the unusual opportunities offered them by Hitler's irreligion? The first essay in nuclear warfare, however, originated in a Christian country. And as for the more recent tests that scatter long-lived, man-eating isotopes throughout the biosphere—any woman of healthy intuitive powers could have told the scientists long ago that they were playing with worse than fire.

But who cares for female intuition? Most modern Xanthippes behave reasonably: rather than scold, they shrug, and leave Socrates to theorize and experiment at his pleasure—though, of course, reserving the right to blame him afterwards when things go wrong. And who cares for poetic intuition, except perhaps women? Certainly neither priests nor scientists do. A sentimental pagan glory may attach to the name of 'poet', despite the Church, and despite scientists; but what he says carries no weight. He is not rational, but intuitive.

The word 'intuition' must be used with extreme care. Intuition, like instinct, is a natural faculty shared by both sexes—instinct being the feeling which prompts habitual actions. You see a wriggling in the grass; instinct tells you (foolishly perhaps) to retreat. You burn your finger; instinct tells you (also foolishly perhaps) to dip it in cold water. Intuition, however, has no concern with habits: it is the mind working in a trance at problems which offer only meagre data for their rational solution. Male intellectuals therefore tend to despise it as an irrational female way of thinking. Granted, fewer women than men have their intuitive powers blunted by formal schooling; yet, oddly enough, only men who have preserved them unspoilt can hope to earn the name of 'genius'.

Genius has been mistaken for the obsessional industry that often goes with it; but to be a true genius, whether as a poet or scientist, implies thought on a profound intuitive level—the drawing upon an inexhaustible store of miscellaneous experience absorbed and filed away in subterranean cellars of memory, and then making a mental leap across the dark void of ignorance. The nucleus of every true poem is a single phrase which (the poet's intuition tells him) provides a key to its eventual form. But this nucleus is as much as he has to work upon consciously.

All scientists ratiocinate; few have the intuition that will carry them safely across the dark void into some new field of research. If it were not for occasional geniuses—minds which first think intuitively and then rationalize their findings—science would still be back in the Dark Ages. Kekulé the chemist, who discovered the aniline complex, and Rowan Hamilton the mathematician, who invented quaternions, did so by sudden visionary flashes— Kekulé in a waking dream; Hamilton while walking idly one morning across a Dublin park. Later, these inspirations were built into the scientific system, and acclaimed as triumphs of reason. Unfortunately Kekulé, Rowan Hamilton, and the rest applied their intuitive powers to abstract rather than human problems. The exploitation of their findings in the chemical and electronic industries has therefore made life more rational than reasonable.

Rational schooling on the shallow level (as a discipline imposed on all students, whatever their bent) discourages intuitive thought. Our civilization is geared to mass-demand, statistically determinable, for commodities which everyone should either make, market, or consume. Good citizens eat what others eat, wear what others wear, behave as others behave, read what others read, think as others think. This system has its obvious economic advantages, and supports vast populations; but crime and sickness due to maladjustment are rationally glossed over as being inseparable from a pursuit of the majority good. Our technologists can do little better than provide the wretched, maladjusted minority with tranquillizers, drink, prisons, mental hospitals, and teams of social workers.

Maladjustment is due, largely, to conflicts between rationalization and human instinct. City dwellers are forced to live by artifice, rather than by natural appetite. And every year the urban dragon swallows up more small towns; every year wider agricultural areas are industrialized. Not that old-fashioned country-folk are demonstrably happier than well-adjusted city-dwellers—who have grown so used to their surroundings that they find the taste of fresh milk and farmhouse bread positively repulsive, and feel ill at ease in antiquated crooked houses. But humane, creative thought, which depends on intuition, withers under the abstract rule of urban reason.

Myself, I left the city long ago and, whenever I return on a visit, find medicine, art, literature and entertainment still further rationalized. Too few physicians practise the intuitive diagnosis that used to be expected from every medical man while medicine was still a calling rather than a business. Too many young painters have decided that there is no escape from commercial art but to go non-representational; and non-representational art, once the prerogative of wild men, has therefore turned academic. Literature is a trade: 'creative writing' courses supply the know-how. Organized entertainment rests on a pseudo-science of audience-reaction—an axiom of which is that the public should have its drama, sentiment and humour as hygienically and economically processed as its food.

Our predicament is technological maturity linked with emotional immaturity. While the scientific world needs intuitive thinking for further progress, the world of politics demands a purely rational approach to life, and rejects all reasonable intuitions of a humaner sort. Efforts to save mankind from near-suicide made by the United Nations and lesser philanthropic groups are too impersonally expressed to be of much avail; nor have women been given an opportunity, even at this late stage, to exert an influence commensurate with their numbers and wealth. The truth is that politicians, salesmen, priests, teachers and scientists are (often against their private conscience) forcibly banded together in the public interest against all who demand personal liberty of thought. Thus, if catastrophe finally halts the blind progress of rationalization. . . . But this is a favourite field of science-fiction, and better left untrod.

Meanwhile the few remaining poets are pledged, by the age-old loyalty which they owe their Muse-goddess, to resist all pressure from mechanistic philosophy. I should not claim, as Shelley did, that poets are the 'law-givers of mankind'; but some still uphold the principle of imaginative freedom. Socrates was perhaps aware of this peculiarity when he banned poets from his humourless Republic—I even wonder whether it may not have been the cause of Xanthippe's quarrel with him. Did a dialogue, unrecorded by

Plato, take place perhaps between Socrates and an angry, unyield-
ing poet, Xanthippe's lover—in which the honours went elsewhere?

I am no outlaw by temperament; I simply suffer from a poetic
obsession which an increasing number of reasonable people share
with me. Poetry, for us, means not merely poems but a peculiar
attitude to life. Though philosophers like to define poetry as
irrational fancy, for us it is a practical, humorous, reasonable way
of being ourselves. Of never acquiescing in a fraud; of never
accepting the second-rate in poetry, painting, music, love, friends.
Of safeguarding our poetic institutions against the encroachments
of mechanized, insensate, inhumane, abstract rationality.

8

The Lost Atlantis

(1967)

Atlantis is, I think, the most romantic place-name in English literature as it was in Greek and Latin: perhaps because, unlike Paradise, the Land of Perpetual Youth, the Isles of the Blessed and so on, it has always claimed a genuine geographical existence. I fell under the Atlantian spell as a small boy by reading an early example of science fiction, in the Jules Verne tradition, called *The Crystal City under the Sea*. It described a visit by diving-bell to an immense glass palace where the primitive Atlantians had retreated from the Deluge that overwhelmed their country, and where a few of their descendants still somehow survived in cultured ease under fifty fathoms of Atlantic Ocean. I believed it whole-heartedly.

It was Solon, one of the 'Seven Sages', a tricky Athenian merchant of the seventh century B.C., who after taking to politics and somehow winning a reputation of veracity and virtue, not only put Atlantis on the map—I mean this literally—but wrote its epic history. A couple of centuries later the philosopher Plato picked up the story and used it as a main theme in two of his Socratic dialogues. And because Plato, his master Socrates, and his pupil Aristotle eventually became buttresses of the whole European academic system, the Atlantis theme has remained in the public eye ever since. It is remarkable how many professional mediums remember previous incarnations as priestesses there.

New theories about its geographical position are constantly proposed. The latest such venture comes from an American: Dr. James Mavor of the Woods Hole Oceanographic Institute who has now boldly identified the continent of Atlantis with the Aegean island of Santorin, originally named Thera, which was shattered in the late Minoan period by a monstrous volcanic eruption. He has supported his theory by quoting Professor Galanopoulos's very reasonable suggestion that the widespread Minoan Empire based on Crete was destroyed by the Thera eruption when enormous waves from only sixty miles to the north wrecked all its fleets and coastal cities. Professor Galanopoulos is a Greek seismologist. Dr. Mavor seems also in all probability to have read an anonymous article published in the London *Times* of February 19th, 1909, and titled 'The Lost Continent', where Crete is first identified with the submerged Atlantis. Nevertheless, I believe him to be mistaken.

According to Greek historical tradition, Atlantis was situated neither in the Atlantic Ocean nor in the Aegean Sea, but in the low-lying Libyan coastal plain that stretches far inland behind the shallow Gulf of Sirte—see any contour map of North Africa. Four thousand years ago a great part of this region was flooded by salt water from the Mediterranean, but by Solon's day the main surviving evidence of catastrophe was a group of salt lakes, the largest of them called Lake Tritonis, lying near the foothills of the Atlas. These lakes have since shrunk to the salt marshes which formed part of General Rommel's famous Mareth Line of the Second World War. That this huge region was at one time highly populated is proved by the great number of neolithic flint tools and arrowheads which still strew its desert sands.

To suggest that Thera or Crete was Atlantis is clearly off target. Not only were Thera and Crete never more than small crowded islands, but in Greek classical times the surviving Atlantians were described as a primitive North African people settled not far to the west of their original home. A careful study of two or three ancient Greek myths would have greatly helped Dr. Mavor in his understanding of the Thera eruption. For instance, the myth of Typhoeus, or Typhon, meaning 'stupefying smoke', who was the largest monster ever born. Our authorities are respectable: the poets Hesiod, Homer and Pindar, and the mythographers Apollodorus and Hyginus. From the thighs downward Typhon was a mass of fiery snakes and his outspread arms reached a hundred leagues in either direction, shrouding the sun. The terrified Olympian Gods fled from him to Egypt where they disguised themselves as animals; but Almighty Zeus, whom Typhon had hamstrung, later recovered sufficiently to drive his enemy to

Sicily and throw Mount Etna on top of him. Typhon however, according to Homer, continued to belch fire and smoke from his couch beneath the crater. Zeus, we are told, went to Egypt disguised as a Ram; which clearly refers to the Oracle of Ammon in the Libyan Oasis of Siwwa where Zeus was so worshipped, the Oracle having apparently been founded by Minoan refugees. Typhon's hamstringing of Zeus probably refers to the destruction of King Minos's Palace at Cnossos, excavated some forty years ago by Sir Arthur Evans, and, as Professor Galanopoulos suggests, the commercial collapse of the Minoan Empire.

Before the eruption in about 1500 B.C. Thera had been a roughly oval island, with a limestone ridge, of which the highest peak is now named Mount Elias, running towards the centre from the south-east. But all that survived of the middle part of the island was an enormous crater filled by sea water; so that Thera became a narrow crescent, nowhere more than three miles wide, with the gap between its western tips sketchily joined by the islets of Therasis and Aspronisi ('white island'). The crater, now a harbour, has sides 2,500 feet high in some places, and nowhere less than 1,200 feet, though to the north it is broken by a mile-wide gap with soundings of nearly 1,200 feet. Thera has been subject to volcanic eruptions throughout modern history. In 197 B.C. one of these threw up a new volcanic island now called Old Kammeni, in the centre of the crater, when according to the historian Strabo flames shot up from the sea for days. Little Kammeni appeared nearby in 107 B.C. and New Kammeni as late as A.D. 1707. Meanwhile in A.D. 1650 a violent submarine explosion inundated the eastern coast and disinterred two hitherto forgotten cities named Perissa and Kamari, evidently of Minoan date, though no archaeologists were present to examine them.

The islands of Therasis, Aspronisi and a large part of Thera are still covered with a thick layer of white volcanic ash, a soil which, as visitors to Vesuvius know, is marvellously adapted to the cultivation of the grape. The present excavation by Professor Spyridon Marinatos of Athens University on the south coast of Thera, near the modern seaside resort of Akrotiri, lies deep under vineyards. Preliminary digging points to a large Minoan harbour city, half a square mile in extent, which must have housed thirty thousand people. Dr. Mavor, who was Professor Marinatos's guest for a week there, is not in any way responsible for the venture. Some remarkably well preserved wooden houses were

found, they say, three stories in height, like the street-façade
shown on a plaque from Cnossos, and contain quantities of
furniture. No skeletons, jewels or precious metals, however, have
so far come to light: which suggests that the inhabitants had been
given warning and got away in time. I remember, some sixty
years ago, reading a contemporary newspaper account of the Mont
Pelée explosion on the island of Martinique, according to which
an old Carib woman had informed the Governor that a cold spring
on the mountain was flowing with hot water, which showed that
the Goddess of the mountain was angry with him. Thermal
springs are still common on Thera: and the priests of Thera may
well have had similar foreknowledge of the eruption, besides
earth tremors, and finally warned the inhabitants to flee with the
divine images while they still could. The island clearly possessed
a huge fleet to support so large a population and the refugees
probably steered for Egypt—to the great Minoan entrepot of
Pharos. Whether or not they reached it is unknown, because
Typhon's power was even greater than they can have supposed.
The force of the eruption, estimated as five times greater than that
of Krakatoa, sent mountainous waves rolling across the Mediterranean. These not only wrecked Cnossos and numerous other
cities of Crete and Southern Greece, but also reached Egypt and
submerged the Pharos harbour works which were twenty-five
acres in extent and built in massive polygonal masonry. When
King Menelaus visited the island on his way back from the
Trojan War, three or four centuries later, he is said by Homer to
have found it a mere breeding place of seals. The harbour was
not rediscovered until 1916, by Gaston Jondet. Among the deities
who fled to Egypt from the rage of Typhon were Athene and
Poseidon, both of whom are recorded in Greek myth to have been
born near Lake Tritonis. Their priesthoods must surely have
preserved traditions of the swamping of Atlantis some six hundred
years before.

A Libyan Atlantis makes perfect historical sense; an Aegean
one makes none at all. Agriculturists never emigrate unless forced
by a natural disaster, which may be a desiccation of the land by
over-cultivation, as in ancient Central Asia or modern Oklahoma.
Or unusually heavy rainfall, such as formed Lake Copais in
Boeotia sometime in the thirteenth century B.C. Or violent storms
such as swamped a large part of the Netherlands in the twelfth
and thirteenth centuries A.D., forming the Zuider Zee; or that

turned Earl Godwin's fertile island in the English Channel into the dreaded Goodwin Sands. But Atlantis is far more likely to have been submerged by a submarine eruption in the Western Mediterranean which inundated the Libyan lowlands. These seem to have formerly extended northward far into the Gulf of Sirte.

Many details in Plato's account of Atlantis, such as the sacrifice of bulls on pillars, the race-courses, and the hot-and-cold water systems in Atlas's palace prove (as I pointed out fifteen years ago in my *Greek Myths*) that the Minoans, not the neolithic Atlantians from Libya, were being described. Nor does Libya have the mountainous coastline with which Plato credits Atlantis. He records that Atlantis lay beyond the Pillars of Hercules and consisted of an enormous kingdom with a chain of fruit-bearing islands separating it from a further continent unconnected with ours. And that the Atlantians canalized and cultivated a huge central plain fed by water from the hills that ringed it completely except for a seaward gap. One day, however, greed and cruelty overcame them, and with Zeus's permission the Athenians defeated them single-handed and destroyed their power. At the same time the Gods sent a deluge which in one day and one night overwhelmed Atlantis so that its harbour works and temples were buried under a waste of mud and the sea became unnavigable. Plato's account of the Athenian victory over the Atlantians, by which were meant the Minoan Cretans who had extended their influence to Egypt and Italy, appears in Greek myth as the story of Theseus's killing of the Minotaur (apparently a Western Semitic king of Cnossos who represented the Bull-God El) in his labyrinth. But this historically credible victory cannot have been won until immense waves from the Thera eruption had wrecked the Minoan fleet and harbours.

Plato's detail of the vast numbers of elephants found in Atlantis must belong to the earlier story—and if Athenians figured in it they will have been worshippers of the Goddess Neith or Anatha, who became 'Athene' only after some of her people had migrated to Athens. One misleading detail in Plato's account is the siting of Atlantis beyond the Pillars of Hercules; from which it has been deduced that the country was situated in the Atlantic Ocean. Corrective information was later, however, supplied by the historian Diodorus Siculus who records an early Libyan legend that the Atlantians, whom the Amazons (matrilineal Libyans who worshipped Neith) had defeated in ancient times, lived to the

westward of Lake Tritonis and had their capital city on Cerne, a
coastal island now generally identified with Agadir at the base of
the main Atlas chain. He adds 'and it is said that, as a result of
earthquakes, the parts of Libya towards the ocean engulfed Lake
Tritonis, making it disappear'. Since, however, Lake Tritonis
still existed in Diodorus's day, he probably meant 'as a result of
earthquakes in the Western Mediterranean the sea engulfed parts
of Libya and formed Lake Tritonis'. Though Diodorus's legend
of Lake Tritonis cannot be dated, he makes it precede the 'Ama-
zonian' invasion of the Aegean islands and Thrace, an event which
we know took place about 3000 B.C. and was repeated nine centuries later at the time of the Atlantis disaster.

The engulfment of Atlantis caused a grand dispersion of neolithic farmers in all directions: westward to the Atlas and beyond,
southward across the Sahara, eastward to Egypt; all these refugees taking the Atlantis myth with them. It is found in West
Africa among the Yorubas.

Solon got his legend from the Libyan priests of Saïs in Lower
Egypt. His epic poem about Atlantis is unfortunately no longer
extant. But the Atlantis and the Typhon myths had, it seems,
already become conflated, which would be natural if these priests
of Saïs were descended from survivors of two similar floods
caused by volcanic action. Their account may well have been also
influenced by imported myths of other disasters, especially Noah's
flood, for which archaeological evidence was found some forty
years ago at Ur by Sir Leonard Woolley. This flood had been
caused by a torrential rain in the Armenian mountains to the north
of Mesopotamia; the Euphrates overflowed and drowned immense
numbers of peasants. The Greek myth of Deucalion and Pyrrha
is a variant of Noah's flood, apparently brought to Greece by
Semitic refugees but coloured by native myths of the Boeotian
Greek flood that formed Lake Copais.

The Atlantian horde which crossed into Spain and travelled to
the North are commonly known either as the 'Beaker A people'
or as 'the passage-grave builders'. Their descendants seem to
have forgotten the original situation of Atlantis; because the myths
of each refugee tribe placed it under the seas that bounded its new
home. Thus the Cornish described their 'Lyonesse' as having
lain between Cornwall and the Scilly Islands. Also, the Welsh
spoke of the 'lost Cantrevs of Dyfed' as having formed part of
Cardigan Bay; and near Harlech, where I spent my childhood, a

Roman breakwater at the mouth of the river Artro was explained as part of the broken sea-wall which let in the flood. The Irish, Bretons, Portuguese and French placed their own Atlantis, respectively known as *Hy Brasil*, *Ys*, *Mayda* or *Ilha Verde*, and *Asmande* or *Ile Verte*, in the Atlantic. Until recently, Plato's muddled story tempted scientists to look for it on the Atlantic Ridge which stretches from Iceland to the Azores before bending south-eastward to the islands of Ascension and Tristan da Cunha. Modern oceanographic surveys now, however, make it clear that apart from these former mountain peaks, the entire ridge has been under water for sixty million years. Nevertheless, a legend fathered (in a play by Thespis) on the Satyr Silenus who is apparently a caricature of Solon, describes a Continent across the Atlantic full of splendid cities and peopled by huge, happy, long-lived inhabitants. Had someone once managed to navigate the Atlantic, reach Mexico, and return? Professor Cyrus Gordon's recent authentication of a sixth century B.C. inscription found in Brazil a century ago and hitherto considered a forgery makes this possible. Graeco-Roman speculations about the existence of America were made in turn by Eratosthenes, Pomponius Mela, Cicero and Strabo. Seneca even foretold its rediscovery, in the second act of his *Medea*. This passage is said to have greatly excited the young Columbus; though Norsemen from Greenland had mapped North America as far south as the Carolinas a century or two before his day. And 'Brazil' owes its name to the Irish and Portuguese legend of Hy Brasil.

So while wishing Professor Spyridon Marinatos a successful dig, I contend that an archaeologist's main task is to preserve, date and photograph finds and leave the task of interpretation to the few trained anthropologists who can still disentangle myths and think in primitive religious terms. It is regrettable that Schliemann bungled his excavations at Troy both for want of modern technical equipment and from having a greater interest in loot than in history and that Sir Arthur Evans sometimes cheated in his presentation of his Cnossos finds. But it was the careful study of Greek myths which told both of them where to look.

9

Reincarnation

A year or two ago, a London Sunday newspaper read mainly by English working people published a questionnaire in which the editor asked whether they believed (a) in heaven and hell, (b) in reincarnation or (c) did not know. To his surprise the *yes* answers for reincarnation led handsomely over those for heaven and hell. Of these readers, except in agricultural areas, hardly one in twenty attended religious services, even irregularly; and if large numbers sent their children to Sunday school, this was mainly to get them clear of the house on an afternoon traditionally sacred to marital rites. The American attendance rate, on the contrary, has risen spectacularly in the past two generations and is now claimed to have reached more like 11 citizens in every 20. Reincarnation, in fact has not made much headway in the States, heaven and hell still being an unalterable dogma in church, chapel, synagogue and mosque—with, of course, such generous modifications as purgatory and limbo. American orthodoxy has been encouraged by a gentleman's agreement between business and religion; for most institutions and organizations hold that such beliefs produce a more reliable type of worker in all grades. A small minority of America's reincarnationists, mostly converted by theosophists trading as popular astrologers, were given a boost in 1956 by the publication of *The Search for Bridey Murphy*. This, you will perhaps remember, was the story of how 'Ruth Simmons', a young Colorado housewife, gave a hypnotist named Morey Bernstein many verifiable details of her previous incarnation as a Belfast Irishwoman living about 150 years before.

A correspondent of *The Christian Century* commented at the

time, 'I met a man in a Des Moines beanery who had a copy of *The Search for Bridey Murphy* under his arm. I looked up from my plate of beans and asked how he liked the book. He answered, without much enthusiasm, "All right." When I asked him if he thought there was any truth in it, he said, "Well, I don't know," but added, "I'd rather believe in it than nothing. Hell, I don't want just to die. I'd like to have a second chance." In that, I am sure he spoke for a lot of people and came close to the Christian Gospel and its teaching of eternal life. The interest in Bridey Murphy is an outward reach for a spiritual world of some sort.'

And yet this correspondent had greatly understated the case. Admittedly, reincarnation is not a familiar part of Hebrew belief in the hereafter; but a notable exception was made in the case of the prophet Elijah, who, according to *The Second Book of Kings*, had been carried off by a celestial chariot and who, according to *The Book of Malachi* iv. 5, would reappear on earth just before the coming of the Messiah. Hence Jesus himself quotes the *Malachi* text, in *Matthew* xi. 10-11, while identifying John the Baptist with Elijah. The crucial importance of this point has seldom been stressed. When Jesus was asked by the captain of the temple guard, shortly before the Crucifixion (*Mark* xi. 28), 'By what authority doest thou these things?' he replied with a counter question, 'The baptism of John, was it from heaven or of men?' He meant, 'Was my installation by John as the Messiah, in a lustral cere- mony at which the traditional coronation psalm was recited (*Mark* ix. 1-11), divinely inspired or not?' Had the captain denied John's inspiration, he would have infuriated the pilgrim crowds who identified this martyred hero with Elijah. They knew that none but a prophet was entitled to perform the coronation ceremony; they also knew that the acceptance of any new prophet, apart from Elijah's reappearance in the last days, had been banned by an edict of the Sanhedrin some two hundred years previously. Jesus was now claiming a right to purge the Temple courts in accordance with Zechariah's Messianic prophecy (*Zechariah* iii. 7 and xiv. 21); but the genuineness of his Messiahship depended on Elijah's reincarnation as John the Baptist—another lonely and persecuted prophet. No honest theologian can therefore deny that his acceptance of Jesus as Christ logically binds every Christian to a belief in reincarnation—in Elijah's case, at least.

The English masses have fallen away spectacularly from their nineteenth century Protestantism and prefer to believe in some form of reincarnation. This is partly because the 'upper classes' have long used religion to keep the 'lower classes' in their proper places, as in the popular hymn:

> The rich man in his castle,
>   The poor man at his gate,
> God made them, high or lowly,
>   And ordered their estate.

Partly, also, because the Christian concept of heaven had been frozen too early by the ecstatic Revelation of the other St. John. His paradise was not, as the Essenes held, a terrestrial park well supplied with rivers, fruit trees and gentle winds; it was a first century A.D. Oriental court perpetually engaged in ritual homage to a potentate sitting in judgment over countless trembling souls. These were allowed no choice between eternal fires of hell and eternal choral singing—neither of which tempts the average British citizen. By the way, our pagan ancestors, taught to believe in a chilly, barren, homeless hell lying to the far north, were delighted by the first Christian missionaries' description of hell as an enormous bonfire. 'We will keep warm,' they are said to have cried joyfully. And (by the way again) Gehenna, the original Hebrew hell, was not at first preached about as if it were a real place. The prophets used it as a metaphor taken from Jerusalem's perpetually smoking municipal rubbish dump in the valley of Hinnom.

Reincarnation rarely came up in England as an alternative to heaven and hell until Tudor times, when Shakespeare's fellow playwright, Christopher Marlowe, put it into the mouth of Dr. Faustus. Faustus, you remember, had sold his immortal soul to the Devil in exchange for all that he most desired in this world. The final scene in the play shows Faustus' last night on earth. He hears the clock strike 11 and, knowing that the Devil is due to claim his fee at midnight, appeals in vain for God's last-minute pardon—for a shortening of his eternal sentence even to 100,000 years. Then he laments that the Christian faith allows him no hope of reincarnation. As a scholar, he has read about Pythagoras, the Greek mystic who preached the gospel of 'metempsychosis,' or reincarnation, to the Sicilians of Crotona.

> Ah, Pythagoras' metempsychosis! were that true,
> This soul should fly from me and I be changed

Into some brutish beast: all beasts are happy.
For when they die
Their souls are soon dissolved in elements,
But mine must live still to be plagued in hell.
Curst be the parents that engendered me:
No, Faustus, curse thyself, curse Lucifer
That hath deprived thee of the joys of Heaven.

The clock striketh twelve.

Pythagoras, surnamed Mnesarchides ('one who remembers his origins'), was born about 582 B.C. on the Aegean island of Samos and seems to have belonged to the Pelasgian Orphic cult, which flourished thereabouts. He announced himself as a reincarnation of the Trojan hero Euphorbus. This choice has long puzzled scholars. It may have been merely metaphorical, because Euphorbus, meaning 'he who eats the right food' (Pythagoras is known to have been a food faddist), was the son of Panthus, meaning 'loving thought', and won fame as the Trojan who drew first blood when the Greeks landed at Troy. Euphorbus also dealt Achilles' comrade, Patroclus, his mortal wound—Hector merely gave him the *coup de grâce*—which was the turning point in the Trojan War. As a Pelasgian from Samos, Pythagoras' sympathies would have been pro-Trojan; the city of Troy claimed Pelasgian founding fathers. He, it seems, believed that reincarnations took place at regular intervals, such as 207, 216, 440 and 462 years—mathematical attempts to regularize the unpredictable. But later, Pythagorean metempsychotics settled for 1,000 years or 3,000, or some other round number.

Most moderns aspire high in their preincarnations. Queen Elizabeth, Napoleon, Joan of Arc, Julius Caesar, St. Theresa and Shakespeare are common choices—claims which, if made persistently enough, condemn many harmless, over-imaginative people with practical relatives to the funny farm. A friend of mine, an English psychiatrist, recently had under his charge two patients, each of whom claimed to be the Virgin Mary. One was quite young and the other middle-aged. He introduced them to each other to see what would happen. The elder reacted instantly, 'Hail Mary, my spotless daughter! I am your mother, St. Anne, who bore you immaculately.' The younger embraced her new mother with enthusiasm.

Fervent belief in reincarnation, when a symptom of mental unbalance, is caused, as a rule, by the patient's dissatisfaction with the dull routine of life. A visitor once asked an inmate in an English institution,

'How goes it?'

'Thank you, sir; I suppose I'll get through my present struggle in the end. But this week has been almost as bad as Waterloo. That was a deuce of a battle, if you like! We English couldn't trust our Belgian allies, and Old Nap had veteran troops with him. If Field-Marshal Blücher hadn't arrived just in time with his Prussians, I think we'd have been knocked out. I happen to remember that day very well indeed. You see, I *am* Lord Wellington.'

'But it was touch and go for the French, too, wasn't it?'

'Oh, yes, *mon Dieu*! Our luck was out that day and I wasn't feeling any too good myself—ate too many fried *pommes de terre* the night before. Stupid of me. As you may have guessed, I happen to be Napoleon.'

'But you just said that you were Wellington!'

'Yes, of course, but that was by another mother.'

Memories of incarnation are seldom any more to be trusted than these. The saddest case I knew personally was a woman who believed that she had once won the Kentucky Derby and was, indeed, still a race horse. One morning, she fell down some steps and got water on the kneee, but hastily went to bed, concealed the injury by complaining of toothache and even made a dentist's appointment for having all her teeth extracted. The fact was that she had read somewhere that trainers always shoot race horses with water on their knees. I do not offer these cases as an argument against the theory of reincarnation, but only against a confusion of past with present. One practical problem that reincarnationists have to face is that the recent enormous increase of population means a shortage of well-travelled ancient souls for new infants to house. The problem of finding enough that date from 207, or 462, or even 100 years ago is already insoluble—unless a human soul can be reincarnated in the animal kingdom. Or unless souls like those of Napoleon, Joan of Arc, St. Peter, Queen Elizabeth and the rest are capable of several contemporary rebirths—a concept that seemed illogical even to those two Virgin Marys.

The primitive belief in animal preincarnations seems to have been caused less by a man's vague facial resemblance to some bird or beast than by the institution of totem clans. These can be studied even now in Africa, Central Australia and elsewhere; and we know that clan members often impersonate their totem animal at changes of the moon. It is still a schizophrenic habit in West Africa to leave the kraal and prowl about as a leopard or snake or crocodile, convinced that after death the soul enters the body of one's totem animal. Relics of such totemism appear in early Greek mythology. We can trace the goddess Athene's sacred owl to the owl totem of a primitive Pelasgian clan that survived near Athens until classical times. The Pelasgian goddess Hera—Juno in Latin—had a peacock sacred to her and was said to have been born either at Argus, mythically connected with Hundred-Eyed Argos, apparently a Pelasgian peacock totem, or on the island of Samos, where Pythagoras was born. This may explain Pythagoras' reputed claim to have once been a peacock. The Latin poet Ennius later declared that Homer, born on near-by Chios, had made the same claim. Both Homer and Pythagoras may have been 'mindful of their origins' as peacock totemists, though using the peacock in the metaphorical sense still current among the Arabo-Persian Sufis. The peacock, which has the ugliest feet and the most beautiful head feathers of any known bird, is for them an emblem of perfectible man battling against his earthly nature. This is perhaps why the peacock is also said to have been a favourite preincarnation of Pythagoras' close contemporary, Buddha. It is likely that the Pelasgians took their name from a totem clan of storks—*pelargos* in Greek—birds that enjoyed the same sanctity as now preserves them in Holland. In northern Greece, stork-killing carried the same penalty as homicide.

What happens to souls after death is a question that has puzzled man ever since he first became capable of conscious thought. Conscious thought implies a desire to survive as long as possible and, therefore, a fear of death and, therefore, because one can dream vividly about people long dead, the conjecture of spiritual survival. Much the same after-world is described in all five continents, and contrastive paradises and hells derive, it seems, from visions produced either by hallucinogenic drugs or by nearly drowning, or by starvation, or by severe illnesses, or by other causes that temporarily deprive the brain of oxygen and allow dream fantasy full play. Many ancient peoples, however, have believed that the answer to 'Where do we go from here?' is closely linked with the complementary question, 'From where do we come?' Thus, any genetic peculiarity in a child, such as a large nose, red hair or a particular aptitude for some craft or skill, will suggest that he is the reincarnation of an ancestor remembered as having the same traits. Moreover, families that have for centuries specialized in, say, flint knapping, or wood carving, or drumming, or medical diagnosis, tend to bequeath craft memories to their children in a way that rules out merely environmental explanation. This evidence of particular, as opposed to racial, inherited memory naturally buttresses a belief in reincarnation. I read in a scientific report recently that when planarian worms have been given pieces of other worms to eat, particular memories of the defunct are transferred to them. I wonder if that is why, in certain West African kingdoms, every new king is made to eat a piece of his predecessor's heart: to digest the royal tradition, as it were?

So we come to India, where Brahmin priests use the doctrine of metempsychosis to control public morals as successfully as their Western colleagues use heaven and hell, and where the dark, primitive Dravidians of the south have gradually converted their northern conquerors to a belief in animal reincarnation. Nevertheless, these Brahmins carefully combine it with their original Day of Judgment view, preaching that whoever breaks their moral code will be sentenced, after death, to be reborn as an ass, pig, dog, monkey or as some even less esteemed creature. The general Brahmin theory is that one is whirled continuously around on the wheel of necessity, passing through a huge variety of forms before returning to the divine source. The later Indian theologians estimate their number as 8,400,000.

The theory of metempsychosis intrigued many British soldiers, engineers, planters and civil servants who had worked in India under the British raj, though it had already reached the professional classes at home through the compulsory reading of Greek classics at the universities—especially of Plato, who accepted Pythagoras' faith in Dionysus, god of the hallucinogenic mysteries at Samothrace, Eleusis, Corinth and elsewhere. Dionysus was worshipped as a redeemer who persuaded men to purify their lives: so that their souls might rise, each time, a little higher on the divine scale and eventually be freed from the same wheel of necessity and return forever to the mystic goddess, Persephone. Plato's *Republic* contains the vision of Er, son of Armenius, who fell sick, was mourned for dead and, on recovery, described his visit to the infernal place of judgment, where souls reassemble after a stay in hell or purgatory and there choose new human or animal forms for rebirth. Er saw Orpheus changing into a swan and Thamyris, a blind Thracian bard, into a nightingale. All these souls then drank of Lethe, the river of forgetfulness, and shot away, like stars, into their new bodies. Er had not, evidently, learned of an alternative to Lethe that has recently been found inscribed on certain gold Orphic tablets from Samothrace, tied around the necks of Sicilian corpses. This alternative was to give a secret password to the guardians of a secluded well in the underworld—probably overhung by the hazel tree of wisdom—at the same time, attesting their purity of heart and demanding to be made heroes in Persephone's paradisal court.

A Brahmin friend of mine from south India, who is now Westernized enough to take an objective view of metempsychosis, wrote to me recently:

'For us Brahmins, Brahman is the supreme principle, like the Western "God". Today the central core of Hinduism is how a man can liberate his soul from the bondage of human birth and death, and unite with Brahman. Buddha, after his enlightenment, recalls his previous existences:

'One, two, three—a hundred thousand births, many an aeon of the world's disintegration, many an aeon of its reintegration. . . . In my varied former existences, I remembered such and such was my name, my sept, my class . . . and my term of life. When I passed thence, I experienced other existences, wherein such and such was my name. Thence I passed to my present life, in which I recall my diverse past existences in all their details and features'.

'Once, when I was 12 years old, I lay exhausted on a coir cot after days of fever. It was a hot afternoon and our large family sat in the cool of the veranda after the meal, the younger men dozing, the women falling into lazy rhythms of mechanical household tasks and the children playing draughts nearby, half listening to the women's talk. At this hour, very old people would wander from house to house and exchange gossip. As they talked about legendary figures or told stories of their younger days, the persuasive lilt of voices drew us into a world of magic. The sun helped the enchantment by making us drowsy and suggestible.

'A beautiful young woman named Kamala had shyly joined

us. She was a new arrival in our village, having recently married the schoolmaster. The sadness of Kamala's eyes attracted me. She always talked softly and slowly, as if trying to recall forgotten memories. That afternoon, she told my grandmother how happily married she now was. She stressed the word "now" because of having had a cruel husband in her last incarnation. He had beaten her daily, and though she adored their child, one day she could stand his behaviour no longer. Hugging the infant to her breast, she had walked to a deep well and drowned them both. Kamala shuddered as her story ended. She was worried that she might not have a child in her new incarnation—a child by an affectionate husband, for a change. After studying her face closely, I believed her story. A year or two later, I decided to test it by making secret inquiries in the distant village that she had named. There I found that the suicide story was true and that the husband had recently died. Kamala had never tried to meet him again since her death.

'Many similar stories came my way, always about unhappy previous lives. Some were factually verifiable, but in no case did anyone claim to have reached old age or died a natural death. Though I could not mistake the sincerity of the narrators, who always spoke of the past with detachment, neither could I persuade myself that they had been personally active in the scenes they described.'

My Brahmin friend has here, unwittingly, perhaps, accounted for the widespread Indian belief in metempsychosis. As a child, Kamala may have been half-asleep one day at the village gossip hour and overheard the suicide story from a visitor. Which brings up the famous case—I think it was reported by Jung—of the ignorant servant girl who talked Hebrew in a hypnotic trance. She was discovered to have been formerly employed by a rabbi, who had recited the Talmud aloud at night in his study downstairs. Her drowsy mind had acted like a tape recorder and she remembered reams of rabbinical comment, though not in the least knowing what the words meant. Kamala's mind may have acted similarly, except that the story was told in her own language, so that the meaning had impressed itself on her. And just as American or English children will cast themselves imaginatively as the heroes or heroines of fairy tales, so Kamala had identified herself with the drowned woman and used the reincarnation theory to support her claim.

So we return to Bridey Murphy, whose story was obviously not fiction invented by Ruth Simmons. My guess is that she had overheard in childhood some old woman, perhaps her grandmother, retelling what she had heard from some other old woman. The tape recording made by Morey Bernstein points clearly in this direction, because though, under hypnotism, she talked with a brogue in describing her supposed preincarnation, the language she used was of too late a date to have come from Bridey herself. My eye balked at the words "camisoles" and "candy" in the year 1806, the date that Ruth gave, which was far too early for camisoles, especially in Northern Ireland—the first recorded mention of them appears in *The Gentleman's Magazine*, published in London ten years later; and "candy" as a general term for sweetstuffs is an American, not an early Irish, usage. Which means that we are hearing her story at second or third hand. So I am not surprised to learn that St. Theresa's Church at Belfast, where Bridey claimed to have been married, was not built until 1911; and that Queen's University, where her husband is said to have taught, was still Queen's College in his day, not having been raised to university status until 1908. Morey Bernstein wrote *The Search for Bridey Murphy* as an exposition of the paranormal powers of the mind under hypnotism, but succeeded in proving only what was already known; namely, that hypnotism can uncover lost memories— among them, casual conversations overheard in sleep.

The receptive mind, of course, is occasionally granted visions of the past, as many well-attested ghost stories have proved. But these phenomena seem to depend on the so-called 'gramophone theory' of ghosts, meaning that any excessive emotion of terror or grief can be impressed on a building and reawakened years later in the mind of a sensitive visitor, especially if the weather and the hour correspond with the original occasion.

In 1926, I wrote a poem called *The Castle*, which recorded a childhood nightmare of being unable to escape from a ruined castle court.

> Walls, mounds, enclosing corrugations
> Of darkness, moonlight on dry grass.
> Walking this courtyard, sleepless, in fever;
> Planning to use—but by definition
> There's no way out, no way out—
> Rope ladders, balks of timber, pulleys,

A rocket whizzing over the walls and moat—
Machines easy to improvise.
                              No escape,
No such thing; to dream of new dimensions,
Cheating checkmate by painting the king's robe
So that he slides like a queen;
Or to cry, 'Nightmare, nightmare!'
Like a corpse in the cholera pit
Under a load of corpses;
Or to run the head against these blind walls,
Enter the dungeon, torment the eyes
With apparitions chained two and two,
And go frantic with fear—
To die and wake up sweating by moonlight
In the same courtyard, sleepless as before.

One afternoon, sixteen years later, I visited Berry Pomeroy Castle in Devonshire. This was during the Second World War, and I found it closed to visitors, except in the mornings; but a worn track ran under the main gate and I wriggled in. Though overcome by a nameless horror, I resolutely visited the dungeons, until I could stand the strain no longer and hared back to safety. Two days later, my wife and I were visited by Mr. Beer, husband of my local typist. We gave him tea and he casually asked whether I knew the Berry Pomeroy Castle. Yes, indeed I did. 'Well, what do you make of this?' he asked, showing me a photograph, and added: 'I don't know how this woman came into the picture. I didn't see anyone around at the time. It looks like she's leading a dog on a string. I was there last Sunday morning with the wife. Would you like to keep it as a curiosity?'

The photograph showed a tall, thin woman in fourteenth century costume, walking past the gate that I had wriggled under—and leading a small ape on a chain. When Mr. Beer had gone, I burned the photograph. It was too horrible. But, fortunately, my wife will testify to the woman and the ape. I recalled the Elizabethan phrase 'To lead apes in hell'. Shakespeare used it in *Much Ado About Nothing*—meaning to be a passionate woman cheated of her sex life. And I concluded that Mr. Beer, a simple soul, had felt the presence of that unhappy woman in the castle court and somehow impressed the picture on his sensitive camera plate. But, if so, who was she? She had nothing to do with me.

Years later, I read that Isabella of France, Edward II's widow, had spent some years at Berry Pomeroy. As a young woman, after providing the throne with an heir apparent, she had been neglected by her homosexual husband in favour of his boyfriend, Piers Gaveston. Eventually, she deposed him with French help, procured his murder and put her son, Edward III, on the throne. He did not, however, prove grateful, but in the end sent her off, under guard to various castle keeps remote from London; until, after many years of 'leading apes in hell', she took the veil of the Order of St. Clara. Had I been an Indian, I might well have claimed a preincarnation as Isabella. But being myself, I accounted otherwise for my feelings of fear at Berry Pomeroy and for *The Castle* poem. As a child, I had spent most of my summer holidays in North Wales, near Harlech Castle, which had been built in the thirteenth century by Edward II's father: an immense, scary, moated pile, closely resembling Berry Pomeroy. We children were always afraid of getting locked up there at nightfall by the deaf old castle-keeper, Mr. Richard Jones, while we were playing hide-and-seek in its towers and dungeons. In fact, Mr. Beer's photograph had been no more than a strange coincidence.

A story: A devout widow once got in touch with her dead husband at a spiritistic séance. A loose liver, he had finally been shot by a jealous husband. The widow at once recognized his voice and said anxiously, 'Oh, darling, how are you? I've been so worried. That dreadful hell. . . .' 'I'm fine?' he answered. 'I'm in clover—literally. My! You'd love it here. Beautiful blue river, glorious green meadows, sun blazing down and me surrounded by the most beautiful cows you've ever seen in your life—so sleek and graceful and charming!' She gasped and ventured doubtfully, 'Oh, I *am* so relieved, Charles! But, honestly, I hadn't realized that there were any *cows* in heaven.'

'Who told you that I was in heaven, stupid? I'm stud bull at a farm of pedigree Jerseys beside the old Mississippi. Having a whale of a time, too.'

The simplest and most obvious argument against metempsychosis is that memories of preincarnation depend on the human mind, that the mind depends on its brain, that the brain depends on its body and that the body depends on its racial history and genes. It is difficult to accept that Pythagoras actually remembered having been, as he claimed, a merchant and a prostitute; or that, Empedocles, the fifth century B.C. Sicilian, remembered having been a simple village girl at one time, a mindless fish at another and a bodiless bush at a third. But Pythagoras may easily at some time or other have imagined himself a merchant or a prostitute by feeling a sudden flash of sympathy for members of those un-mystical callings. And Empedocles may have stood still in a forest one day, rooted to the spot by meditation, and felt like a bush; or have swum thoughtlessly in the sea and felt like a fish.

Human reactions to danger are often archaic instincts, meaning inherited memories, as when a bomb falls through the roof of a building and explodes and the shock survivors absurdly try to scratch a hole through the tiles with their nails—because their remote ancestors would have acted like that in some stage of the human evolution from three-eyed lizard to hominoid. Neverthe-less, the common flying dream is no proof that the dreamer was ever a bird; or, indeed, that any of his ancestors were, since palaeon-tologists deny this link in our evolutionary chain. It seems to be either metaphorical of a wish to fly away from our present cir-cumstances or else—since time is only a convention and memory works both ways; either as reminiscence or as prophetic anticipa-tion—of a future age when human beings will develop wings, as birds once did, and dispense with balloons, planes and rockets.

10

The 'New English Bible'

Dr. C. H. Dodd, Director of the *New English Bible*, explains that the Revised Version (1881–95) had not ousted the King James Bible from Church use by the time that its own copyright was about to lapse, though fresh textual discoveries had already put certain passages out of date. In 1938, therefore, the University Presses of Oxford and Cambridge, as copyright holders, decided to forestall rival publishers by asking scholars to submit specimen pages of a new Revised Version. These specimens did not pass muster, war broke out, and no more was heard of the project until May 1946, when the Church of Scotland made a bold move. Her General Assembly sent a memorandum to other Protestant Churches, suggesting that the King James Version had grown too archaic for further amendment and that a new authoritative translation should be published in current English for the 'wider public'—meaning, perhaps, non-churchgoing Christians. They persuaded the Church of England, the Methodist Church, the Congregational Union, the Baptist Union, the Presbyterian Church of England, the Society of Friends, the Churches in Wales, the Churches in Ireland, the British and Foreign Bible Society and the National Bible Society of Scotland, to form a Joint Committee which would undertake the new translation—on condition that the two presses subsidized it.

Panels of scholars were thereupon set up for the Old Testament, the New and the Apocrypha. They commissioned specialists to draft rough translations of entire books, and then discussed these around a table, verse by verse, until a closer rendering had been approved by vote. The second draft went to a panel of literary advisers, who met around another table and suggested improvements in style. The third draft went back to the scholars, who satisfied themselves that their intricate work had not been undone and, in cases of doubt, disputed with their advisers the conflicting claims of scholarship and current English. Where agreement could not be reached, the decision was left to a triumvirate, who prepared a fifth draft for approval by the joint committee. Their New Testament is at last on sale, gaily bound and elegantly printed, and has been greeted with a Special Service of Thanksgiving at Westminster Abbey, to which each Church sent representatives.

Was this service not somewhat premature? After all, no one can hope to understand the Gospels (as the Evangelists themselves insisted) without first studying the Law and the Prophets; and, since the Revised Old Testament lagged four years behind the New, we may have to wait a long while for these to appear in the same edition. And, despite their acceptance of the memorandum, the Churches now admit that their work can only supplement, not replace, the King James Version. Morever, though a wider public may be persuaded by 'Bible Year' propaganda to buy half a million copies of this New Testament—for a celebrated court case and the commendation of a Bishop recently sold over a million copies of *Lady Chatterley's Lover*—will they ever take it to their hearts, as their ancestors took the King James Bible? The answer, I fear, is: they cannot, and will not.

Almost every good translation of the Bible—such as Jerome's Latin *Vulgate*, Luther's German Bible, Bishop Morgan's Welsh Bible, and the Bibles of Tyndale and Coverdale—has been undertaken by a single highly gifted zealot. Tyndale was executed before he could complete his task, but he set the English style which his friend Coverdale borrowed (1535), which persisted in Matthew's Bible (1537), the Great Bible (1539), and the Bishops' Bible (1568), and which lives on in the King James Version (1611). A sacred book must be all of a piece, as though written by the hand of God Himself; and this can hardly happen unless a man of strong character, wide knowledge, and natural eloquence, working only for the love of God—perhaps under threat of death—sets his seal on it. If scholars afterwards correct the inevitable errors, they will at least jealously preserve his rhythms and diction.

Yet it is now as when Homer complained that four stalwarts of his own day could hardly budge from the ground the boulders that

Hector and Ajax tossed about in battle. Modern ecclesiasticism cannot tolerate a Tyndale. He will no longer be strangled and burned at the stake, as in 1533, but simply ignored. If a new translation is needed, the invidious task of authorship must be shared among a number of highly placed Protestant theologians, whose majority decisions will flatten out any intrusive personal style.

The *New English Bible* is thus a literary freak: a book without a writer. The scholars who made the first rough translations did not write it. Nor did the panel of advisers. Nor did the chairmen who invited suggestions and counter-suggestions. Nor did the secretaries who took down the texts voted upon. Nor did the editorial triumvirate. Nor did the Director, Dr. C. H. Dodd, Oxford's foremost exegetist and a man of immense learning, but certainly no master of English prose. What the Presses needed, if they were set on missionizing lost Christians, was a professional writer who, sitting down alone and undisturbed, would work out a translation not merely verse by verse, but chapter by chapter: keeping his English at a continuous high level, varying the rhythms, making the sense inescapable and the style irreproachable, carrying each chapter through several drafts, and then allowing two or three learned and sympathetic friends to suggest amendments.

Granted, even an ideal modern English translation, the main virtue of which would be its immediate intelligibility, could not compete in holiness against the King James Bible. Those solemn Tudor cadences, divided into poetic verses, combine with an antique vocabulary to slow down the reading pace and promote religious awe. How memorably the sermon on the Mount begins!

1 And seeing the multitudes, he went up into a mountain: and when he was set, the disciples came unto him:
2 And he opened his mouth, and taught them, saying:

No writer could improve on that today. However, the Church of Scotland had argued: 'Better read the Bible as if it were a newspaper than not at all. Though archaisms may preserve sanctity, they also obscure truth.' Very well. In that case the Joint Committee should have been realistic. People read newspapers for information and pleasure, not as a religious task. And since subeditors pass no news items unless brief, simply written, and self-explanatory, their rule should have been followed. True, the New

Testament cannot be offered to the average newspaper reader without drastic revision and copious annotation. But we are now living in the Late Christian Era, when fewer than five so-called Protestants out of every hundred are regular churchgoers or Bible readers. Most of them, indeed, still feel sufficient religious nostalgia to get married by a priest, have their children baptized, and arrange a church funeral; yet it is not the archaic language of the Bible that daunts them so much as their ignorance of its historical and doctrinal background—which the new translation does nothing to dispel. Moreover, what they are now given is pulpit English, an uneasy compromise between ancient and modern, rather than current English.

See what the panels offer in exchange for that haunting introduction to the Sermon on the Mount:

> When he saw the crowds he went up the hill. There he took his seat and when his disciples had gathered around him he began to address them. And this is the teaching he gave:

Any efficient sub-editor would have reduced its length by a whole line, striking out five 'he's' and making it clear that Jesus did not escape up a hill in order to address the disciples in private, but took his seat on a convenient hillock and preached thence to a crowd. As the passage stands, *them* refers only to the disciples. It should run, rather:

> Becoming aware of the crowds, Jesus seated himself on a hillock, and when his disciples had joined him, preached as follows:

Or take a sonorous King James passage:

The
First Epistle General
of

JOHN

Chapter I.

He describeth the person of Christ, in whom we have eternal life, by a communion with God: to which we must adjoin holiness of life, to testify the truth of that our communion and profession of faith, as also to assure us of the forgiveness of our sins by Christ's death.

1 That which was from the beginning, which we have heard, which we have seen with our eyes, which we have looked upon, and our hands have handled, of the Word of life;

2 (For the life was manifested, and we have seen it, and bear witness, and shew unto you that eternal life, which was with the Father, and was manifested unto us;)

3 That which we have seen and heard declare we unto you, that ye also may have fellowship with us: and truly our fellowship is with the Father, and with his Son Jesus Christ.

4 And these things write we unto you, that your joy may be full.

Contrast this with the jerky *New English Bible* rendering: one of the two passages selected by the Presses to advertise their venture:

The
First Letter of
JOHN
Recall to Fundamentals

1 It was there from the beginning; we have heard it; we have seen it with our own eyes; we looked upon it and felt it with

2 our own hands; and it is of this we tell. Our theme is the word of life. This life was made visible; we have seen it and bear our testimony; we here declare to you the eternal life which

3 dwelt with the Father and was made visible to us. What we have seen and heard we declare to you, so that we and you together may share in a common life, that life which we share

4 with the Father and his Son Jesus Christ. And we write this in order that the joy of us all may be complete.

The gratuitous sub-title, *Recall to Fundamentals*, might serve for an editorial in some Diocesan Review but helps no one to identify the recurrent 'It' of verse 1. Puzzled readers, seeking guidance from the King James synopsis, will find that this graceless 'It' (perhaps the most undistinguished word in our language) refers to none other than Jesus Christ as the Incarnate Word of God! And the chopping up of a long Greek sentence has introduced a confusing new subject, 'our theme'. The translations also use the word 'life' five times in five lines, where the King James Version is content with three, and where only two are needed. Nor do they explain whether 'John' is John the Baptist, John the Apostle, or John the Elder.

An intelligible version in current English would run to little more than half the length:

Letters Ascribed to John, son of Zebedee

I
Manifesto presenting Jesus of Nazareth as
the Incarnate Word of God.

This is to testify that the Word of Life uttered by God at the Creation took form as Jesus the Anointed King of Israel, whom we, his followers, were privileged to see, hear and touch while he lived on earth. It will cause us supreme joy if all who read these words enter the spiritual fellowship which our new understanding of eternal life permits us to share with God through His son Jesus.

A literary adviser who suggested so free a handling of Holy Writ would, of course, have been frowned upon by his panel. Though a proper translation from New Testament Greek into English sometimes demands the recasting not merely of phrases and sentences, but of paragraphs, the Joint Committee had ruled that the Biblical verses must keep their original order; and that no additions must be made to the text, even where its sense was defective; nor any words omitted, even where they were repetitive.

Then take the King James rendering of *Luke* v. 12–14:

12 And it came to pass, when he was in a certain city, behold a man full of leprosy: who seeing Jesus fell on his face, and besought him, saying, Lord, if thou wilt, thou canst make me clean.

13 And he put forth his hand, and touched him, saying, I will: be thou clean. And immediately the leprosy departed from him.

14 And he charged him to tell no man: but go, and shew thyself to the priest, and offer for thy cleansing, according as Moses commanded, for a testimony unto them.

Contrast this with the *New English Bible* rendering:

12 He was once in a certain town where there happened to be a
man covered with leprosy; seeing Jesus, he bowed to the
13 ground and begged his help. 'Sir,' he said, 'if only you will,
you can cleanse me.' Jesus stretched out his hand, touched
him, and said, 'Indeed I will; be clean again.' The leprosy
14 left immediately. Jesus then ordered him not to tell anybody. 'But go,' he said, 'show yourself to the priest, and
make the offering laid down by Moses for your cleansing;
that will certify the cure.'

What is the unenlightened reader to make of this incident? It would
have been only fair to explain that the man cured was not a leper—
true leprosy reached Palestine from Syria in King Herod's days,
centuries after the Mosaic quarantine law had been promulgated—
but a sufferer from some lesser skin disease described in *Leviticus*,
such as scaldhead, ringworm, psoriasis, or a vitiligo (like Miriam's)
psychosomatically induced. Since Mosaic 'lepers' were barred
from towns and villages, 'town' should be rendered 'township'.
'In a certain town there happened to be a leper' mischievously
suggests that he had broken quarantine; it also omits the implica-
tion of *behold*, that Jesus first noticed him. 'Bowed to the ground'
transforms the man's convulsive prostration into a slow, courteous
reverence. 'Sir' is not at all the way for an abject sinner to address
God's representative; and 'Indeed I will' is wrong, since *will* in
modern English implies a resolve, not a wish. Observe the sequence
of *y*'s—lepros*y*, immediate*ly*, any*body*—and the juxtaposition of
offer*ing* and cleans*ing*, accidents which offend the ear. 'Jesus then
ordered him not to tell anybody' needs qualification, being at
once contradicted by 'But go show yourself to the priest'. 'Sacrifice' should be 'sin-offerings'. To certify a cure, the 'leper' had to
produce two sacrificial lambs, a quantity of flour and a measure of
oil (or, if he was poor, one lamb and two doves); but these sin-
offerings were not brought to the Temple until seven days after
his ritual purification. The modern reader deserves something
like this:

In one township, a vitiliginous man caught Jesus's eye and
threw himself on the ground, crying: 'My lord, you could cure
me, if you wished!'

Jesus touched him. 'Then be cured,' he said, and as the rash began to fade added: 'Tell no one of my part in this cure. But go to a priest, show him that your skin is clear, obey his instructions, and get ready the sin-offerings ordained by the *Book of Leviticus.*'

Since the Gospels were written in provincial Greek by semi-literate Aramaic-speaking saints, and have been edited with often shocking carelessness, the question arises: how far should errors be corrected? Because an inattentive early copyist of *Matthew* xxvii. 9 misread a proper name, must the modern reader search through *Jeremiah* for an important and relevant prophecy which occurs in *Zechariah* alone? The *New English Bible* withholds even the marginal correction found in the King James Version. And because sacred pictures always show Jesus carrying the whole cross, not the cross-piece only (as demanded by the Roman penal code), must this mistranslation be perpetuated?

The Presses advertise their scholars' attention to newly discovered papyri, but I find little evidence of it. I first looked up *Galatians* iv. 14 (a convenient instance), to see whether use had been made of the eldest and best text from *Chester Beatty Papyrus* 46 which, as it happens, corresponds with the Byzantine text used in the King James Version. But no: the translators had preferred an inferior Western text, and gone out of their way to present Paul's self-confessed infirmity as a physical one—though the King James' marginal reference rightly equates it with the 'thorn in my flesh' (II *Corinthians* xii. 7), a familiar Old Testament phrase implying an uneradicated moral weakness. In *Matthew* vii. 6, I read: 'Do not give dogs what is holy; do not feed your pearls to pigs.' Yet Henry and Renée Kahane of Fordham University showed three years ago that these injunctions are parallel and directed against sacrilege rather than folly. They mean: 'Do not give sacrificial meat to dogs, nor throw crumbs of shew bread before swine.' Wherever I looked, it was the same. A need for unanimity among the rival Churches, some of them fundamentalist, had always prevented the translators from effectively modernizing in the way they were commissioned to do. They had patched an old garment rather than woven a new one; though warned by the highest possible authority what the result would be.

I have heard since from an Oxford professor, with a seat on the *New English Bible* Committee, that Jeremiah's 'O for a lodge in a

garden of cucumbers!' was conscientiously translated by a modern-
ist on his team as 'ah, for a hut in a gherkin allotment!' Unfortunately, though *gherkin* is Dutch for a small cucumber, English
usage insists on a gherkin being pickled before it can claim to be
such.

11

Mr. Nabokov's
democratic eclecticism

Mr. Vladimir Nabokov, who has published a four-volume translation of Pushkin's *Eugene Onegin*, is a precisian in the rich Russian
language and further claims to have become a precisian in the
equally rich and even more widely dispersed English language.
Nobody could deny that he has a capacious English vocabulary, a
good ear for dialogue and for verse cadence, besides great skill in
handling long complex Ciceronian sentences so gracefully that his
reader's attention seldom wanders. I therefore regret to see him
quarrelling with Mr. Edmund Wilson, one of the ablest prose-
writers in the United States, however gross the provocation.

Ne sutor supra crepidam judicaret, but on this occasion neither
shoemaker sticks to his 'last': each has invaded the other's ambience. My own obsessional precision appears in these inverted
commas—or *commata* if Mr. Nabokov prefers the Grecian plural—
around 'last'. 'Last' is a mistranslation of *crepidam*, now wrongly
governed in quotation by *ultra* 'beyond', instead of *supra*, 'above'.
The Younger Pliny's proverb, jokingly mishandled by Shakespeare
in *Romeo and Juliet*, refers to the sewing-together of sandal soles
which, unlike shoes or boots, require no last: thus a Roman sneak-
thief could steal himself a pair from the Public Baths after a mere
glance at their length, without first trying them on for comfort.
The proverb means, in fact, that a man whose craft is limited to
sole-making should not judge the merits of anything worn above
ground-level. Mr. Wilson may have a grounding in Russian, but
as a sandal maker and sandal wearer only; and languages, like

shoes, should not be treated in slip-shod fashion, that is to say without having both of the user's feet securely and comfortably housed within them.

Since, on the other hand, English is not Mr. Nabokov's mother tongue, he might well have followed Joseph Conrad's example of achieving so pure a *literary* style that it set a standard even for us carelessly-speaking natives; or else have been content with Mr. Niccolo Tucci's Russo-Italian way of keeping the faint foreign flavour in his English, which amounts to a *captatio benevolentiae*. We islanders seldom trust Europeans who speak our own language without a trace of accent or who write it over-well, such as Conrad and André Maurois. I have even known an Englishman to be turned down by the Foreign Service for talking French in too Parisian a style: 'Not a reliable type, my dear fellow: obviously suggestible, don't you know.' But Mr. Nabokov has much more than a grounding in English—which gives him an immense advantage in this duel with Mr. Wilson—and his one error lies in arrogating a native-born's right, first asserted by Lewis Carroll's Humpty Dumpty, to do what he likes with the language.

'When I use a word,' Humpty Dumpty said in rather a scornful tone, 'it means just what I choose it to mean, neither more nor less. . . . The question is which is to be master—that's all. They've a temper, some of them—particularly verbs. *They*'re the proudest—adjectives you can do anything with, but not verbs.'

Mr. Nabokov's English education has been mainly American, and taking advantage of the late Henry Ford's abrupt dismissal of history as bunk, and flouting the tradition, preserved even by Humpty Dumpty, of a uniform language-level, he announces himself as an 'eclectic democrat.' 'I do not care if a word is "archaic" or "dialect" or "slang": whatever suits me, goes . . .'

No, pray, it does not go; or not very far. He ought to recognize that the reader's brain is a sensitive electrical receiving machine and cannot readily accept messages on more than one wave-length at a time, however high its fidelity. Hence Mr. Edmund Wilson's poor reception of Mr. Nabokov's vocabularistic diversity. I should prefer the form ecleptic to eclectic; it conveys more violence.

Someone has just translated a newly discovered Hebrew text into what purports to be the language of the King James Bible:

'O Lord, Thou showerest novel horrors over this earth, and its agonized cry rises up to Thee.'

Here my black-Protestant brain boobs, unconvinced by the English. Consulting Cruden's *Concordance of the Holy Scriptures*, to verify my suspicions of the language-level, I find that *shower* as a verb does not occur in the King James version, nor does *horror* as a plural, nor does *novel*, nor does *agonized*; *its* should be *her*; and *rises* should be *riseth*, to match *showerest*. My martyred hero Tyndale would have written:

'Alas, O Lord, why lettest thou this new horror of darkness overspread the earth, that being in an agony we cry upon thee and make lamentation?'

How far Pushkin himself felt himself bound by the language-level convention, I cannot pretend to know: but surely an English translator of his poems should respect it? We English mix our language-levels only for comic or satiric purposes:

Beshrew thee, my sonsy wench, thou are a proper little bit of all right, by my blooming halidom...

is a rhetorical trope known in England as *gorblimey* (sc. God blind me!). The term also covers the sporting of a hat or jacket which seems out of key with the rest of one's clothes. Mr. Wilson was justified therefore in protesting against Pushkin's hero's alleged possession of a 'girl *pal*' unless the context was altogether *gorblimey*. *Pal*, a seventeenth century Romany word for 'criminal confederate' was borrowed by mid-Victorian English public schoolboys to mean 'confederate in idle pranks'. Two generations later it meant 'crony' or 'comrade'—hence Lord Kitchener's 'Pals' Battalions recruited for the First World War—and could be applied to a girl with whom one was on comradely rather than on erotic terms:

Be my pal,
Dear old Sal,
For you know I shall
Remain your loving pal,
Moreover....

—rhyming with 'the banks of the Regent's Canal'. Maybe 'miss' is the right word for the *Eugene Onegin* context; it certainly belongs to the correct period and exhales the required aura of 'unpleasant flippancy', rather than either criminality or being a good sort. Pushkin, a contemporary of Keats, could hardly have envisaged a 'pal'.

Mr. Wilson objects to Mr. Nabokov's use of *loaden*, which, although unimpeachably the Old English past participle of *load*, should be avoided, except in either dialect or gorblimey verse, because the nineteenth century used it as an affectedly poetical synonym for 'loaded' or 'laden'.

Scrab is another ink-horn word; once used by Caxton but, apart from a single airing given it by Emerson in 1890, found only in dialect contexts since before Pushkin's time. *Scrabble* has a better history, but for the recently invented game.

Dit, for *ditty*, was once used by Edmund Spenser, who loved obsolescent forms, but never again until Mrs. Browning whimsically picked it up. Even as a useful rhyme for *wit*, *tit*, *kit* and *cit*, it (*dit*) seems hardly worth resuscitating.

Curvate is not in the *O.E.D.*, and we do not know Noah Webster's source for its use.

What distresses me most in Mr. Nabokov's defiance of Mr. Wilson is his seemingly casual but altogether wanton invention of *youthen* as a synonym for *rejuvenate* or *make youthful*. He is violating another accepted English convention: that one may resuscitate moribund dialect words, as Mr. Nabokov does with *shippon*, anglicize French, German, Italian, Spanish or Russian words that lack exact English equivalents, or form new words from the Latin and Greek—though mule-words such as *television* and *automobile* are as a rule greeted with groans and eventually converted into 'telly' and 'car'—but one should *not* enlarge the small stock of Anglo-Saxon words by spurious coinages. We lovingly hoard, for instance, a few verbs in -en based on nouns, such as *hearten*, *frighten*, *threaten*, *strengthen*; but what is *youthen*? Neither the twelve-volume *Oxford English Dictionary*, nor the six-volume *Oxford Dialect Dictionary*, nor Noah Webster's *Dictionary*, will be found to record such a form. If Mr. Nabokov's *youthen* is to stick in the language until it *agens*, he must first plant it in a song corny enough to become a top-ten pop-hit. By the way, *top-ten* is well on the way to becoming a synonym for *outstanding* or *egregious* and will soon lose its hyphen, as *pop-hit* also will. In fact, if the word *toff* (short for *top-hat* or *tophat*) is any guide, *pophit* shortened to *poff* will mean a song that one would rather not hear more than once.

In any case Shakespeare, though he has hugely enlarged the dictionary, was content to write in *The Merchant of Venice*:

> In such a night
> Medea gatheréd the inchanted hearbs
> That did renew old Eson

not:

> That youthen'd ancient Eson.

Admittedly Keats, whom Mr. Nabokov admires, was an eclectic democrat in his romantical refurbishing of the Classics. For example, Endymion's reaction to the Moon Goddess's unexpected embrace smells of the livery stables rather than of Mount Latmos:

> By the soft completion of this face,
> Those lips, o slippery blisses, twinkling eyes,
> And by these tenderest milky sovereignties.

We Grecians know that the true Moon-Goddess's eyes gaze calmly, without a twinkle; her bright lips never drool saliva; her virgin breasts secrete no Junoesque milk. But the language-level here is not democratically eclectic: for *breasts* Keats uses *sovereignties*, rather than *tits* to rhyme with *dits*.

The same with his:

> perhaps a careless nurse
> May have crump'd up a pair of Dian's legs
> Or warped the ivory of a Juno's brow.

Here again, Diana is not presented as a goddess of swift-striding gait and flashing feet, but as the same good-time Hampstead girl with the pin-up face and the elegant pair of legs. I find *crump'd* for *crumpled* odious in the context—to *crump* more usually means to eat with a sound recalling that of pigs or horses. I also regret Keats's use of *gloam* for *gloaming* in *La Belle Dame Sans Merci*, though Mr. Nabokov praises it. Keats invented *gloam* himself; but at least it was only a noun, not a verb, and has failed to enter the language; and he could offer as good a precedent for the verb '*crump*' as Mr. Nabokov can for the more useful and pleasant *rememorate*.

I admire Vladimir Nabokov, at all events, for his refusal to toe any line whatsoever except his own; and a slight semantic failure at the close of his tirade has left me with a most sympathetic early portrait of him as a curly-haired boy-dreamer imprisoned in a velvet-lined musical-box which played only Tchaikovsky's hideous, banal and insulting music at him.

12

A 'Goy' in Israel

(A talk delivered at Zoa House, Tel Aviv, to the Israel and Commonwealth Association, January 19th, 1959.)

What does it feel like to be a *goy*? Most modern Jewish fiction, or autobiography disguised as fiction, answers the complementary question 'What does it feel like to be a Jew?' The *goyim* who surround each protagonist in these very similar dramas are described objectively; but the Jewish reader and the author himself can only guess what goes on behind their masks. Are they cruel, insensitive, or merely ignorant?

I am a *goy*, and the son of *goyim*: several generations at least on both sides of the family. It has recently become the fashion in the United States for young non-Jewish intellectuals to ransack their yellowing archives in search of a Jewish great-great-grandmother. The other day one of the Lowells of Boston told me with sparkling eyes that he actually *has* a Jewish great-grandmother. I cannot make any such claim. My father's pedigree contains several mediaeval Kings of England, albeit through an illegitimate line, several Spanish Kings maternally descended from the Prophet Mahomet and—since we Graveses married into several Irish families—any amount of legendary Irish kings and heroes. No Cohens or Levis, not one! I did have a German great-grandmother named Schubert, but unfortunately she came of solid Lutheran stock.

Perhaps a closer investigation of the Spanish strain might be rewarding. Philip II—I think it was he—once decided that all males of Jewish ancestry should wear a hat of peculiar design to

H

distinguish them from men of honest Christian lineage. He did
not specify 'Aryan', because most of the great Southern aristocrats
boasted of their princely Moorish blood. The next day Philip's
Court Jester appeared before him with three such peculiar hats.
'Who are to wear these, Fool?' asked the King. 'Why, nuncle,' the
Jester answered, 'this one is for me, that one is for thee, and t'other
is for the Grand Inquisitor!' So the hat was never heard of again.
. . . At all events, write me down as a *goy* and as a Protestant *goy*:
than which nothing in the world could be more *goyesque*. Naturally,
my family started with Catholicism, but a direct Graves ancestor
was one of the two Roundhead colonels appointed by Parliament
to guard Charles I's sacred person at Holmby House in 1647,
when he had been captured; and from him descends a long line
of Anglo-Irish Protestant rectors, deans and bishops until I break
the sequence.

An early rabbi once declared that the worst day in Israel's long
history was neither that on which the ten tribes were carried off
into captivity, nor those on which Solomon's and Zerubbabel's
Temples went up in flames. It was the day when a group of
seventy-two Alexandrian Sages (whom for some unaccountable
reason we *goyim* call the 'Septuagint', or 'Seventy') translated
your Hebrew Scriptures into Greek. That makes sense. Israel's
very personal religious archives—containing frequent confessions
of her backslidings into idolatry, and gloomy records of her casti-
gations—passed into enemy hands; with the eventual result that
Christian *goyim*, who cannot pretend even to be sons of Abraham,
claim the God of Israel as their God and the Scriptures as their
own Holy Writ; denying you stiff-necked and rebellious Jews any
hope of the eventual salvation that your own Prophets had held
out to you! And the Moslem *goyim* refuse you admittance to the
Cave of Machpelah at Hebron, bought with solid cash, where
Abraham, Isaac and Jacob are interred!

An equally bad day for us *goyim* was that on which the Latin
Bible first appeared in English translation. The Puritanism which
this publication induced proved a severer blow to us than King
Harold's defeat at Hastings in 1066, or the revolt of the American
colonies in 1776. Puritanism set my ancestors off their balance—
because the Bible (here at least I agree with the Catholic priesthood) is a most dangerous book for private reading by people
of limited education—and England has never recovered from
the widespread mental disorder that resulted. The real trouble

lay in having adopted a cult which did not make simple, homely national sense.

For several centuries before all this Protestant Bible-reading started, Catholicism had been a way of life rather than a religion, a prolongation of as much Graeco-Roman culture as the barbarians had spared; and fitted Europe like an old shoe. The heel might be split, the sole might let in water, but it was wearable. The princes of the Church had allied themselves with temporal monarchs, grown rich, studied Classical rhetoric, attended to their ritual duties; but interfered little with pagan holidays, customs, and popular traditions. If the people kept quiet, paid tithes, and reverenced the clergy, that was religion enough: masses were said in Latin, which they did not understand, and the priest discouraged any close interest in theology—promising that he would see them all safely to Heaven.

In 1534, when Henry VIII broke with Rome, he did so for political, not religious reasons. In fact, he was orthodox enough to have won the title 'Defender of the Faith' from the Pope himself. But Henry would never have dared make the breach, had he not been supported by a large body of Englishmen who, while secretly studying the Bible in English, suddenly realized the immense difference between the teachings of Jesus recorded in the New Testament, and contemporary Church doctrine. They looked upon the Pope as anti-Christ, and his open sale of indulgences for sin shocked them. Hitherto their knowledge of the Scriptures had been carefully regulated. The priest chose only the more edifying passages for his commentaries; now at last both Testaments lay at their private disposal.

Soon a multitude of non-conforming sects sprang up. Since the monarchy lagged behind these in theological speculation, and maintained the Divine Right of Kings, civil war became unavoidable. And representatives of such extreme Independent sects as Anabaptists, Old Brownists, Traskites, Anti-Scripturists, Familists, Soul-Sleepers, Questionists, Seekers, Chiliasts and Sebaptists— formed the fanatic Puritan spearhead. King Charles' imprisonment and execution followed as a corollary.

It was old Christian dogma that the Mosaic Law, entrusted by God to the Jews, remained valid only until the Messiah came— that the Messiah had come in the person of Jesus the Nazarene— that though the New Testament was inspired by him to replace it, the prophecies contained in the Old were authoritative proof of his destined Messiahship—that Christians were a New Israel, successors of the Old Israel which had denied Christ and been therefore rejected by God. So my Protestant ancestors, in order fully to understand their New Testament, pored over the Old, and came to remarkable and unsettling conclusions. Some, finding Jesus to have declared that the Law of Moses would never pass away until the end of the world, now regarded Jewish ritual obligations (so far as they could be observed without a Temple or priesthood) as still binding on Christians. For instance they wanted to keep the Jewish Sabbath instead of the Christian Sunday which the Christians had borrowed from Mithraism, along with Mithras's Nativity Feast on December 25th, adoring shepherds and all. They also thought it wicked to eat blood-sausage, and would not remove their hats in church.

The most famous Independent of all, John Bunyan, author of *Pilgrim's Progress*, went further. He could find no evidence in the Bible of any curse on the Old Israel, and was plagued by a desperate conviction that, not being of Jewish stock, he would be burned to cinders by God's avenging angels at the Battle of Armageddon. These Independents, among them the Pilgrim Fathers who had sailed to New England before the Civil War, lived in constant terror of damnation, as it were keeping Yom Kippur all the year round; and their so-called Sabbaths, instead of being days of rest and joy, spread a profound gloom over the week. Even Jesus, whom the mediaeval Catholics had softened into a gentle, kindly presence, born of a gentle, kindly, semi-divine Virgin-mother—a revival of the ancient European Sea- and Moon-goddess—menaced them in dreams with continual reproaches and threats. They did not accept the ethical Law as a sweet burden, like the Pharisees, but made it a yoke of iron; and learned to hate the irreligious Catholics even more than they hated Jews. Instead of confessing their sins to a sympathetic priest, paying a small penance for a light-hearted absolution, and then cheerfully sinning again, the people acquired individual consciences and thus a soul-destroying sense of guilt. Merry England, which implied a romantic Virgin-worship (now heretical), perished with Cromwell's victory at Naseby in 1645. The Crown has been Protestant, by law, since 1688.

A story about Protestant, Catholic and Jew goes to the very root of the matter. After the last war, an American aircraft-carrier was being paid off and dry-docked. Gradually all the drafted men and

officers went ashore, then most of the regulars. At last nobody
remained aboard but a small maintenance crew and three naval
chaplains. On their last night of duty, these three foregathered
in the otherwise deserted ward-room, and the Catholic said: 'Well,
gentlemen, we must say good-bye. But first let me testify to your
very correct behaviour. Neither of you has interfered in the least
with the spiritual welfare of my flock, and for that I wish to express my gratitude.'

The Protestant chaplain spoke next: 'Yes, gentlemen, this has
been a very happy ship. And she owed a great deal of her happiness
to the way we three pulled together, side by side, each without
retreating an inch from his own religious convictions. I thought
it most courteous of you to allow me a free hand in organizing the
sports and pastimes of your flocks as well as mine; and not for the
world would I have taken advantage of your generosity.'

The rabbi spoke last. 'Well, my friends,' he said, after a pause.
'It has certainly been a most interesting experience, and I think we
three succeeded in avoiding any serious friction—you sir, wor-
shipping God in your way; you, sir, in your way—and I in His!'

What does it feel like to be a *goy*? Embarrassing, for careful
students of religious history. The trouble began with Saul of
Tarsus—later Paul—who once, when in danger of his life from an
angry pilgrim crowd, claimed Jewish birth. He certainly became a
Jew by adoption early in his career, but according to the Ebionites
(the austere apocalyptic section of Nazarenes) was the son of
Greek parents; and the Ebionites can hardly be suspected of
deliberate falsehood. His story of having sat at the feet of Gamaliel,
Israel's Supreme Court Judge, is implausible, if only because
Gamaliel required of his picked law-students a deep and accurate
knowledge of the Hebrew Scriptures; whereas Paul, in his
Epistles, quotes only the Septuagint, even where the Greek
wrongly differs from the original Hebrew text. Paul's father was
probably a Syrian-Greek God-fearer, the God-fearers being a
Gentile fraternity who accepted the Ten Commandments and
were well disposed to their Jewish mentors, but who 'bowed in
the House of Rimmon'—meaning, that they refused circumcision
and obedience to the whole ritual Law, for fear of offending their
Greek, or Roman, or Syrian city authorities. Those Jews controlled
a great volume of Roman trade, and also international trade with
Parthia, India and beyond. The God-fearers wanted a share of
this, and the Jews accepted them as business associates, though

without the unquestioning trust that they reposed in proselytes who accepted the full burden of the Law.

To judge from a confession of Paul's in the Epistle to the Galatians—'to the Jews I became as a Jew', it seems that he underwent circumcision—a *sine-qua-non* for his secret-service work as an *agent provocateur* employed by the Sadducees (collaborators with Rome) against the Nazarenes to whom all Romans were unclean blasphemers. The Acts of the Apostles frankly describes how Paul, after assisting in the murder of a Greek-speaking Nazarene named Stephen, used this breach of the peace as an excuse for getting the Jerusalem Ebionites arrested and imprisoned; and how, after a spectacular conversion to their faith at Damascus, he once more changed his coat and, three years later, went about collecting God-fearers into a rival religious society of his own. Still later, when accused of defiling the Temple, he declined to be judged by the Supreme Court of Israel, which was famous for its lenity. Suddenly disclosing his Roman citizenship, he appealed to the Emperor: well aware that no honourable Jew would dare to give evidence in a religious case judged by Nero. Nor would any pupil of Gamaliel's, or any Jew with the least pride in his race, have made such an appeal. Paul's 'Christian' Church became completely separated from the Jerusalem Church of Ebionites and other Nazarenes. The Jerusalem Church was presided over by Jacob of Bethany, an ultra-pious Temple priest, whom Christians call 'St. James the Less', and whose judicial murder, according to Josephus, brought about the downfall of the Roman-appointed High Priest Hananiah II. Jacob's Nazarenes regarded Jesus as the Messiah, but otherwise remained no less loyal to the Law and the Prophets than Jesus himself had been. Paul presently claimed that Jesus' crucifixion totally annulled the Mosaic Law, and that an act of repentance and a confession of belief in his Messiahship was the only needful passport to Heaven. Mystical accretions—some of them, like the Trinity doctrine, now given a Gnostic origin, others borrowed from paganism—expanded the Pauline faith. Yet Paul's adoption of the Jewish ethic, as whittled down and reconciled by the God-fearers with obedience to their Roman overlords, stuck; and is still Christian dogma for Catholics and Protestants alike.

When Judaism had been proscribed and nearly battered out of existence, the Christians escaped by joining the hue and cry against their parent faith, accusing the Jews of Jesus' murder, and rewriting the Gospels to present him as an original thinker who detested the Pharisees, knew better than Moses, and was honourably treated by Pontius Pilate, the Roman Procurator. To substantiate the Trinity doctrine, they even went so far as to make Jesus identify himself blasphemously with God.

The Puritans could hardly repudiate St. Paul, whose epistles and life-story formed part of their Bible, and get back to the authentic Jesus. They chose a position somewhere between the Jews and the Catholics; but the diversity of their sects, and a great difference in opinion even within the Established Church of England, where they formed the Low Church party, made this 'somewhere' an unhappily vague position. Catholicism never admits any sects; one is either a believer or a heretic.

To us English, all Jews were a mystery for over four hundred years before Cromwell invited them back. They had been expelled in an access of religious hysteria: being accused of numerous unexplained crimes—especially the ritual murders of children, laid at their door, it seems, by members of a primitive pagan cult surviving in East Anglia, who actually committed them. Thus Shakespeare, who pilloried Shylock, the villainous Jew, in his *Merchant of Venice*, is unlikely ever to have met a Jew—unless perhaps a Sephardic physician attached to the Spanish Embassy in London. The tradition of wicked Jews who spat at Christ being endorsed by the Gospels, a Jew was a safe target; and Shakespeare borrowed his story from the Venetians, who had cause to be jealous of their Jewish trade rivals. An unusual feature in the case is Shakespeare's sympathetic understanding of Shylock's troubles.

Cromwell invited the Jews back for political, not religious reasons. They brought modern banking methods to London from Holland, and the City's present financial strength rests squarely on the foundations they laid. Their descendants have met with little trouble since those days, always showing gratitude and loyalty to England. Yet although, a century ago, religious toleration reached a point where Jews could be enrolled in the British nobility, and one even became Prime Minister and founded the 'Primrose League' (the most true-blue Conservative institution of all) it would be foolish to pretend that they have been fully assimilated into British social life. Jewish dietary laws, and the yearly reminder at Pesach that their true home lay far away, made this impossible. They remained guests, albeit honoured guests.

Anglican church services are very odd, if one pauses to consider them. It cannot be honestly denied that Jesus was a descendant of King David, rather than King Alfred; or that he was born in Judaea of a Jewish mother, rather than in Wessex of an Anglo-Saxon one; or that he was acclaimed King of the Jews, rather than King of England. Yet he is always thought of as a blond, fair-skinned Anglo-Saxon wearing a Greek robe, like that of Socrates; and so are all his disciples—except perhaps Matthew, the converted tax-gatherer and, of course, Judas. The oddest part of the service, as I look back to my country childhood, came when the local squire and his lady, the village worthies and their wives, and whoever else of the common herd attended Matins on Sunday, sang the Psalms of David: identifying themselves with the Israelites of old, and boasting of God's help to them in Egypt and the Wilderness. How unconvincing the psalm of the Babylonian captivity sounded from those bucolic Gentile lips!

> By the waters of Babylon we sat down
> And wept when we remembered Zion.
> As for our harps, we hung them up
> Upon the willows that were thereby.
> How can we sing the Lord's song
> In a strange land?

If only they could have celebrated King Alfred and the Danes, or the Battle of Agincourt, or something in their own glorious past! . . . I last attended an Anglican service (to please my mother) during the First World War, which the Church chose to support as a 'Crusade Against Evil'. One of the psalms for that Sunday was *Cur Fremunt Gentes?* or 'Why do the Gentiles so furiously rage together?'—an unanswered question which, since I had already come to suspect the Gospel denials of Jesus' orthodox Judaism, provoked a bitter smile.

My mother, a saintly woman, educated as a German Lutheran, pitied our Jewish neighbours for their miserable stubbornness and —a great tactical mistake—went out of her way to show them kindness. They did not repel her, but they must have read her like a book. . . . How much guilt underlay this self-enforced pity is problematical: but I do know that the chief motive forces in Protestant charity, when directed by the well-placed towards the needy or underprivileged, is guilt. The origins of our British Welfare State can be traced to a sense of guilt in comfortable nineteenth century Protestant homes; charity was showered on ragged victims of the Industrial Revolution. It took the form of soup-kitchens, free education, and the vote—as a result of which the former governing class are today being slowly but surely evicted from their ancestral snuggeries. The famous Balfour Declaration purported to be an act of gratitude for the loyal services of Jews in the First World War, especially for Chaim Weizmann's free gift to the British of chemical formulas that greatly assisted the Ministry of Munitions. But the very looseness of the wording 'A National Home in Palestine' is psychologically suspect: it suggests a sense of guilt struggling with Protestant orthodoxy.

A couple of generations ago other Puritans, John Bunyan's successors, began to worry that they might not be the people celebrated in the Psalms of David. Yet the Church preached a New Israel chosen by God after the Jews rejected Christ. 'Well, who *are* these Jews?' some troubled inquirer pondered and, on consulting his *Encyclopaedia*, found that they were the tribes of Judah and Benjamin, plus a few Levites and Simeonites. The rest of Israel had been carried into captivity and never released. 'But an Israelite, except in a fanciful sense, must be descended from Abraham, Isaac and Jacob,' he argued, 'and Englishmen cannot sail under false colours!' Then a happy thought struck him. 'We Christians are those lost tribes!' Hence the extraordinary pseudo-historic theories of the British Israelites, a sect which included a number of wealthy and influential Britons, among them (it was said) the late King George V, Head of the Protestant Church. He hopefully called his heir 'David', but David chose to be named Edward VIII; and a beautiful dream ended in tears.

*　　　*　　　*　　　*　　　*

While still a Protestant in faith as well as ethical conditioning, I could not feel at ease with Jews; but so soon as I grasped the historical implications of being a *goy*, and took pains to undo all the knots in which my youthful mind had been entangled, everything changed. In fact, a negative anti-anti-Semitism became a positive pro-Judaism. When the State of Israel was proclaimed, I rejoiced; and imagined myself home at church in my childhood, where the same squire and his family, and the same village worthies, were singing cheerfully:

'When the Lord turned again the captivity of Zion,
Then were we like to them that wept!'

—but not meaning a word of it. . . .

So at last you Jews won what you had always prayed for: a return to your own land! I foresaw that 'What it feels like to be a *goy*' would soon acquire a new sense. A *goy*, in relation to Jews dispersed all over the world, who are living on sufferance as guests in a generally hostile environment, is one thing; a *goy* in relation to a small though dynamic *nation* of Jews, based on their original homeland, is another thing altogether.

Until that miraculous day, most European Jews were taught from earliest infancy: 'Be careful! Never listen to the *goyim*! Swallow insults, keep the Law! Be patient; you are one of God's Chosen, and precious in His sight. One day He will make us a nation again!' It was a superiority complex, and difficult for a sensitive *goy* to understand. Though he might be welcomed in a Jewish home and treated like a king, with all the extravagant hospitality of which perhaps the Irish alone are equally capable, he felt inferior and guilty; because he had not suffered a million slights and snubs and insults; and because he had been faithful to his national destiny. Often twenty generations of his ancestors had been around in those parts; but the Jews had been denied an ancestral home three times as long. Pity was not what he felt towards them, nor envy—it was a certain awe. And the Protestant in him said: 'Not surprising; the Bible says that they are God's Chosen People.' Even St. Paul in his Epistle to the Corinthians had blurted out: 'What advantage then hath the Jew? Much, chiefly that to the Jews were committed the holy oracles of God.'

Of course, a 'but' followed; nevertheless. . . .

Ten years after the Lord turned again the captivity of Zion, your Government invited me to visit Israel. I answered in hot sincerity that it was the greatest honour ever paid me. Whatever vicarious guilt I felt for the persecution of your ancestors by mine, was at last officially purged. Here in Israel I am a *goy* in the new, different sense. The *awe* remains: that Israel is a nation once more, and not a sentimental show-piece either, a mock-antique, but a strong, proud, energetic, well-disciplined nation—one that continues to welcome homeless Jewish immigrants into an already crowded country, and establish them as useful citizens.

When I heard of your recent war with Egypt, I smiled a quiet

historical, neutral smile: such as came to my lips the other day
when I saw a 'still' from the film *Solomon and Sheba*, showing
Solomon's army in flight before a squadron of Egyptian uhlans.
In 1926, I was Professor of English at Cairo University, and saw
something of the Egyptian Army. Officers were then selected for
advancement by weight; and if one of them did not like the look
of a subordinate, he would force open his mouth—and spit in it!

*   *   *   *   *

My sense of awe has been heightened by the realization that
Hebrew is again a living spoken language—the same Hebrew from
which our vernacular Old Testament was translated at third hand,
through Latin and Greek. And the blood-curdling life-histories of
those who came here as ragged refugees, and can now hold their
heads high again, seem to me a sufficient guarantee that the New
Israel will endure. A friend named John, an officer in your merchant
navy, though a member of a *kibbutz* at Caesarea, told me: 'At first,
my wife and I talked German in the home, but somehow we slid
into Hebrew; it keeps us in touch with the children.'

John, by the way, hates being parted from his family by going
on distant voyages, and has no natural love of the sea. 'Then whatever made a sailor of you?' I asked.

'Dire necessity. All my family at Warsaw went into the gas-
chamber, except me. But they helped me to escape, and I managed
to buy the papers of a Polish sailor killed in 1939. I assumed his
identity, and the Germans drafted me into their merchant navy. A
week later I contacted the British secret service, so I did not have
the crime on my conscience very long. Later, I was in a British
prisoner camp on Cyprus, for smuggling arms to Israel. But I never
cared to change my occupation. We have a shortage of sailors.'

'And your salary?'

'High enough, though I don't handle any of it. Everything goes
to the *kibbutz*. Really, I'm an individualist, but the *kibbutzim*
were needed to handle and organize immigrants, and I naturally
show my gratitude, now that I'm well established. Besides, I have
few wants except books, and the authorities indulge me in those.'

Colonel T. E. Lawrence, whose official biographer I was,
thoroughly approved of the Balfour Declaration, and wrote to me
before he died in 1935: 'It is a problem of the third generation.'
If he meant 'the third generation from now' (for your Rothschild
settlements had already attained a fifth or sixth generation of

'Sabras'), he was wrong, Unlike Moses, who kept Israel forty years in the Wilderness, you have not needed to await that third generation. The first generation has speeded up history.

Most *goyim* are surprised to find that religious observance is not compulsory here; that indeed, the orthodox are a minority and many Israelis seem to be free-thinkers. But you may remember what answer Hillel, President of the Sanhedrin, gave the young Roman who impertinently asked to be taught the Law in the time he could stand on one leg. Hillel quoted Leviticus: 'Thou shalt love thy neighbour as thyself!', adding: 'The Law and the Prophets amount only to that.' And Hillel discouraged all mystical speculations about the nature of God; he held that the task of loving one's neighbour was exacting enough for most men. Despite minor disputes inseparable from a nation still in its pioneering days, loving your neighbour is the main task you Israelis have chosen; or so I judge from visits to five *kibbutzim*, where friends of mine are members. A little free-thinking, short of active anti-clericalism, can surely be forgiven.

Our British Welfare State rests on a theory of social justice and fair shares for all. But 'Fair Shares for All' does not encourage overtime, or doing without luxuries so that as many poor fellows as possible can benefit from one's own industry. 'Love thy neighbour!' is a positive injunction—like 'Six days *shalt* thou labour!' 'Fair Shares for All!' is negative.

What advantage therefore hath a Jew? Much: chiefly that unto the Jews were committed the holy oracles of God! And, though there have been saints in every land, and under every religion, Israel was the first nation to make brotherly love and mercy head the list of moral virtues. So, if asked to pronounce on the knotty question: 'What is a Jew?', I should answer: 'Anyone who feels himself a Jew and will faithfully obey that Levitical text.' All other considerations seem to me legalistic and unworthy of Israel's historical role.

13

Forgotten loyalists

It will be news to many Americans that the 1776 rebellion, by the thirteen colonies against Parliament, was no less a Civil War than the 1861 rebellion, by the Southern States against Congress. Heroic legends of the losing side in the Second Civil War are still current throughout the South, and a sense of dire national tragedy darkens such names as Gettysburg and Manassas. The First Civil War, on the other hand, has too often been painted in gay colours as an unanimous uprising of patriotic American farmers and backwoodsmen against a tyrannical foreign power. But. . . .

. . . But in 1776, the Loyalists, though not brilliantly organized like the revolutionaries, or 'Liberty Boys', were just as numerous, and drew their strength from the well-to-do, solid law-abiding classes of America. If their case earns no sympathetic mention in school or college text-books, this is because at the Peace of 1783— imposed on the British by their European foes, whose armies Congress had hired to stave off military defeat—all surviving Loyalists were forced either to emigrate or to abjure the allegiance for which they had sacrificed everything.

No sane person regrets, of course, the emergence of the United States from that fratricidal struggle; but I invite any ordinary law-abiding American—who loves his country, contributes generously to national defence, and hates gangsterism, graft, lies—to put himself in the place of a typical Loyalist.

You, Sir, are a leading citizen of a small township lying some twenty miles from Boston, and drive over twice a week to see friends and buy stores. Your ancestors came here in search of the religious freedom which you still cherish. You own a prosperous farm—the family seat for more than a hundred years. You speak English, dress like an Englishman, use English money, and are governed by English law. You feel proud that England has triumphed in the recent Seven Years' War—thus freeing Massachusetts from the threat of French invasion and the raids of scalp-hungry braves, and opening the Middle West to development. Your Royal Governor is Massachusetts-born, and on good terms with his Assembly.

American politics are an extension of English politics; you have Whigs and Tories as in London, where a Tory government now holds office. Your Whigs believe that to oppose unfair Parliamentary measures is to defend the general rights of Englishmen. So you believed, too, under a former Whig ministry. 'But, thank God, I can see little enough to quarrel about,' you say. 'We enjoy almost all liberties that the English enjoy, and many that they lack. Royal Charters let us govern ourselves by whatever laws the Assemblies frame, short of treating with foreign powers. True, Parliament prohibits heavy industries over here, yet why should that vex us? In New England, we have developed profitable light industries, and could not find labour for the heavy sort unless by importing negro slaves—a ruinous expense, this climate being too severe for coloured people. True, also, we may not trade directly with France, Holland or Spain; yet why should that vex us, either? Our smugglers fetch any goods we need that are not supplied by England.'

Trouble began in 1765, when Parliament passed the Stamp Act to cover the costs of American defence. 'A just measure,' you observed at the time. 'Remember how Pontiac and his Indians raided the borders of Virginia, Maryland, Pennsylvania and New York, and what damage he did? The English Commander-in-Chief appealed for American aid, and met with a wretched response. Some Assemblies would not help at all. Only Virginia sent troops worth their salt, but without paying them. In the end, regular infantry were left to win the two-year war, single-handed. If we cannot be bothered to defend our own frontiers, why won't we allow the regulars a trifling sum for this hazardous task? The Stamp Duty amounts to a mere quarter-dollar a year per head.'

At the same time, the English tightened up their Preventive Services. 'Reasonable enough. Smuggling has grown so widespread that English manufactures can't compete in our markets against goods dumped here by former enemies.'

You were shocked when the Boston mob from Fish Street and neighbourhood made the Stamp Act an excuse for ugly riots. Leading smugglers, naturally, were behind the movement. Also a group of unqualified lawyers, who saw their livelihood taken away by the Act—because all legal documents needed stamps, and none but the qualified might handle them. The mob pillaged mansions belonging to the Comptroller of Customs, the Deputy Registrar of the Court of Admiralty, and the Chief Justice himself, though he was known to have thought the Act impolitic. Similar outrages were reported from Rhode Island, Connecticut and New York.

English manufacturers had a million pounds sunk in American trade, so parliament withdrew the Stamp Act. 'Maybe,' you said, 'it was an error to impose internal taxes on the Colonies. After all, we are not directly represented by Parliament. But how can our defence be paid for otherwise, if the Assemblies will vote nothing?'

The Chancellor of the Exchequer decides to raise funds by external taxes, and in a manner that should benefit law-abiding people. He imposes a duty of threepence a pound on tea, a drink to which every American and Indian is addicted. The Boston smugglers, under 'King' Hancock, have piled up huge stocks of Dutch tea, and sell it at a shilling a pound; now you will buy your Bohea twopence a pound cheaper, tax included, since smuggling and the post-war slump have hit the East India Company so hard that they must drop the wholesale price to sixpence. 'Checkmate, Hancock!' you think. 'You have piled up half a million dollars since the War ended; and it was your lawless crews who led the recent riots. Now you'll sell at a loss.'

You are wrong! Hancock, being allied with the 'Sons of Liberty', a group of radical Whigs, engages their leader, Samuel Adams, to avenge him. This gentleman, having often failed in business (notably as manager of a malt house) afterwards served awhile as Government tax-collector, escaping imprisonment for fraud only by the help of powerful friends—Hancock among them. He is a shrewd lawyer—though his mother, conscious perhaps of his defective character, made him swear never to practise. Aware that the Boston garrison are forbidden to intervene in civil disturbances unless blood has been shed, Adams leads fifty

Liberty Boys, disguised as Indians, aboard the tea-ships—
where they throw £15,000 of cargo into the harbour and escape
arrest.

'Committees of Correspondence', managed by Samuel's cousin,
John Adams, take sympathetic action in other ports: they either
prevent the tea-ships from unloading, or else store the chests in
damp cellars. John Adams is an honest man; but you deprecate his
friendship with such well-known rascals, as you also deprecate the
ardent debates on liberty now so fashionable in Boston. Why should
men who bear a grudge against decent society, men who have
failed in business or been dismissed by their employers, invoke
John Ball, Wat Tyler, Oliver Cromwell, John Hampden? 'Those
heroic Englishmen,' you exclaim, 'had a right to speak in Freedom's name; they were oppressed, we are not. Too many apostles
of Liberty, like your atheistical outlaw John Wilkes, mistake it for
licence.'

In March 1774, alarming news reaches you. Parliament has
passed the Boston Port Act, which will close the docks and
paralyse trade until the East India Company has been reimbursed.
'The Liberty Boys provoked this,' you say, shaking your head,
'but it will drive them to even worse excesses, and invite punitive
action.'

The Sons of Liberty do indeed take reprisals against all whom
they suspect of sympathizing with Parliament. Sounded one day
by one of their delegates, you style yourself a neutral on politics.
They will not allow that. 'Take your choice,' they say. 'Either join
us, or join the tarnation Tories!' Many neutrals are terrorized into
supporting them, though not you. Why bow the knee to Samuel
Adams? He graduated in your year at Harvard, and there's little
you don't know about his character.

Barns of inoffensive Tories are fired, their cattle driven off,
their families stoned, their houses robbed, and they themselves
obliged to choose between conforming or starving. Often, a Tory
caught alone is beaten up, tarred, feathered, and led in ridicule
from township to township. Government servants get the worst
treatment; and even ministers of religion suffer for their faith. One
has bullets fired through his windows; another has his pulpit
nailed up; a third is confined to the pound, as if he were a stray
dog or pig, and fed with red herrings thrown over the gate, in
mockery of his alleged love of the redcoats. Victims need not
trouble to bring complaints before a magistrate; no witness will

dare appear. Nor do all ministers remain loyal to their King. Congregationalists embrace the Libertarian cause inflaming hatred against more respectable sects. You have yourself passed a Congregational place of worship and heard the preacher ranting inside on the 'Demon Bishops' of England—how every tenth child born is ravished from his mother's side, along with the tithe pig and the tithe calf, to glut their monstrous appetites.

As yet no Americans, even the wildest of them, think that the thirteen Colonies should elect a Federal Government and declare for national independence. As late as October 1775, Thomas Jefferson writes to a friend: 'We cannot in this country conceive that there are men in England so infatuated as seriously to suspect people here of a wish to erect ourselves into an independent state. If such an idea really obtains amongst those at the helm of affairs, one hour's residence in America would eradicate it. I never met one individual so inclined; but it is universally disavowed.'

Yet the Tories accuse the Whigs of plotting a 'Great American Republic'. 'Are not you Whigs in open mutiny?' they ask. And the angry Whigs protest: 'We are no mutineers, but His Majesty's loyal Opposition!'

Hundreds of persecuted Tories have fled to Boston, and found lodgings near the Barracks. You hold on at the farm, boycotted by your neighbours, hoping that the political atmosphere will improve. It gets worse. Finally, you sell your standing crops and cattle at a great loss, lock your doors, board up your windows, pile a few belongings on a wagon, and escape with your wife and children.

Terrorism prevails in other States, where also Committees of Correspondence have gained strength. 'Surely Mr. Governor Hutchinson should arrest the ring-leaders and use force?' you ask. Unfortunately, the garrisons are too small to take punitive action— being here not to overawe Americans, but to protect them from Indians and foreign armies. So Liberty Boys fear nothing, and can laugh at redcoats. Samuel Adams has warned the Governor that he will avoid fatal clashes only by withdrawing his troops to a fort in the harbour; and he weakly agrees.

New England newspapers conform to the rebels' wishes, lest their type be seized and their presses smashed. Everyone knows that the stories which they print about the 'brutal and licentious soldiery' are untrue. Redcoats have been strictly forbidden to assault native Americans, whatever the provocation, and therefore show disciplined patience in the face of constant insults and injuries. Walking peacefully down the street, they hear from behind them: 'What cheer, lobster scoundrels?' or 'Hullo, you red-herring rascals!', and receive a shower of stones and filth. Their assailants scuttle away. You have yourself seen impudent youths mobbing a sentry as he guarded the Customs House or Magazine. One grabbed his bayonet, a second knocked off his tall Grenadiers' hat with a stick, a third threw mud at his white buckskin accoutrements. The youths encouraged one another: 'Don't be skeered, lads! He's a bloody-back coward, like the rest.' You did not intervene, for fear of being denounced at Liberty Headquarters. That night, you could have expected a knock on your door, and a group of masked visitors waiting on the front-step.

Thomas Paine, a young troublemaker dismissed from the English Preventive Service after leading an abortive wage-strike, has emigrated to Philadelphia where, in January 1776, he publishes *Common Sense*, a pamphlet that discusses the evils of hereditary kingship and the absurdity of little England's claim to govern an entire continent. 'In no instance hath Nature made the Satellite larger than its primary Planet; but England and America reverse the common Order of Nature.' *Common Sense* sells edition after edition; and the idea of Independence spreads like a forest fire, now that Parliament has ordered a blockade of all American ports until the colonists regain their senses.

Soon, Liberty Boys are stealing arms from distant magazines, and dismounting the cannon that defend our harbours. Moreover, financed by Hancock and his associates, they offer fifty pounds apiece in gold for each British soldier—plus twenty dollars in silver if his Tower musket is in good repair—who will desert King George and drill the newly-formed rebel levies. They also offer protection against any sergeant's party sent to arrest him.

The Boston garrison find life intolerable; but the Government, being short of funds, hesitates to dispatch reinforcements. Instead, the Prime Minister promises to exempt from tax such colonies as will make a reasonable contribution to their country's defence. This offer comes too late. Already there has been fighting at Lexington; and the battle of Bunker Hill follows. American troops even invade Canada, trying to win over the French *habitants*.

King George makes an eleventh-hour peace move: he appoints General Howe and Admiral Howe as his commissioners. Too late again! The Declaration of Independence, drafted by Mr. Jefferson, has been signed; and Congress will not receive them, since they are empowered only to accept submission and grant pardons. Congress, standing on the Common Rights of Man, forms a Federal Government. But King Hancock, who hoped to be elected Commander-in-Chief, must swallow his chagrin when Colonel Washington is appointed.

The choice of Washington is a gesture towards the Southern States. That Southern aristocrats, though uninfected by Libertarianism, feel resentful of England, they showed at the time of the Stamp Act. Their tobacco monopoly no longer benefits them; for prices have fallen in spectacular fashion, ruining many planters. Virginian gentlemen want to sell abroad at their own price, instead of being robbed by avaricious London brokers. Of the humbler people down South, thousands are transported felons, or the descendants of such, and hate their mother country.

The Libertarians, styling themselves 'patriots', have out-manoeuvred you by always striking first, while you waited for the English to act. Why did you not form active counter-revolutionary clubs ten years ago, and scare smugglers and gangsters into obedience? Why not? Because you were law-abiding! Now they threaten you with fines, jail, exile, confiscations, and even death, if you defy *their* laws. Do you remain a Tory? Or do you desert your friends and risk getting branded as a traitor if Congress is beaten?

A hard choice. Lexington showed that American farmers are a force to be reckoned with. The redcoats sent there to arrest Samuel Adams and King Hancock, failed in their object and, though they dispersed the militia on the Green, were harassed the entire length of the return march by deer-hunters hidden behind walls or trees, who slipped off as soon as any movement threatened them. The redcoats lost three hundred that day. Those Americans, who lost only a hundred, may not be parade-ground soldiers, but they are past masters in the use of the musket—as the English learned again at Bunker Hill.

Yet deer-hunters will not stand up to regular troops in a pitched battle or siege. The strong forces now sent over by Parliament can occupy seaports and riverports and maintain the blockade indefinitely. But for Washington's bold stroke at Trenton, his command would have melted away in the winter of 1776, when most terms of engagement expired.

War enters its second year. General Burgoyne's surrender at Saratoga teaches General Howe, the Commander-in-Chief, the folly of committing regular troops to fight in wooded country, far from their lines of supply. He plays safe. 'This damned ugly business will last until both sides bleed to death!' you sigh. A second embassy arrives; their peace offers exceed the Libertarians' wildest hopes. Congress, however, swayed by Samuel Adams and his partisans, again scorns conciliation: 'This war began with Parliament's disbelief in our capacity to defend America's frontiers. See what havoc we have inflicted on the best army in Europe!'

Nevertheless, American generals are losing three battles for every one they win. The Bostonians suffer frightful casualties in their ill-conceived attack on Penobscot. Libertarian fervour cools, trade and industry decay, Continental paper money falls to a thirtieth of its face value. War is carried into the Southern States—Georgia, Virginia, the Carolinas. At Richmond and Norfolk, the entire tobacco crop, earmarked for paying Congress's French allies, has been burned. Mutinies break out in the revolutionary army, whose officers at last employ the same rigorous discipline that made the Boston mob sneer at the 'Bloody-backs'. Gaps in Washington's ragged ranks, mainly consisting of Protestant Irish immigrants, are now filled by English and Hessian deserters, negro slaves freed on engaging for three years' service, criminals set loose from jails. To encourage a better class of recruits, handsome grants of real money and land must be offered. One Southern State promises every volunteer 'a healthy sound negro between the ages of ten and thirty years, or sixty pounds in gold and silver, at the soldier's option.'

And you? Destitute and unemployed, you have grudgingly joined one of the twenty-five Loyalist regiments now in the Royal service—a force little smaller, and certainly more American, than the thirty thousand which Washington is struggling to keep under arms! Samuel Adams has been castigating his generalship as weak and dilatory, though well aware that his ill-fed, ill-equipped, and ill-assorted men are in no state to march.

At last, you hear news of General Cornwallis' surrender at York Town—brought about by sickness, short rations, the landing of a strong French expedition and the English fleet's failure to arrive in time. This disaster convinces King George that victory in America can be bought at too dear a price.

Peace is signed. The United States of America becomes a sovereign nation, and you have lost all. You tear the facings from your English uniform and weep.

14

Do you remember Albuhera?

The infantry regiment has become an uneconomically small unit for purposes of training, administration and fighting. Or so the Army Council is convinced. They plan, we gather, to let our regiments—some of which date back to the reign of Charles II—blur their identities in Regional Brigades. Officers and men will be cross-posted from one unit to another, as casually as civil servants change their Ministries. Commonsense to the logistician; plain nonsense to the fighting soldier.

It is the highly emotional regimental traditions, hoarded down the centuries, that alone account for smartness on parade, disciplined patience during civil disturbances, courage on the field. Recruits at the Depot are not taught British history, or even British Army history, but Regimental history, with battle honours as its reverent chapter headings.

Will a Sherwood Forester happily transfer his heroic allegiance to a newly created 'North Midland Brigade'? Surely not? There is still more fraternal feeling between the six 'Minden' Regiments, who wear roses in their caps on August 1st to commemorate their fantastic routing of two French cavalry corps in 1759—or between the Fusilier regiments who stormed the Heights of Albuhera in 1811—than between any regional groups.

Not long ago I had the honour of an early morning stroll around Jerusalem with the Prime Minister of Israel, Mr. David Ben Gurion. I asked him: 'Do you remember Albuhera?' At once ex-sergeant D. Green of the Royal Fusiliers, First World War veteran, stopped dead in his tracks and warmly shook my hand. 'So you're a Royal Welch Fusilier!' he cried. . . . He had not forgotten that our two regiments had been so mauled at Albuhera that the victorious survivors—one of our companies commanded by a corporal—formed a common mess and swore perpetual friendship.

What saved the Channel Ports at the First Battle of Ypres in 1914, when a second-lieutenant straight from Sandhurst could be killed leading a battalion of fifty men (mainly cooks, transport men, drummers, and the Battalion orderly room clerks) in a desperate counter-attack? Not even patriotism allows a battalion to suffer so. Patriotism is good enough for losses of two or three men out of every ten; only regimental pride can raise the proportion to nine. Britain cannot afford to sacrifice this heroic reserve of strength. Nearly a century ago, Lord Cardwell forcibly married several pairs of regiments for administrative reasons, and caused losses in morale that it took over a generation to repair. The proud Fifty-Second Foot, for example, was forced to pool battle honours with the Forty-Third, and rename itself 'Second Battalion of the Oxfordshire and Buckinghamshire Light Infantry'. Much the same mistake was made—though admittedly with greater discretion—two or three years ago.

It is always an open secret which pub or pubs in a country town are the best, which college or colleges in a university are the best. Not necessarily the oldest or largest or wealthiest; but the ones where the atmosphere is most alive, generous, free. So with regiments: all are good, some are indispensable. The Gloucesters, for instance, with their double cap-badge won when their senior surviving officer ordered the remnants of his command: 'Rear Rank, About Face! Fix Bayonets! Charge!' Cut them to pieces, wear them out with sleepless nights, forced marches, constant shelling, refill their ranks with raw recruits: they always remain superb. So do the Die-Hards. I could name a dozen more, but why give offence by omission?

If administrative convenience must be studied, let the merely good regiments be disbanded with honour, but build up the indispensable ones into brigades or half-brigades under their rightful names. If we ever have to fight a new infantry war— which is a moot point—the rightness of this decision will be proved in another Minden, or Albuhera, or Inkerman, or Waterloo.

15

The pirates who captured Caesar*

The old-fashioned historical novel popularized by Sir Walter Scott has its charm, though neither Scott nor his imitators troubled to throw their minds back fully into the past. Thus the nineteenth century *Zeitgeist* broods over the Waverley novels and Bulwer-Lytton's *The Last Days of Pompeii*, and even over Charles Reade's *The Cloister and the Hearth*, which was written with far greater historical care. The tradition of dressing up one's own contemporaries in togas, farthingales, or kirtles and placing them on the appropriate stage is likely to die hard: one Tudor novel of the Twenties makes a young noblewoman greet a young nobleman at the Field of the Cloth of Gold with: 'I do hate parties, don't you?' More recent publications invent detailed ancient instances of modernistic sexual abandon: a fashion started by Kathleen Winsor's *Forever Amber*, and since refined by busy students of the late Dr. Kinsey. Every new art fashion derived from archaeological discoveries—in Tutankhamen's Egypt, in Minoan Crete, in Etruria—soon provides its crop of costume novels, all without any authentic three-dimensional characters to make them readable.

The only excuse I have ever found myself for writing a historical novel is that an obviously untrue or inadequate treatment has been given a real story by the original annalists. If I feel convinced that something very different happened, yet cannot prove it, a suggested restoration in fictional form is tempting. But the novelist needs to be two jumps ahead of the academic historian, know as much as he does, and invent nothing anachronistic or factually disprovable. It is hardly enough to retell accepted history

* *The Young Caesar*, by Rex Warner.

with dramatic embellishments; there should be a ghost clamouring for justice to be done him.

Novels of historical restoration are severely limited in subject. To treat of English scenes between (say) 1350 and 1650 raises difficult linguistic problems—tushery and pshawdom always rear their horrid heads. How much easier when one can, as it were, translate Anglo-Saxon or Norman-French into simple modern English! But even that demands the effort of *thinking* in the original language, as I have done in Greek, Latin, and sixteenth century Spanish while writing various novels of my own; most authors shrink from the effort. A still worse limitation is that few historical periods contain enough striking individuals (as opposed to types), or sufficient documentation about their personal habits, to justify a novel.

Rex Warner, for instance, has written *The Young Caesar* as a sort of *History Without Tears*, rather than as a costume novel—I suppose because he had read a film-magnate's recent pronouncement 'Togas are out!' and because Caesar had no exploitable psychopathic kinks or dark secrets, and never even behaved with humanly attractive inconsequence. He was clear-headed, realistic, fearless, abstemious, unsuperstitious; a resourceful politician; a generous friend; a vigorous womanizer who never allowed his liaisons to hamper his career, but used them to shrewd practical purpose; an aristocrat who understood the word in its literal and now forgotten sense of governmental capacity; a consummate strategist and logistician; a leader who secured the absolute devotion of his troops by never asking more of them than he was willing to undertake himself. Historians have not traduced his character, nor has Mr. Warner unearthed any new material about him. Moreover, Caesar's authentic despatches survive and are worse than useless to a novelist who chooses the pseudo-auto-biographical device: being so succinct and limpid that they discourage imaginative embellishment. Mr. Warner ought to have been warned by Cicero's remarks in his *Brutus*:

'Caesar wrote admirably; his memoirs are cleanly, directly and gracefully composed, and divested of all rhetorical trappings. And while his sole intention was to supply historians with factual material, the result has been that several fools have been pleased to primp up his narrative for their own glorification; but every writer of sense has given the subject a wide berth.'

If I were reviewing *The Young Caesar* as serious history, I should check every reference against the original texts, but it does not merit that treatment. Here is Mr. Warner's account of Caesar and the pirates who held him to ransom off the Mysian coast:

'In particular, I disliked their boastfulness and the contemptuous manner in which they used to speak of Rome. . . . I used to call them dunces, ignoramuses, illiterate peasants and all sorts of other abusive names, all of which they deserved. . . . In a civilized world, I informed them, they were quite intolerable; and, though in recent years Rome had, because of her own troubles, slackly permitted them to grow in strength, a time would certainly come when every pirate ship would be driven from the seas. They regarded these remarks of mine as exceedingly amusing and when I added that, so far as they themselves were concerned, I proposed, as soon as I was released, to have the whole lot of them brought to justice, they thought this the best joke of all. Indeed, their sense of humour was as imperfectly developed as were their intellectual faculties.'

Caesar then chattily describes how, having purchased his release, he went to Miletus, raised a fleet, and soon captured his captors. The story ends:

'With regard to my prisoners I thought that it would make a clean end to the expedition and would also redound to my own personal credit if I were to have them executed immediately at Miletus, where already, as the result of my exploit, I was enjoying the greatest popularity. However, on second thoughts I decided that it would be more tactful to refer their case to the governor of the province, from whom also, it seemed to me, I was entitled to receive some consideration and some reward. So I brought the prisoners to Pergamum and left them there under guard. I myself went on as fast as I could to Bithynia by the same road as that on which, seven years before, I had first travelled to that country.'

This breaks one of the main rules that bind a historical novelist: because Mr. Warner's story does not square with the facts given by the two main authorities, Plutarch and Suetonius. Plutarch records that Caesar took the captured pirates to Pergamum, and that when Junius, the Roman governor of Asia, postponed their punishment, he returned 'and crucified them himself, as he had often jokingly threatened to do while he was their prisoner.' Mr. Warner has also missed the real point of the story. Suetonius writes:

'Caesar was not naturally vindictive; and if he crucified the pirates who had held him to ransom, this was only because he had sworn in their presence to do so; and he first mercifully cut their throats.'

The language which Mr. Warner puts into Caesar's mouth is both inelegant and sadly out of key. Caesar could never have used the pleonastic phrase 'quite intolerable', nor did he tautologically call the pirates 'dunces, ignoramuses and illiterate peasants' but, according to Plutarch, 'dunces and barbarians'; and he threatened them with crucifixion, not merely with justice.

As for his alleged comment: 'their sense of humour was as imperfectly developed as were their intellectual faculties'—try putting that into Latin! *'Nullum habuerunt sensum umoris'* would mean no more than: 'they had no sensation of sexual potency'. The modern concept 'sense of humour' appears first in James Russell Lowell's *Democracy and Other Addresses* (1886); and is there defined as 'that modulating and restraining balance-wheel which we call a sense of humour'. Caesar would have been sufficiently conversant with Greek dramatic usages to remark that those pirates missed the tragic irony of his smiling threats; as he was also sufficiently sure of himself to forgive Catullus his damaging satires, and to take no disciplinary measures against troops who sang bawdy songs about him on the occasion of his Gallic triumph. But neither he nor any other Roman of rank, however *jocosus*—which meant 'witty at other people's expense'—allowed the least sense of humour to modulate or restrain his ambitions. Hence the Civil Wars; hence the Ides of March; hence the Roman Imperial cult.

16

A significant lecture at Mount Holyoke

(1956)

This is written from Majorca, which tourist agents call 'The Island of Love', adding that the sun always shines in Majorca, and that it is always summertime here. Don't be misled! It is always summertime here because we put the clock one hour back several years ago—for daylight saving—and have never since put it forward again; this is very hard on my sun-dial which is always an hour wrong now. And, yes, the sun certainly always shines in Majorca, except at night or during an eclipse, but his beneficent rays for the past month have filtered through thick cloud, which is very hard on American and British tourists who have brought along only light summer clothes. And, yes, I am sure there is love in Majorca, as elsewhere, why not?—even though that wretch D. H. Lawrence, who came here once on a visit about thirty years ago, had scathing things to say about the inefficient manner in which Majorcan girls made it. This I thought very hard on the respectable Majorcan girls who were not allowed to do any necking or petting even with their accepted *novios*, even in the presence of faithful chaperons. But perhaps D. H. Lawrence generalized from the not so respectable girls whom he met in the quayside bars, where they sat waiting for foreign sailors and novelists.

I am asked as a 'distinguished visitor', announced for a lecture at Mount Holyoke early this coming February, to give a brief account of what I shall say, or rather (because this will appear when the date has already passed) what I shall have said in my lecture. But I think it is unlucky to make prophecies. Here in

Majorca we always say about future plans, 'If it please God—*and* the mayor!', and since I haven't visited the United States for eighteen years, before World War II indeed, it's hard to believe that I'm really going there. By air, too, putting my pocket sun-dial backwards an hour (cf. II *Kings* xx. 11) four or five times en route! So please excuse me!

What do distinguished visitors normally say when they lecture? Significant things, I suppose. But from whom, or from what, are they to be distinguished? And of what are their speeches significant? Ah, that's a beguiling word, is 'distinguished'. And so is 'significant'. Around the house where I write this nonsense roam scores of cats of both sexes, no sex, and all colours. Never mind about their sex-life or their fur; but among them is a tom-cat distinguished from all the others because he has one blue and one white eye, and gets all the best throw-outs in consequence. His eyes are held to be significant. Significant of what? Someone's grandmother says that they are significant of good luck.

This has started me thinking about the Epeirot recruit from Dyrrhachium who enlisted in the Byzantine Army in the middle of the fifth century A.D. He was a tough, shrewd, energetic peasant and distinguished from all the other tough, shrewd, energetic peasant recruits that year, because he had eyes of two different colours. His name was Anastasius, but they nicknamed him 'Dicorus', which is the Greek for that peculiarity. Well, you can guess how it was. The captain of his company didn't know half his men by sight or name but always recognized Dicorus; and as Dicorus was always clean on parade and alert on sentry duty, and held the correct religious views, the Captain naturally promoted him to corporal, and then to sergeant. The Colonel, similarly, did not know half of the sergeants by sight, but Dicorus was easily distinguished by his eyes; so because he had a crisp word of command and kept his section in good order, the Colonel made him sergeant-major. One day an Inspecting General remarked: 'A very fine body of men, Colonel. I suppose you owe a lot to that sergeant-major of yours—fascinating, his eyes, eh? Significant, even. My old grandmother always used to say that two eyes of different colours are lucky. I'm going to take him on my staff in the "Silentiaries" '—meaning the Lifeguards.

Meanwhile, Dicorus had been studying *Frontinus* and *Vegetius* and *Army Regulations*. He made a good Staff Officer, and went up the tree quickly, because he was a distinguished man, and had significant eyes. Indeed, everyone thought, when the Emperor Zeno died, that Dicorus was obviously the man to fill the vacant throne and marry the Empress Ariadne. So he became the Emperor Anastasius, but they continued to call him 'Dicorus', because he was the only Emperor ever to have eyes of different colours; and all their grandmothers had always told them what a lucky sign this was. He made by the way, a most unsuccessful Emperor and all his successors for the next thousand years had both eyes of the same colour.

When I arrive (if I arrive), you'll have found me distinguished by my height, broken nose, unruly grey hair, and mumbling English accent. I shall also, perhaps, have raised the question of poetic significance in my lecture about *Legitimate Criticism of Poetry*. I think of choosing two or three 'great' poems which, though they are supposed to be well out of the reach of sublunar criticism, any decent young woman with a heart in her breast and a light in her head secretly knows to be punk. My task is to confirm such young women in their opinions by showing how these 'great' poems came to be written, for all the wrong reasons, of course; and to suggest a few charms for use against the dragon of Compulsory Literary Orthodoxy—'CLO' for short—who haunts the text-books on both sides of the Atlantic, and who can't tell poetry from pink pills.

Mind you, as a law-abiding family-man I have nothing against orthodoxy as such. The Campus Dragon that regulates the dress and deportment of alumnae is certainly a most benignant one, and a protection to distinguished visitors who distinguish themselves in lecture halls by uttering significant significances. But CLO is another matter. Personally, when I was at college, I resisted all attempts to teach me what I *must* admire, and have done so ever since. I have, in fact, wandered in the wilderness, forty years—as long as Moses did, in fact, and still resist CLO. This is not to say that, with modern prison techniques of brain-washing (starvation, purges, electric shocks and persistent grilling), I couldn't be forced into literary orthodoxy. But so far I have kept at large; and I hope that I can persuade all young women with hearts in their breasts and lights in their heads not to be defeated and devoured by CLO: persuade them not to harden their hearts and dim their lights, but always resolutely to distinguish good from bad, however 'great', and when anything is offered them as 'significant', always ask pertly, 'Significant of what?'

17

Tyger, Tyger

Tyger, Tyger burning bright
In the forests of the night,
What immortal hand and eye
Dare frame thy fearful symmetry?

Christopher Burstall, a TV interviewer from the B.B.C., visited my
Majorcan home last year to cross-examine me on why people felt
so strongly about Blake's *Tyger, Tyger*. Later it proved that the
main object of his programme had been to ask school-children the
same question; so that my more detailed answer was cut to a
couple of minutes. I never watched the performance, but a tape-
record remained and after excising my *uhs*, *ahems*, coughs and
aposiopeses* (the polite rhetorical term for failing to end a
sentence) I found that I had said, or meant, more or less as follows.

*   *   *   *   *

* INT: What makes *The Tyger* work so strongly for you?
R.G.: I think it's that uh it has what you might call a dream quality.
And um in the case of schizophrenes such as um Blake, um um
INT: What's the main quality about *The Tyger* which makes it have such
a strong effect on so many different people, do you think?
R.G.: It's difficult for me to answer that because—I read it first when I
was young, when I was very impressionable, and uh so much a part
of me in a way that it's difficult to think of it in any objective way or
guess what effect it has on other people. It's certainly a very strong
poem. And uh—I've been thinking about it recently and it seems to
me that uh Blake was certainly in his uh in a state of schizophrenia at
the time. And uh one notes in—in the case of schizophrenic personalities, one very strange characteristic which is that they uh part of
their life is uh as a normal...

I first read *Tyger, Tyger* when I was young and impressionable. It became so much a part of my poetic experience that I find it hard to be objective about its effect on other people, though I realize now that Blake had been writing in a typical state of schizophrenia. This is what lends the poem the vivid quality of a waking dream. Often schizophrenics cannot distinguish between the matter-of-fact world and their own imagined one. Nobody has yet discovered the cause or cure of this illness but the symptoms often include, as in Blake's case, visions of devils or angels, an illusion of enormous spiritual superiority over other minds, aggravated by persecution mania, wild blasphemy or indelicacy and intense loneliness. Blake's *Island in the Moon*, for instance, written in the same period as *Songs of Innocence* and *Songs of Experience*, brutally satirizes a genteel late eighteenth century philosophic society which included his patron Linnell. Despite the gusto of its hilarious and often bawdy dialogue and songs, the satire is still under control. It reminds us of a reckless drunkard driving a car at full speed through traffic along a narrow country road: we hold our breaths in horrified admiration.

The tiger appears frequently in schizophrenic visions: it steals for instance into the naïve jungle paintings of the Douanier Rousseau. Morbid psychologists have come to use it as an emblem of what they call the Dionysiac principle, meaning that of manic abandon to physical ecstasy; probably because, according to Greek mythologists, the drunken god Dionysus brought tigers back with him from his famous expedition to India at the head of his Maenads and Satyrs. The River Tigris, by the way, is said to have been renamed in celebration of this feat. Blake contrasts his Tyger with the peaceful and passionless lamb, and though the noble lion is said (by a common misquotation of *Isaiah*) to lie down with the lamb in the Kingdom of Heaven, no such claim has ever been made for the heartless tiger.

Blake's 'Did He who made the lamb make thee?' repeats the theological question which Omar Khayaam the Persian had asked and settled to his own satisfaction some eight centuries before. To represent God as an almighty and eternal Man, Khayaam pointed out, is to credit him also with bestial human traits inappropriate to a God of Love; which makes the metaphor fallacious. But Blake, with his non-conformist Protestant education, was still saddled with this metaphor of man's physical creation in God's mage, and it haunted him. How to reconcile a God of Love with a

God of Destruction? Omar confessed at the close of his *Rubaiyyat* that he repents of many sins but still hoped for Divine mercy since 'he never argued that the One was Two'. But Blake has not yet solved the problem, which stalks him like the Tyger itself as he dreams open-eyed in broad daylight. His Tyger is, in fact, the concept of God as Evil.

The word *dare* throughout the poem seems to be in the wrong tense. Its past tense is either *dared* or *durst*, never *dare*. Blake uses the present tense as though watching the creative process still at work. And as I pointed out in a lecture given at Oxford in 1965, *Tyger, Tyger* makes poor prose sense, especially with its unbridged gap between the second and third stanzas.

> And what shoulder and what art
> Could twist the sinews of thy heart?
> And when thy heart began to beat
> What dread hand and what dread feet?

The stanza refers to God's creation of the Tyger, but what part do His feet play? Is Blake thinking of a potter who puddles clay with his feet, or is he thinking of a smith who works his forge-bellows with one foot? The word 'feet' is left in the air. However, on referring to the original work-draft, included in Blake's 'Rossetti MSS.' of 1793, which also contains some *Songs of Innocence*, I found the answer. He had originally included the feet as messengers, not artificers:

> What dread feet
> Could fetch it from the furnace deep
> And thy horrid ribs dare steep
> In the well of sanguine woe?
> In what clay and in what mould
> Were thy eyes of fury rolled?
>
> Where the hammer, where the chain?
> In what furnace was thy brain?
> What the anvil? What dread grasp
> Dare its deadly terrors clasp?

On re-reading this draft, the first stanza clearly dissatisfied Blake, not only because *deep* and *steep* were rhymes that came too close

K

to *beat* and *feet*, but because the over-literary 'well of sanguine woe' made one line too many. So he deleted the whole stanza, though the tiger's furious eyes clearly formed an even more important part of the original vision than its camouflage of stripes. He replaced the eyes, however, in a less haunting couplet:

> In what distant deeps or skies
> Burnt the fire of thine eyes?
> On what wings dare He aspire?
> What the hand dare seize the fire?

The natural tiger is, after all, a monstrous, untameable cat, and a most illuminating sequence of cat-drawings appeared recently in the *Sunday Times*, and I believe also in the *New York Times*, to illustrate the effect of schizophrenia on the graphic arts. They were by Louis Wain who, when I was very young, had become the most famous comic artist in England. He never drew anything but comical cats—cats in almost every condition, position or occupation. Wain's cats appeared in the popular papers every week and almost every day. Cats were his obsession, but eventually they grew too much for him. A phantom King Cat, like Irusan in the Irish legend of *Suibhne Gelt*, transformed itself into a Tyger, sprang and pinned him to the ground. I remember the shock of terror and grief when I heard, as an adolescent, that Louis Wain had been chained up in a lunatic asylum.

Wain had begun as a simple commercial artist, with no obvious signs of the mental illness that was to destroy him. When it struck he began painting cats in Van Gogh style, though so far as I know, without any acquaintance with Van Gogh's not yet famous paintings. Wain's King Cat glowers at us terrifically, like Blake's Tyger. In what clay and in what mould were its eyes of fury rolled? After a few years, Wain's schizophrenia followed the usual course towards pictorial disintegration. The same cat-face continues in vague outline but gradually adopts the schematic style of drawings found in pictures drawn under the influence of lysergic acid (L.S.D.); until at last only careful reference to the earlier sequence indicates the shadowy presence of the King Cat, which finally disappears altogether like the Cheshire Cat in Lewis Carroll's *Alice in Wonderland*.

Louis Wain's acute vision in what we may call his Van Gogh period closely corresponds with Blake's in *Tyger, Tyger*. Van

Gogh, too, had been a dull enough painter until his schizophrenia developed and was accompanied, like Blake's, with religious hysteria and persecution-mania. Van Gogh's famous *Chair* and *Sunflowers* seem to come right out of the canvas at you, and are to most ordinary pictures as feverish dreams are to pale daylight fancies. The main difference between Blake and Van Gogh was that Van Gogh killed himself before reaching the schematic or so-called 'psychedelic' phase symptomatic of L.S.D. art. Blake, whose case was not violent enough to qualify him for a lunatic asylum, survived as a writer of rambling Prophetic Books in which his claims to moral perfection and angelic inspiration were fully pressed. The schizophrenic's incorrigible habit of confusing universal abstractions with characters in his private life is shown by the appearance, in an illustration to *Jerusalem*, of the evil demon 'Skofeld', wearing chains. 'Skofeld' is John Schofield, a drunken private soldier who in 1803 had tried to arrest Blake on the charge of using seditious language. Blake himself appears among these moral abstractions: as having the spirit of Milton enter into his foot, and as heroically dethroning the Arch-Demon Urizen, who apparently symbolizes Rationality ('your reason'). In effect (to use psychological terms) the schizophrenic process in artists or writers proceeds from frequently untalented craftsmanship and continues through a period of intense, if disordered, vision to the patient's final severance from society and a growing disintegration of images accompanied by increased fluency in obsessional performance.

James Joyce's literary career is a more recent instance. His early autobiographical books, *Dubliners* and *A Portrait of the Artist as a Young Man*, and his poems *Chamber Music*, read conventionally enough if one allows for the oddity of the Edwardian Irish scene that they describe. They even won him a Civil List pension. *Ulysses* starts on the same simple level but, after a few chapters, clear symptoms of schizophrenia appear, growing stronger and more marked as the book advances. Joyce had much the same illusion of superior power as Blake (though without his religious warmth), the same reckless impiety and the same sense of persecution. He eventually put himself under the care of the Zurich psychiatrist Dr. Breuler, and after escaping to Switzerland from Paris at the outbreak of the Second World War, died there in a catatonic trance. Dr. Breuler wrote that Joyce was the unusual case of a schizophrenic becoming sufficiently aware of his mental condition to direct it consciously into art. Yet the eventual result, *Finnegans Wake*, is memorable for its schematic patterns rather than for any clear message that they convey.

It is easy to criticize the faulty craftsmanship of *Tyger*, *Tyger*, as I did in an Oxford lecture, especially the stanza:

> What the hammer? What the chain?
> In what furnace was thy brain?
> What the anvil? What dread grasp
> Dare its deadly terrors clasp?

'Chain' seems introduced largely for the sake of the rhyme, chains being used in mensuration and mechanics rather than in smithcraft. And grammatically the antecedent of 'dare its deadly terrors clasp' is 'anvil'; which no working smith clasps. The famous last stanza is not altogether clear either:

> When the stars threw down their spears
> And watered heaven with their tears,
> Did he smile His work to see?
> Did He who made the lamb make thee?

Blake does not indicate whether the stars threw down their spears in bellicose mood, or simply let them fall from their grasp in grief. Yet these anomalies, including the confusion of tenses already noted—with 'dare' in the present tense, but 'could', 'was', 'did' and 'made' in the past—increase the nightmare tension of the poem. To repair them would be to show Blake's mind in a less unbalanced state than it was and so falsify his theme. Yet to saddle readers with an unresolved nightmare is not, I suggest, a responsible poet's task. Khayaam, faced with the same problem, struggled (as he put it) through the privative month of Ramadan; and when it had ended left his readers awed but at peace with God. Blake, it seems, felt twinges of guilt at having written more seditiously about his Maker than he would have dared write about His Majesty King George III.

The following lines occur in the Rossetti MSS. under the date 1793:

> When Klopstock England defied,
> Up rose William Blake in his pride,

For old Nobodaddy aloft
Farted and belched and cough'd
Then swore a great oath that made heaven quake
And call'd aloud to English Blake.
Blake was giving his body ease
At Lambeth beneath the poplar trees.
From his seat then started he
And turned him about, thrice times three,
The Moon at that sight blushed scarlet red
The stars threw down their cups and fled . . .
If Blake could do this when he rose from a shite
What might he not do when he sat down to write?

In the *Everlasting Gospel* he dared question Jesus's chastity, and the Virgin's:

The morning blushed a fiery red
Mary was found in adulterous bed. . . .

Here, it will be noticed, he uses his own exalted *Tyger, Tyger* imagery for obscene purposes. The Tyger's apparition may have come in self-punishment; his eventual loneliness was caused by his having either insulted his friends or scared them away with his wanton blasphemies. He wrote, sometime between 1808 and 1811:

Cosway, Frazer and Baldwin of Egypt's lake
Fear to associate with Blake.
This life is a warfare against evils;
They heal the sick: he casts out Devils.
Hayley, Flaxman and Stothard are also in doubt
Lest their Virtue should be put to the rout.
One grins, t'other spits and in corners hides,
And all the Virtuous have shown their backsides.

Hayley, for two of whose books Blake engraved the illustrations, was a patient and generous patron. But Blake turned on him too:

When Hayley finds out what you cannot do
That is the very thing that he'll set you to.
If you break your neck it is not his fault
But pecks of poison are not pecks of salt,

> And when he could not act upon my wife
> He hired a villain to bereave my life.

He also wrote songs of marvellous tenderness, another common characteristic of schizophrenetics; but that was in his better days.

18

Five score and six years ago

I have never been a schoolmaster, although my father tried to steer me that way. He was a poet, famous as the author of Irish songs, including 'Father O'Flynn', 'Trotting to the Fair', and 'The Jug of Punch', now often mistaken for folk-songs. He was also a school inspector under the then English Board of Education with the poet Matthew Arnold among his elder colleagues. Both earned their bread and butter from education, both made it their lifework to improve conditions of Government-supported schools—especially for the teachers. My father's main triumph was to win Government permission for laying out school playgrounds where children could learn football and other organized games instead of fighting and throwing stones at one another in the street. Since National education in England was then controlled only at the elementary level, it was on the reading and writing of English that Matthew Arnold and his colleagues concentrated.

Naturally my brothers and sisters and I got the backwash of our father's grammatic exactitude. He used to wince dramatically at our lapses. 'So me and Clarissa picked strawberries like you said we could.' (Wince.) 'You mean, my dear Robert: "So Clarissa and I picked strawberries as you said we might." *Like you said we could*, my boy—I agree that Shakespeare used "like you said" at least once, and of course any grammatical absurdity is permissible in popular drama, but "like you said" has always been regarded as slovenly among the educated. No, I didn't doubt that you *could* pick strawberries; which is why I told you that you *might*.'

I have grown up like my father, I admit. My children speak well enough, but recently I had to discipline a granddaughter for

saying 'different than'—a usage which now seems to have gained
an unshakable hold on the States and which has a long if dis-
creditable semi-literary history in England, beginning about the
time of the Cromwellian Wars. I told my granddaughter '*Compared
than* any of your friends, Antonia, you speak pretty fair English.'
Alas, 'compared than' will soon be as firmly rooted as 'different
than', having already reared its ugly head in Australia. Now, tell
me, am I a snob? And what is good English?

The writing of good English is too often regarded as an intellectual attainment, won by a short course of intense study. This is to
mistake Good English for Success English, a language everywhere
sold by correspondence courses to underpaid business executives
who hope with its help to become overpaid business directors.
Success English is directly descended from Success Latin, otherwise called Rhetoric, the avowed aim of which was to make a bad
cause seem better by a skilful hypnotic arrangement of words.
Yes, of course: Success English has its uses. All leading nations
this side of the Iron Curtain offer as many goods as possible for
sale to all their citizens as a means of stimulating them to produce
more goods for sale abroad; and of course expendability is an
important sales asset, in so far as it staves off market saturation.
Thus Success English in the English-speaking world has become
an instrument of such outstanding economic importance that its
varying degrees of psychological impact are studied with minute
care at the high-research level. A century ago Success English
closely resembled Success Latin in being a well-woven sonorous
Ciceronian-type oratory, a famous example of which has long stuck
in my memory:

'If you want a really fine, unsophisticated family pill, try
Dr. Rumboldt's liver-encouraging, kidney persuading, silent
perambulator: twenty-seven to the box. This pill is as mild
as a pet lamb and as searching as a small tooth-comb. It don't
go fooling about but attends strictly to business, and is as
certain for the middle of the night as a twenty-dollar alarum
clock.'

Modern Success English can be deceptively unrhetorical in tone:
as it were quiet, familiar bed-time persuasion by an uncle or elder
sister to some perpelexed junior, but always with a memorable
last line telling him what he should buy, sell, or be.

Yet for innocent teachers of English, most of whom have had no direct contact with trade, commerce, or industry, and some of whom, like myself, could never sell a sack of grain in time of famine, Success English seems crooked English: the use of language to distract a reader's attention from factual discrepancies, not to say falsehoods. Their task, especially at the more elementary levels, is to teach straight English, both as a moral discipline and as a help to honest communication between friends. The crooked can be no business of theirs.

Now, our language, though the richest in the world, is the least disciplined and therefore the easiest to write badly; there is perhaps no such thing as *talking* bad English, at any rate among those who claim it as their mother-tongue. I am all in favour of dialects: the greater the diversity of dialect the less danger there will be of over-centralization and loss of independent local vagaries and obsessions.

Ideally we should be encouraged to speak our own dialects, though *taught* to write straight English. I hesitate to say 'literary' English because 'literary' has now come to mean affected, lifeless far-fetched, snobbish. And I don't want to call it Oxford English if only because there is an Oxford in Mississippi which cannot compare in semantic correctness with Cambridge, Massachussetts. And because, although Oxford, England, is the home of the authoritative thirteen-volume *Oxford English Dictionary* and its noble companion, the six-volume *Oxford Dialect Dictionary* (each volume weighing some seven or eight pounds), yet both works are collections of *precedents*—not, like the dictionary sponsored by the French Academy, Tables of the Law laying down which verbal forms are correct and which are not.

So let us settle for 'Mandarin English'. As you all know, despite the immense diversity of dialects under the old Chinese Empire, the Imperial Court imposed on all outlying provinces the acceptance of a common written sign-language, in which their officials could report and correspond without misunderstanding. And this became possible because, though spoken Mandarin was a purely Court Language, the signs had the same *sense*, if nothing like the same *sounds*, in every dialect throughout China. There is already a Mandarin-English convention shared by the London *Times* and the *New York Times*, the main news columns of which, apart from occasional spelling differences, are bound by the same rules of grammar and show little vocabularistic variations. This should be made the basis of elementary education. And, of course, teachers of English (like my father) find themselves losing their original dialects and talking Mandarin English as an example to their pupils and families.

English is a vernacular language. 'Vernacular' originally meant a sort of Latin spoken by slaves, *vernae*, of foreign parentage born in Roman households: a pidgin Latin with most of its case-endings and conjugational forms ironed out. English is indeed doubly a vernacular, because Norman-French began as a pidgin Latin, spoken by Gallic provincials conquered by Caesar's un-educated and mainly non-Roman legionaries; and English was a pidgin Norman-French spoken by William the Conqueror's Anglo-Saxon serfs. Nevertheless, for centuries, Latin remained the sole language of culture and government in England and France, Italy and Spain, so that when a national vernacular reached the dignity of acquiring a literature it was subjected to whatever Latin grammatic rules, taught in the monkish schools, were still relevant to it.

Thus even now the grammatic test of written English, written French, and the rest, is much the same: 'does it offend the basic rules of Latin?' Which is why I quarrel with, say, *different than*. One can be *better than*, *worse than*, *other than*—*melior quam*, *pejor quam*, *alius quam*, but one can't be *differens quam*, 'different than', because 'different' means in Latin 'separating from' and one can't be *separating than*. My father's objections to 'Me and Clarissa picked strawberries like you said we could' were also based on Latin rules. The polite convention is for the 'I' or 'me' to come second, not first; and though it is possible in English to say 'It's me' or 'that's him'—by analogy with the French 'c'est moi' or 'c'est lui'—the Latin-conscious French insist that active verbs are governed by a nominative noun or pronoun. 'Like you said' is not Latin: either it is *Ut dixisti* meaning 'as you said' or *Sicut dixisti* meaning 'like as you said'.

Of course in love letters, or family letters, we write as we talk because our correspondents imagine our voice speaking to them and know its inflections so well that they seldom miss the sense. It is quite different when we write to strangers, whom we can't expect to understand our individual usage of words, or even to be glad of a letter from us; so we take great trouble to make our sentences formal and Mandarin-like.

It is not generally realized how far vocal inflexions clarify sense.

In speech we need no punctuation at all. If I say, 'Everyone in the audience shakes his head and thinks I'm a fool', that's one thing; but if I say 'Everyone in the audience shakes his head and thinks "I'm a fool",' that's something very different. Or take: 'The room smelt of onions. I simply had to force open the window and at once felt better.' Which when written down might mean, not that I took the simple easy measure which presented itself for my comfort, but that violence was forced on me by sheer necessity: 'I *simply had* to take forceful action'. Or take the proverb 'Stuff a cold and starve a fever'. When it is written down, the sense of the normal vocal inflexions is lost. Like 'Give a dog a bad name— and hang him,' it really means if you overfeed a man with a cold you're liable to make him so sick that you'll have a fever case on your hands.

Again, 'only' in written prose governs the sense of the word which it immediately precedes: 'I only saw Absalom' should mean 'I only *saw* Absalom, I did not speak to him or hear what he said.' So teachers ought to emphasize the importance for instance, of writing 'I saw only Absalom' or 'I alone saw Absalom' if what one means is not: 'I only *saw* Absalom.' And they should explain punctuation as the means of helping the eye to understand what the ear understands easily enough: giving it an exact musical score to translate into sound.

In mediaeval times the few people capable of reading books spelt out each word aloud, and recognized the meaning by the sound. Not until two centuries ago did the movement of the reader's lips become unusual. And only in the last century have educated people acquired the art of reading up to four hundred words a minute. This rate amounts to about twenty-four thousand an hour. In conversation the voice goes at about one-fourth the speed. And the reading eye is, as a rule, far shrewder than the ear. Are we not all more easily deceived by a telephone message than by a letter?

The craft of writing good English is based on a single principle: never to lose the reader's attention. Since the most obvious ways of losing it are to offend, confuse, or bore him, good writing can be reduced simply to the principle of active care for his sensibilities.

I am told that in the United States the English teachers entrusted with educating younger and relatively under-privileged students and therefore—I deeply deplore this 'therefore'—there-

fore drawing smaller salaries and living in more difficult circumstances, are those who appear to be the most conservative in their
views of what is good English. Clever young university professors
now tend to be liberal and to give the language full rein. But
although I have defined a born gentleman or lady as one who
knows by instinct when to wear the wrong clothes, and the born
writer as one who knows exactly when to take grammatic liberties
with the language, yet I expect universities to be seats of learning
rather than workshops of creative writing. They should concentrate on teaching Good English, Straight English, Plain English,
Mandarin English, not (to borrow a metaphor from non-figurative
art) how to paint with a spray gun or sculpturally harmonize the
random *objets trouvés* of the junk heap. Yet when students are
called upon to analyse and discuss the English classics, these same
liberal professors do not oblige them to write in Classical English
themselves but encourage the use of slipshod, if vivid, colloquial
English.

This is a healthy sign only if it means making a break-away
from the academic English hitherto obligatory for Ph.D. theses.
The 1776 Revolution, which was a protest against the imposition
of English political theory on English colonists with their own
way of life, had this unfortunate result: it led ambitious early-
nineteenth century Americans to look elsewhere in Europe for
their re-education—to France, Italy and especially Germany.
Germany was enjoying a famous period of enlightenment and producing remarkable scientists, historians and philosophers. Their
bellicose madness had not yet begun; they were not even anti-
Semites, but the good boys of Western culture. Unfortunately,
they were saddled with the German language, which had always
been a monolithic one, not an omnium-gatherum vernacular.
Although simple in grammar and accidence, it lacked the fluidity
of English; also it denied its writers the licence that every Briton
and every American claims: to borrow whatever phraseology he
pleases from anywhere he likes and pass it as current coin. The
strong party in the Revolutionary Congress that wanted to cut the
main taproot with England had voted to make German the official
language of the United States; and this would have become law
had not a splinter vote in favour of Hebrew saved English for the
country.

German is a curiously cumbersome language, and, as all delegates to the United Nations become aware, linguistically out of

step with English, French, Italian, Spanish, and Russian. A German delegate in the old League of Nations days at Geneva once barked at the official interpreter, 'Sir, why do you rudely wait until I have finished my sentences instead of translating them phrase by phrase as you do for my fellow-delegates?' 'Pardon, your Excellency,' the interpreter answered, 'but you give me no option. I patiently and soberly for the triumphant main verb, which on putting at the end of your excessively long rhetorical periods you with so much severity insist, to wait am obliged.' American Academic writers, even though they might not, as it were, reserve the final thunder of the German main verb, have learned from German scholars to load their writings with the longest and least necessary words in or out of the dictionary; which produces a mental fatigue encouraging readers to suppose that the theme and its handling are too awe-inspiring for dispute. The Germanic prose style lingers on in psychological and sociological university studies. Their avowed object is to be scholarly, which implies writing in a language that only dedicated scholars can understand, one purged of all collo-quialism, levity, or emotion; and this style has long dominated highbrow literary journalism and even musical and artistic criti-cism, though any creative work with life in it should obviously be discussed in correspondingly live English.

The fact is that honest writers try to give their readers as little mental fatigue as possible. The most frequent cause of badly written English is a confusion of mind due, if not to ignorance, either to emotional stress or to dishonesty. Here I come to a dis-cussion of a particular case which I may be considered unwise to air, but the importance of which few will deny.

The Reverend Edmund Wasson, a Doctor in Philosophy at Columbia University, a Classical scholar and an obsessionist about the English language, was born in 1864. In the late 1930's he published a paper suggesting that one of the greatest stumbling blocks in the attempt to educate the American young was that Lincoln's Gettysburg address had been mistakenly forced on the youth of at least the Northern States as a model of the sublime use of the English language. He denied the speech to be sublime *at any rate as English prose* and suggested that all the numerous grammatical faults and equally numerous misleading, unnecessary, or ill-chosen words which strew it can be traced to distress of mind, a struggle with his conscience, and an uncomfortable feeling that his eulogy of the Federal dead did less than justice to the Confederate dead, who after all, fought only to preserve the rights granted them by the Constitution.

Lincoln's Gettysburg Address
November 1863

'Four score and seven years ago our fathers brought forth on this continent a new nation conceived in liberty and dedicated to the proposition that all men are created equal.

'Now we are engaged in a great civil war testing whether that nation, or any nation so conceived and so dedicated, can long endure. We are met on a great battlefield of that war. We are come to dedicate a portion of that field as a final resting-place for those who here gave their lives that that nation might live. It is altogether fitting and proper that we should do this. But, in a larger sense, we cannot dedicate, we cannot consecrate, we cannot hallow this ground. The brave men, living and dead, who struggled here have consecrated it far above our poor power to add or detract. The world will little note, nor long remember, what we say here. It is for us, the living, rather to be dedicated here to the unfinished work which they who fought here have thus far so nobly advanced. It is rather for us to be here dedicated to the great task remaining before us—that from these honoured dead we take increased devotion to that cause for which they gave the last full measure of devotion—that we here highly resolve that these dead shall not have died in vain, that this nation under God shall have a new birth of freedom, and that government of the people, by the people, for the people, shall not perish from the earth.'

No one, it is clear, can hold a reader's attention, let alone the attention of a large audience, by starting the first sentence with a difficult mathematical problem: 'Four score and seven years ago'. Few of us are capable of instant mental arithmetic. The Federal troops gathered at the cemetery had already been subjected to a two-hour speech by Edward Everett and were now asked to calculate as follows: 'how much is four score and seven years? Answer: eighty-seven. What year are we now in? I guess it's still eighteen sixty-three. Now, that is eighty-seven subtracted from eighteen hundred and sixty-three? Seven from thirteen leaves six: carry one; nine from sixteen leaves seven; carry one; one from eighteen is seventeen—answer: seventeen hundred and seventy-six.' By which time none but practised accountants would have caught up with the rest of the sentence; and even those would have been thrown once more by Lincoln's suggestion that their fathers brought forth a new nation on this continent, conceived in Liberty. It is one of the salient features of American life that only women conceive and only mothers bring forth; besides, 'forefathers' would have been more easily acceptable to Lincoln's literal-minded audience than 'fathers'. Matthew Arnold, on reading the Gettysburg address in an English newspaper, is said to have got only as far as the four score and seven years, the fathers bringing forth a nation, and this nation dedicated to a proposition—rather than to a burning faith or sublime ideal—before he pushed the newspaper aside. It is no more than a coincidence that Arnold held the Chair of Poetry at Oxford exactly a century before I did; but, of course, poetry makes far stronger demands on one's exact appreciation of the sense, power, and interrelation of words than prose does.

Lincoln uses the word 'we' in a confusing variety of senses: 'we' as all Northerners at war with the South; 'we' as all Northerners, less the soldiers who have survived the battle; 'we' as Secretary Seward and himself. He uses the word 'dedicate' six times: sometimes in the sense of 'commit', sometimes in the sense of 'consecrate', sometimes in the sense of 'devote'. He gets involved in an unnecessary swarm of 'here's' and 'great's'. His confused English certainly suggests to me the specific doubt as to whether it is morally right to consecrate a plot for the immortal Federal dead, while leaving the other side to rot unhonoured—as we English did with the Scots at Flodden Field after persuading the Pope to excommunicate King James of Scotland. Which is why he feels it necessary to add in self-defence 'Altogether fitting and proper to do so'. 'Altogether fitting and proper', like its fellow cliché 'this is neither the time nor the place', has entered the apologetic language of Big Business: a grandiloquence used to distract attention from misjudgments and calamities.

A London advertising firm had just lost two important accounts to a rival firm. The boss was forced to retrench by cutting down the staff, though without letting them suspect that business was on the skids. He sent for a highly paid copywriter, his first and obvious sacrificial victim, and told him, 'Mr Cabbage, it is altogether fitting and proper for me to commend the fine work you have done for us in the past few months, and I for one regard your departure as a great personal loss. If therefore you will go to our cashier——.' The copywriter said, 'So you're going to sack me? Don't you like the colour of my hair or my socks or something? If you don't mean that, what the hell is all this in aid of?' The flustered boss answered: 'This is neither the time nor the place, Mr. Cabbage, to ask such a question.'

Now, I am not here to decry Lincoln, but only to agree with Dr. Wasson on the inadequacies, as plain English prose, of the Gettysburg Address. In fact, although inaudible to all but a few front ranks of soldiers, for lack of a loud-speaker, it seems to have been the right speech for the occasion—short, highly emotional, and obviously his own work: not a handout. The audience must have divined that he was struggling against his own sense of guilt at having committed them to a fratricidal war—a guilt a thousand times enhanced by the physical evidence of the crime that now faced him; though indeed the passage of five months had given plenty of time for tidying up the battlefield. They themselves stood in equal need of spiritual justification, even if conveyed only by a distortion of history, and Lincoln did all he could to acquit them of the Curse of Cain.

Yet I think that if a committee of level-headed writers were called upon to draft Lincoln a speech in retrospect—one that should be short, historically unassailable, simple in wording, with enough emotional balm in it to solace the shivering survivors of that accursed day in July, one above all written in straight English prose that could be published in the papers for national reading, they would probably settle for something like this:

Some ninety years ago a noble group of American patriots—our forefathers—chosen spokesmen of thirteen colonies, signed and published a Declaration of Independence, still the prime charter of our Liberties. They protested to a tyrannical king that, having been born free, they were entitled to equal rights not only with his other subjects but with all free men everywhere. This challenge was taken up by their British oppressors and, in the bitter war for freedom that ensued, each former colony played its heroic part. A new Nation had come into being, a Union presently confirmed by a Constitutional treaty of independent states, bound together in loyalty under a central guiding power directed by their own chosen President.

Suddenly however, this same Union, after long showing the

free world its unanimous resolve to preserve popular government against all aggression or interference whatsoever, has been
ignobly flouted by a conspiracy of rebel states. After our urgent
and persistent pleas for a change of heart had been rudely
rejected, we at Washington saw no honourable alternative at
last but to order the rebels' subjection by force of arms.

Here then we stand confronted by records of the hideous
carnage that their obduracy has forced upon us: and I have
come, as your President, to consecrate a part of this stricken
field as a burial plot for the heroic and victorious dead who
fought, not only for the Union but for the spirit of Freedom and
Equality which this Union was created to sustain.

To render your fallen comrades sufficient homage would be
manifestly impossible. They have sacrificed their all for our
ancestral faith. Nevertheless, while dedicating this plot to their
sacred memory, let us at the same time humbly rededicate our
own hearts to the triumphant cause for which they died—and
not in vain. Let us re-establish this loyal Union of Independent
States as the one sure means of defending our nation against
tyranny from without and against rebellion from within. And
may God assist us in the completion of this burdensome and
heart-rending task.

You will notice the real *casus belli* is clearly and openly given
here. No mention of slavery is needed, since the Founding Fathers
had demanded only equal Freedom with King George's other free
subjects, not ranking Negro slaves with themselves—as Lincoln's
'All men are born free and equal' suggests to school children
today. Even in 1789, the year of the Constitution, slavery persisted
in every State of the Union but one; indeed President George
Washington's principal commercial interest was breeding slaves
for the market. Moreover, the Emancipation that Lincoln had
proclaimed was, he himself emphasized, ordered not in the interests of equality but as a war measure in the interest of the Union.
Indeed, he had emancipated slaves only in the States that had
seceded from the Union, not in the loyal Border states; and had
repeatedly declared that the Civil War was fought to save the
Union 'with or without Slavery'. Many years before, we English
had emancipated the slaves in our West Indian Sugar Islands: not
for religious, but for economic reasons. Slave-owners realized that
free labour was cheaper and more effective: they could lay off free

labour in times of falling prices and feel no responsibility for the sick or aged. And it was this realization that made our famous English Liberal leader, the generous-hearted William Ewart Gladstone, speak forcefully against Abolition in his maiden speech at the House of Commons.

By the way, my prize for official prolixity of words goes to the esteemed Warden of the State Penitentiary of Oklahoma—an institution which, I was informed recently, had engulfed the Oklahoma father of two teen-age daughters, wards-of-court, whom he had smuggled into England. He sneaked back home to collect some money to pay their English school fees, but got arrested on the Mexican border. I wrote to tell him how to get in touch with his daughters who, hearing that the British police were after them, had now moved on.

A fortnight later I got the following letter:

Dear Sir:

Your letter of recent postdate is being returned to you in accordance with predetermined institutional rules, for the reason or reasons checked below.

1. ( ) Your name is not on approved mailing list.
2. ( ) Your letter contains more than four sheets of paper.
3. ( ) Your letter is not written in the English language.
4. ( ) Your letter contains what is considered improper language or is not in the best interests of the inmate.
5. ( ) Your letter is not written legibly enough for censoring.
6. (×) Other. Not at Oklahoma State Penitentiary.

Very truly yours.

X. Y. Z.

WARDEN

In England we merely return the envelope to the sender with 'Gone Away' stamped on it.

19

The decline in bullfighting

The popular *corrida* has developed down the centuries from the countryside sport of letting bulls loose in a village square for assembled *valientes* to bait. True, it borrowed a certain pomp from the Royal Spanish bullfight as first celebrated by the Moorish Kings of Granada, in which *rejoneadores*, well-mounted noblemen, killed bulls with lances and, if unhorsed, used scimitars to defend themselves. But *corrida de toros* once meant no more than 'running of bulls'. The original running is still commemorated at Pamplona in Northern Spain during the five-day Feast of San Fermin. A small herd of bulls careers through the streets every morning, on its way to the bullring, and stout-hearted citizens who dare stay out of doors as they pass try to grab horns and twist tails for good luck. Serious casualties always occur.

From this exercise in communal baiting the heroic matador slowly emerged. *Matador* once meant 'knacker'—a professional butcher chosen to finish off bulls after they had been baited to a standstill by mastiffs, picadors, banderilleros and volunteers with capes. Little glory should therefore be given Romero, 'victor of six thousand bulls', whose tercentenary the town of Ronda celebrated not long ago. Romero reached the age of sixty-four without a single goring, which proves him to have been an exceedingly cautious man. Perhaps the first matador in anything like the present-day sense was Cuchares, whom journalists honour when they use 'the art of Cuchares' as a synonym for bullfighting; he seems to have both directed and assisted in the corrida's preliminary phases. Guerrita, the last old-style matador of note, fought towards the close of the nineteenth century and enjoyed killing by the dangerous method called *recibiendo*: that is, he would spit a charging bull on the sword-point.

Modern bullfighting did not start until 1907. Its inventor, Juan Belmonte, has miraculously survived, though battle-scarred from head to feet. Before Belmonte's day, a matador making passes in the corrida's final phase would advance one leg and hold out the red *muleta* at the full extent of his arm, thus allowing a wide interval between himself and the horns. Belmonte narrowed the safety margin to a few inches: standing upright, feet together, and letting the muleta guide the terrible horns just clear of his thighs. Joselito, Belmonte's cousin, adopted these tactics until killed in 1915. Thereafter nobody dared keep the bull at a distance, or skip about while playing him, for fear of being branded as a coward. In this renascence of bullfighting, the many different passes were finally formalized and perfected, and the sport of bullfighting became an art. The matadors soon combined into a powerful guild under State sponsorship. Only an approved member might now take on brave full-grown bulls. To graduate, he went through a tough apprenticeship as a *novillero*, dealing with four-year-olds, or underweight five-year-olds. Then, at last, he took his *alternativa* at an initiatory fight.

For centuries, corridas had been annually staged in celebration of particular religious festivals: such as the Seville Spring Fair, the Feast of San Isidoro at Madrid, the Feast of San Jaime at Valencia, the Feast of San Fermin at Pamplona—all of which lasted several days. These festivals keep their importance; but the city square no longer serves as the bullring, and every big Spanish town has a corrida at least once a week, weather permitting, from April to October. There are several hundred permanent bullrings in Spain.

The years between the outbreak of World War One and that of the Spanish Civil War in 1936, will go down to history as the Golden Age of Bullfighting. Matadors were courageous, audiences responsive, bulls heavy and fierce. Besides Belmonte and Joselito, we had the temperamental El Gallo, the classically elegant Bienvenida brothers, the resourceful Barrera, and the dare-devil Mexicans Carnicerito and El Soldado. Also Marciál Lalanda, who perfected the *mariposa*, an attractive feat of running backwards and moving the cape behind his body from side to side so that the bull constantly changes direction. And the greatest of them all: Domingo Ortega, once an illiterate young *valiente* of Borox near Toledo. He would dominate his bulls by talking to them as he fought, telling them what he expected of them, until the moment came for ritual sacrifice. So far from being the slender, handsome type of matador, Ortega was ungainly, chubby-faced, round-shouldered, and walked with a slouch. Yet he persuaded difficult and evil-hearted bulls to play around him like poodles. Though his jealous rivals said: 'What luck he has in drawing easy bulls!', it happened too often for coincidence. A foreign *aficionado* once shouted, just as Ortega was about to kill: 'Stop, fool! You can sell that beast for a million pesetas as a performing animal!' Now rich, grizzled, revered and highly educated, Ortega made a sensational come-back in his fifties, as skilful as ever.

By the time that World War Two ended, the Silver Age had begun. Its leading figure, Manolete, performed exquisitely with cape and muleta until gored to death at Linares in 1947. Under his rule, graceful passes rather than the business of preparing a bull for slaughter and then dispatching him cleanly, became the matador's main preoccupation. Manolete was, to be frank, a bad *matador*, in the sense that he seldom killed at the first attempt. A popular refrain accused him of not being able to kill a bathroom cockroach. A more serious criticism was that he worked his bulls so close as to give them no room for manœuvre, thus gaining safety by a pretence of recklessness. Manolete performed coldly and unsmilingly, as a famous surgeon might show hospital internes the right way to remove an appendix, and seemed to despise his audience. This broke a Golden Age tradition of warm friendship between the matador and his *aficionados*, who suffered and rejoiced with him, following the niceties of play as if in the ring themselves. Those Golden Age bulls were fighters, and though the required weight of a single beast was fixed fairly low, the average weight of an afternoon's six had always been far higher. During the early 'Thirties I saw bulls scaling five hundred pounds above the legal minimum, and tall enough to look over a six-foot *barrera*. Hardy beasts, too, bred for courage and speed, with huge horns. By the late 'Forties they were being bred as near the minimum as possible, and often confined to paddocks where they took insufficient exercise; so that their weight consisted of fat rather than muscle. When such bulls rush out of the *toril*, they appear formidable enough; but their legs and lungs are weak, and they come up for no more punishment once the *banderillas* have been well placed. Only a few good herds remain, to be used at special corridas.

Some years ago, Antonio Bienvenida publicly exposed the Silver Age trick of cutting four or five inches off a bull's horns and shaving the butt to a point again. This was done half an hour before the corrida began and, the horn tips being then at an unfamiliar angle to the bull's eye, he misjudged distances, much to the matador's benefit. Manolete had all his bulls doctored in this way, though the public never knew it. Among other unethical tricks were using false scales; giving a bull constipating fodder or tranquillizers; and allowing the picadors to cripple him with an illegally long lance-blade. When most of these abuses were officially banned, casualties rose and some matadors quit. But at Madrid, Seville and Barcelona alone can one still hope to see an honest fight.

A prominent matador clears four thousand dollars a performance after paying his own squadron of picadors, banderilleros, capemen and the rest. He seldom contracts for fewer than eighty corridas a season, and may also undertake a winter programme in Mexico and South America. This means big money. And bullfighting is the one sure ladder from the gipsy camp or hovel to the ranks of Spanish society—look at Belmonte and Ortega! Yet no more arduous profession exists, and by the time a *novillero* has been safely enrolled in the guild, he too often rests on his laurels and does as little as possible to earn his fees. He will have taken several bad gorings already, so why court danger? And why waste one's talents to amuse ignorant tourists?

This is the real trouble! The decline of bullfighting may be confidently ascribed to the immense tourist influx. Most of the annual four million would think ill of themselves if they had omitted a corrida from their visit. They do not come to see sport; they cannot appreciate the art; but they want to witness the spectacle. And, as a spectacle, a corrida remains superb: the well-mounted old *alguazils* wearing sixteenth century costume, the slender matadors in expensively braided jackets and tights, the burly picadors with their long boots and wide-brimmed hats, the coloured silk capes, the trumpets, the band playing *paso dobles*, and the black bull suddenly charging out across the sand.... Tourists have cash to spend, and it would be foolish to deny them this romantic vision of antique Spain.

The Spanish Government has helped the bullrings by banning much of the barbarity which once attended corridas. First, the mastiffs were dropped; they had been trained to attack the bull's muzzle and genitals. Next, the gaunt, highly expendable hacks ridden by picadors were provided with thick quilted coats reaching to the knees. A disembowelled horse is a shocking sight, and three or four horses might be massacred by a single bull. But tourists never consider that the internal injuries suffered when a strong bull evades the lance, charges a quilted horse square, and then returns to the charge, may be crueller than a mortal horning. Nor are they encouraged to disbelieve in the protection afforded by the quilt; because if it were not for tourists, the rings would stay almost empty. Even at Seville, the home of bullfighting, not enough seats are sold after the Spring Fair has ended to attract expensive matadors; most foreigners find the city too hot for a summer holiday.

Spaniards no longer wholeheartedly support the National Fiesta. From habit they attend certain corridas of prestige, where the bulls are the best obtainable, and the matadors on their mettle. Otherwise, they watch football matches and see keener sport for less money. The most depressing entertainment in the world is a bad bullfight. Thus, nine times out of ten, the small group of *aficionados* who react immediately to every turn of play with either acclamation or scorn, gets smothered by the vast, excited but puzzled mass. Not that the *aficionados* are always reliable judges. Ortega has said sourly: 'Many *aficionados*, but no experts! When I am in the ring, only two of us know what is happening: the bull and myself.'*

Convalescent after a bad goring, Luis Miguel Dominguin, a fortnight ago, discussed the difficulty of renewing the public's faith in the seriousness of his art. Dominguin, the finest matador still fighting, declared that few Spaniards now know what they really see and feel, but wait to be told next day on the radio, and in the newspapers, what they should have seen and felt. Though he had seldom fought better than on the occasion of his goring, the public responded half-heartedly. Hardly anyone noticed that

---

* I versified this as follows, giving Domingo Ortega credit for the thought, and applying it to the popular criticism of poets:

> Bull-fight critics ranked in rows
> Crowd the enormous plaza full;
> But only one is there who *knows*
> And he's the man who fights the bull.

President John Kennedy picked this up and quoted it at his first press conference after election to the Presidency; but told the press that it had been written by the Spanish philosopher Ortega y Gasset.

he got caught not by clumsiness, nor because of a defect in the bull's eyesight, but by a sudden puff of wind which moved the muleta too close to his body, and drew the horns with it.

Dominguin and Antonio Ordóñez, his brilliant brother-in-law, backed by two or three others, including the Venezuelan Cesar Girón, are trying in amicable rivalry to bring back the Golden Age. Yet how can they succeed? Breeders realize that unless they produce 'comfortable' bulls for unadventurous matadors, they will go out of business. The old hardy stock is almost extinct. The predominantly Spanish audiences of the Golden Age would not tolerate a fighter who shirked, or who let a bull run the fight instead of running it himself. Nowadays, a matador can continue to earn big money, though he has shown no heroism for years and seems unlikely to do so again. Even the most 'comfortable' bull is potentially dangerous, he reminds himself. The foreign tourist will not protest, and the natives who might protest are all away in the football stadium. At Vittoria, the President of a corrida has just taken the bold step of fining a lazy matador and ordering him to leave the ring; but will this scandal ruin the offender's career? It will not.

The other day I watched Dominguin deal with two bad bulls at Palma de Mallorca, before twenty thousand English, French, German, Dutch, Swiss and Scandinavian tourists, reinforced by a detachment from the American Sixth Fleet. He good-humouredly squeezed the last ounce of fight out of these animals. Furthermore, he consented to amuse the visitors with perilous circus tricks: sitting on the lower ledge of the *barrera*, from where he waved the bull past him, and afterwards *telefoneando*, which means negligently leaning an elbow on the beaten bull's forehead, as if phoning an acquaintance. Yet this is the same man who, in the ring with brave bulls and a warm, appreciative audience, fights as nobly and unostentatiously as Belmonte and Ortega ever did. When he and Ordóñez retire, I see little to prevent a further decisive drop from the Silver to the Leaden Age. It will be a victory for Big Business. Too many matadors are in the game merely to enrich themselves, and no *novilleros* of outstanding promise seem to be on the way. But miracles may still happen.

20

The phenomenon of mass-tourism

(An address given in Spanish to the Ateneo Club, Madrid)

I first made Spain my home in 1929, under Primo de Rivera's dictatorship. I have remained here ever since, except for an interval of absence forced on me by the Civil War. The code of chivalry obliges a man to take his leave when arguments arise at the table where he is a guest and he witnesses deeds of domestic violence which he can do nothing to prevent. I returned when the embers of civil strife had cooled enough for me to reassume the political neutrality I had made a condition of my residence here. I may add that during the short visits I make to my own country, I am equally non-political. My four children, who have been born or brought up in Spain, think of it and always will think of it as their home; and so do I. My chief regret has been that they laugh at me for my wretched accent—for which ladies and gentlemen, I beg your indulgence—but then I was thirty-three when I first came here: too late for learning to speak like a native.

I have always been treated by my Spanish hosts with the greatest courtesy and indulgence; I wish I could claim that the English showed the same invariable kindness to foreigners. And although as a writer with no greater burden to carry around than a pen, a bottle of ink, and the paint-brush I use for scoring out badly composed or ill-constructed sentences, I could live anywhere in the world—here is where my heart lies. You can judge therefore that the things I have to say tonight are not rapid impressions of a visitor to Spain, but the conclusions of one who has time enough to mature his judgments on this extraordinary twentieth century phenomenon, mass-tourism.

Old-fashioned tourism was individual. The word, in fact, is derived from the 'Grand Tour' that young English milords were expected to take in the seventeenth and eighteenth centuries through France, Italy and Germany—under the charge of a tutor —with the object of widening their minds. Spain, though not included in the itinerary while the Holy Inquisition remained a threat to Protestants, was fortunate in being first touristically introduced to the British public by an early nineteenth century connoisseur of art, and a true lover of the Spanish people: he was Richard Ford, the author of *A Handbook for Travellers*. By Ford's time, tourism had spread to gentlemen of leisure, if of less distinguished birth, travelling without tutors. (The Swiss Alps were also added to the Tour: Jean-Jacques Rousseau having discovered, to everyone's surprise, that mountain scenery was sublime and beautiful.)

Thirty-five years ago, I emigrated to Spain which had beckoned me since childhood. My elder brother went abroad when I was ten or eleven, and I succeeded to his bedroom, where I found that he had left behind a manual of Spanish conversation. I studied it and decided: 'That is a very clear, clean language. The Spaniards must be a good people. I wish they taught it at my school instead of German and French.' And many years later I discovered my preference—condemned by others as uneducated—for Spanish red wine over French, and Spanish pictures over Italian.

I chose Mallorca on the advice of my friend Gertrude Stein: 'Majorca is Paradise, if you can take it.' What she meant by this, she explained, was that nothing had ever happened in Mallorca but that, unless I had work to occupy myself with, the Serpent would slide out of some olive or lemon grove and my fall would be assured.

Mallorca could already boast of a small British colony—retired civil servants from Asian and African dependencies, who had not dared face either the English climate or the high cost of domestic help at home. This colony was centred on El Terreno, an 'Isabelina' suburb of Palma; and three of the island's six recommendable hotels had been built there. At the other end of the island, moreover, Pollensa Port had become a successor of the Dieppe celebrated a hundred years before by Coleridge as the refuge of 'Delinquent Travellers'; it attracted a libertarian society not only of the epoch's 'Bright Young Things' but of inverts, swindlers, drugtakers and alcoholics, whom their harassed families supplied with a small quarterly remittance on condition that they never darkened their country's shores again. Pollensa was at once warmer, cheaper, and farther away than Dieppe. I decided against El Terreno, where they played bridge all day; and Pollensa, where they played strip poker all night; and settled instead at Deyá, a village on the wild north-west coast. There I learned a basic Spanish, built a house, lived like a rich peasant, and never left the island for six years. It was Paradise, and I found that I could take it.

About 1931, a small tourist boom began, which troubled me despite such advantages as being now able to buy in Palma cow's milk, beef, butter, teapots, kettles, beer and ready-made sheets, none of which had hitherto been procurable. Several new hotels were added to the six; a small golf course was laid out at Alcudia; blurred pictures of film stars appeared in the local press, the Duke of Westminster anchored his yacht off the Palma mole, and the Prince of Wales himself put up at the Formentor Hotel where he composed a bagpipe march, *Mallorca*, for the Scots Guards pipers. But we still had only a single travel agent, the famous Mr. F. G. Short (recently deceased) who, not content with representing both the Royal Yacht Squadron and Thos. Cook & Sons, found time to run a tea-room, an English lending library, and a house-renting agency.

This boom was shattered on July 18th, 1936, by the Civil War. The Island decided against the Republic, and soon army planes from Minorca dropped bombs and leaflets demanding surrender. All the four or five thousand foreign residents, mainly British, including the stupefied remittance men and women from Pollensa, were evacuated by warships: with the exception of a few obstinate old ladies, who refused either to desert their cats or to leave them quarantined for six months in a British port. I went, too, with a single handbag. The Civil War had not long ended before the Second World War broke out. Between them, they kept me away until May 1946, when my family and I had the distinction of being the first civilian passengers to alight at Palma airport. We came by air-taxi, because all frontiers were still closed and no regular air-lines or shipping lines operated—to find ourselves the sole foreigners there (except for the same obstinate old cat-loving ladies), and severe food shortages awaiting us. It was not until 1950, that the situation returned to normal, the frontiers opened, and the tourist trickle grew to a steady stream. I remember a contemporary *New Yorker* cartoon of an old lady who asks a travel agent, 'Whatever happened to the nice cheap little islands in the Mediterranean, which you used to advertise once?'

'All handsome men are slightly tanned' is a British advertising slogan. That all beautiful girls are *heavily* tanned was a new idea, derived from D. H. Lawrence's German-inspired sun cult. Until then, the whiter the skin the lovelier—which explains the Victorian veil, parasol and huge Florentine hat. But tourists' vacations are too brief for developing a tan on rocky beaches or grass. Hence the importance of sand, which does the work within a week. When an English girl returns brown as a berry to her friends, they can *see* that she has been abroad. Beaches are also safest for families. In valleys and on mountains, children constantly break their legs, get stung by vipers, fall into chasms. Besides, the Mediterranean is free of tides, and sand is a cheap, clean plaything. (Of course, accidents do happen: tourists sometimes go to sleep on a beach in the sun, after a heavy meal, and get frizzled up; others drown in three feet of water. Still, on the average. . . .) Mallorca possesses not only a range of high mountains rising boldly from the sea, but two or three hundred miles of sandy beaches edging flat country of no agricultural value—when I first came here, one could walk the entire length and, except at an occasional small fishing village, meet hardly a soul.

Thus, when the European economy recovered sensationally, when air travel became cheap and safe as well as rapid, and tourists could get to Mallorca from London by plane far more easily than they once could get to the cold and rainy beaches of North Wales and Scotland by train, anyone with business vision could have foreseen the brand-new phenomenon of mass-tourism abroad—meaning charter flights, block-booking of hotels, and so clever a rationalizing of ways and means that a fortnight's vacation can cost no more, and sometimes even less, than an individual return air fare. The business now brings five thousand planes a month every summer to a new and vastly enlarged Palma airport, and has encouraged the building of over a thousand new hotels. Spain, I am told, expects twenty million tourists this year, and I can see nothing against the exploitation of these derelict foreshores as 'throw-away' tourist resorts.

Mass-tourists ask little except the same sort of food that they eat at home: the English, for example, scorn any meal that does not include potatoes—to hell with rice and spaghetti! And who wants wine, when he can get beer? They don't object to a little local colour, especially flamenco-strumming by pretended gipsies, and gaudy souvenirs: dolls in provincial costume, inlaid Toledo steel paper-knives, plastic castanets dangling coloured ribbons, leather wine-bottles, olive-wood bowls and boxes, bullfighting posters with their own names printed between those of El Litri and Jaime Ostos. . . . But they shy away from any closer approach to the real Spain than an afternoon at the bullfight which either puzzles or shocks them. The Civil Guards humour and forgive their occasional extravagances of behaviour, so long as they refrain from insulting the national flag, the Catholic religion, public decency, or the Civil Guard itself. The English tourist's most lasting and pleasurable memories are the friendships he has struck up with members of the same group from the same home town; and the bowling-alleys, bars and night clubs supplied by the organizers of the town. Moreover, Mallorca has so relaxing a climate that people who usually sleep seven hours a night find they need ten.

A young girl was overheard to ask another on a London bus: 'Where did you go for your holidays, Marge?'

'Italy: it rained all the time, and the food tasted funny. What about you?'

'Majorca. It was ever so nice.'

'Where's Majorca?'

'I don't know: I flew.'

An American friend who acts as a professional guide here had to take groups out every night on a tour called *Palma de Noche*, which included a ride around the harbour in a motor launch, visits to night clubs and bars, and free champagne. Good Catalan champagne, *brut*, is a splendid drink, but my friend learned to hate tourist champagne, and to hate mock-flamenco, and eventually to hate the tourists and their interminable foolish questions. One day I met him looking happy—for the first time in weeks, and asked him why. 'One of my new group has done the only sensible thing that any of them yet did.' 'What was that?' 'Threw himself out of the hotel window; it will make me a lot of extra work . . . But I'm deeply grateful to him somehow. Often feel like that myself . . .' He went on: 'The only way I can stick this life is to invent stories for them on our coach-tours: there's a ghastly Moorish-style mansion along the Inca Road, built by a retired Austrian businessman under the Republic. I tell my coach-load that's where Alfonso XIII signed his Abdication, and that two Czarist Grand

Dukes use it now as a gambling den, with ten thousand pesetas as the lowest stake permitted; and that Greta Garbo used to be a dance hostess there. . . . The poor morons lap it up like the champagne. There's nothing much to show them in the tourist season, except mountains and the blue sea streaked with white currents. The harvest is already in, the vintage hasn't begun, the olives have hardly formed on the trees, the almond blossom has long disappeared, the oranges are still green, and the soil is too hard to plough . . .'

Where mass-tourism becomes entangled with individual travel, the latter invariably suffers: hotels, planes, ships, beaches, beauty spots, all are monopolized by groups. Once, at the height of our season, a friend of mine had to hurry over from Barcelona because her mother was dangerously ill. Every plane and boat-ticket was sold out. At last she ran into a group bound for Palma, one member of which had been taken to hospital; she took this woman's place, paying not only her fare, but ten days' pension and sight-seeing.

Tourists are good animals. The most easily domesticated, the Majorcans agree, are my compatriots, of whom three hundred thousand are expected this year. They never argue over prices, or stray into private gardens to pick fruit or flowers, or sunbathe nude in public places, or produce soap and razor and shave themselves in public fountains—like some other nationals. Nor do their girls come here expressly to be seduced by handsome, black-eyed matadors or gipsy dancers. Last summer, a German girl complained of rape, and of having been threatened with murder if she would not consent. The victim, an honest mason, was immediately thrown in jail on the ground that the tourist is always right. It appears that the girl had snuggled up to the mason by way of revenge on her fiancé, who had gone off elsewhere. The mason, unaware of the circumstances and astonished by the girl's behaviour (which he mistook for love at first sight), had no language in common with her except some very elementary French. He babbled: '*Tu es . . . tu es . . .*', and then, unable to think of the *mot juste*—'*belle*' being insufficient—rolled his eyes and squeezed her still tighter. The mason expressed surprise that she yielded so completely, but the quick-witted judge before whom the case came, released him. It was proved that the girl's knowledge of French was equally limited: she had understood *tu es* as meaning *tuer*—a threat to kill her!

Mallorca is fortunate perhaps in its lack of exploitable historical attractions; mass-tourism and individual travel need not get confused. Bellver Castle is ancient, well-proportioned, and placed in a dominant position above Palma harbour. But never having stood a siege in all its history, it has won no fame except as a former prison for Liberals, Protestants, and other notorious evil-doers. Apart from the conquest of the Island in 1229 by King James of Aragon, a Peasant Revolt in the fifteenth century, and Captain Bayo's brief and disastrous Catalan invasion in 1936, no memorable passage of arms has ever happened here. And of the Moors hardly a trace remains beyond a few walls of the Almudaina, the King of Mallorca's Palace—now the Captain-General's residence; a dry and derelict Arab Baths, and the City Mosque converted into the Church of San Miguel. Since the City Fathers of Palma long ago destroyed their mediaeval city walls and gates in the name of Progress so little of historical interest remains to show the tourists, that the natives have been tempted to com-memorate a curious episode of 1835: a visit paid them by George Sand, the novelist, and her lover Fréderic Chopin, who spent a few unhappy weeks (hating, and being hated by, the inhabitants) in the white-washed cells of an abandoned monastery at Vall-demosa. Chopin, sick of consumption, haunted by his Polish-Catholic guilt of adultery, and perishing of cold in one of the severest Majorcan winters recorded, hired a piano, wrote a Prelude or two, and once witnessed a local folk dance. This has been made the peg on which to hang a tremendous legend, exploited daily for the benefit of twenty or thirty tourist coach-loads, with visits to the Chopin Museum Cell, the famous piano (the authenticity of which remains dubious), and dances performed by a professional troupe in nineteenth century costumes. Well, it makes a good outing.

From Valldemosa the buses rumble along the spectacular coast road—three hundred metres above the sea at one point—and pre-sently disgorge their load at Son Marroig, where the Archduke Luis Salvator of Austria lived so long and eccentrically. The tourists are told of lovely Catalina Homar, for whom the ageing Archduke professed a pure and romantic love, and who died of leprosy (contracted during a pilgrimage to the Holy Land aboard his yacht, the *Nixe*) in a house built for her on the rocky headland, guarded day and night by enormous wolfhounds. . . . In fact, Catalina was a very efficient peasant-girl, with a face like a boot and limbs like clubs, who supervised the Archduke's vineyard and won him gold and silver medals for wine at International Exhibitions, and who died of a disease less glamorous even than leprosy.

On their way from Son Marroig to the orange-growing town of Sóller, the buses come hooting through Deyá, and halt outside my house. I can hear the loudspeaker inside: '*A gauche ancien olivier caracteristiquement tortu; aussi LA BAIE DE DEYÁ; à droit demeure le célèbre écriveur* [sic] *americain Robertson* ...' Fortunately the rocks from which we swim are inaccessible to buses, nor is our village easily exploitable by the mass-tourist.

The next day they will visit the Artificial Pearl Factory at Manacor; and afterwards the Caves of Drach, where guides will tell them over the public-address system in three languages what the stalactite and stalagmite formations look like—the Tomb of Napoléon, the Arab Tent, the Frigate. . . . They will listen, from the dark shores of a subterranean lake, to the *Barcarolle* played by an orchestra rowed past in a boat lit by fairy lights; and then spend nearly an hour waiting for another boat to take them across to the exit, in batches of twenty. . . . The only fault that can be found with these caves is that they contain no mammoth or other bones, no prehistoric paintings of horses, bulls, or gazelles. . . . But nor, for that matter, will any cave in Spain or France be so blessed in another fifty years' time. The daily exhalations of carbon dioxide from the lungs of several hundred tourists is, I am told, rapidly flaking off the colours.

*   *   *   *   *

Why should I, a poet, come to a learned society and talk about tourism? Because poets are (or should be) practical people, aware of what goes on around them, and uncommitted to any political or economic or institutional bias. If they have any one interest in life, it is the preservation of *báraka*—a word you Spaniards have borrowed from the Moors, though using it in a more limited sense. *Báraka* derives from a Semitic root BRK, present in the Biblical name *Barak* and in the Phoenician *Barka*—the city of Barcelona is, of course, called after Hamilcar Barca, Hannibal's father. *Barak* or *barka* or *báraka* means 'lightning'. Since lightning is a phenomenon everywhere attributed to the gods, *báraka* connotes the sudden divine rapture which overcomes either a prophet or a group of fervent devotees—whom it unites in a bond of love: it can therefore stand for the blessedness acquired by holy shrines and other places where the spirit of God has plainly been manifested. The poems of Ramon Llull, who wrote his famous *Amic y Amat* in our village in 1283, and those of St. John of the Cross also, have *báraka*. The word has Hebrew equivalents; but the Jews prefer to derive *báraka* from a root meaning 'knee', and therefore devotion to a deity whose worshippers kneel when they pray.

This religious metaphor invites lay uses. If a family has settled down peacefully in a house of their own choosing, every room acquires a domestic, rather than an ecstatic, *báraka*, of which the children become conscious and which spells 'home'. *Báraka* can thus be applied to relics, keepsakes, and other assurances of blessedness. An Arab village woman will prize the dented brass cooking pot that has done service for a generation or more, as having *báraka* and producing far tastier food than the brightest spun-aluminium saucepan in the bazaar.

The problem of tourism is, in my opinion, mainly one of preserving a country's *báraka*. What I felt about the Spanish language as a child, and what I felt about Spain itself when I first came here, was a sense of *báraka* unsurpassed by any other country I had visited. And tourism, though I have joked about it this evening and conceded its great benefits to the national economy, can (if allowed to follow along the lines dictated by international big business) be no less damaging than a civil war: in its destruction of national *báraka*.

John Kenneth Galbraith and his fellow-economists in the United States have emphasized that the old American ideal of thrift, which implied producing durable goods and using them with affectionate care until they can be bequeathed to children and grandchildren, no longer thrives even in the backwoods. Instead, expendability is preached: the manufacture and consumption of goods not meant to last for more than a short season. If a new appliance proves to have an uneconomically long life, it must be replaced by a shorter-lived substitute. With care, you may perhaps keep this year's model working for several years; then something will snap, and nobody will offer to repair it. That these practices keep the wheels of industry turning, and salesmen busy, cannot be denied; but when nothing lasts long enough to become an integral part of a man's life, the principles of artificial obsolescence affect his friendships, loyalties, loves and his tastes in literature and art. The American way of life has now gained a firm foothold in Europe.

M

Anything made by hand has a certain glow of life. Factory-made objects are born dead—however apt their design, however sound their construction, and must have life breathed into them by affectionate use. A veteran typewriter of which you have grown fond seems to reciprocate your feelings, and even encourage the flow of thought. Though at first a lifeless assemblage of parts, it eventually comes alive. And so did an automobile in thriftier days. As for cameras—any good photographer is horror-struck by the loss of a camera that has grown to be part of himself: even if he buys an identical model, there will be a delay of anything from six months to two years before it learns to take his own inimitable sort of picture. Scientists cannot explain such phenomena, and therefore dispute the facts. Let them! *Báraka* will never become a scientific term.

Báraka in literature and the creative arts is of the utmost importance, since the word originally meant 'divine inspiration' or 'blessedness'—a quality which the most daring intellectual experiments, or works most shrewdly designed for the current market, cannot possess. The new economists, respecting a citizen's inalienable right to buy what he wants (or thinks that he wants), let the question 'Will it sell?' rule commercial production. Yet *báraka*—the quality of life in poems, or stories, or paintings, or sculptures, or music, as well as in lesser crafts—is never granted to a man more concerned with selling than with making.

Thus for me, the problem of tourism may be reduced to the question of how much *báraka* you are prepared to forfeit for the comforts of modernity. Modernity has its obvious advantages. I do not sigh for the reign of Philip II, when the Englishman Dr. Andrew Boorde declared that he would rather travel five times to Rome than once to Spain; nor for the reign of Charles III, when a rich young English traveller, Swinburne, described the hardships of travelling as follows:

'We are obliged to carry not only our beds, but bread, wine, meat, oil and salt from one great town to another; for we seldom meet with anything in the inns but bare walls, and perhaps a few eggs, which are sold at an unconscionable price. If we chance to find a few unbroken chairs, we esteem ourselves uncommonly fortunate; yet it is astonishing how dear travelling is in this country. As much is asked for giving you houseroom, as would purchase a good supper and lodgings in the best inns in most

other parts of Europe. As our health is excellent, and conse-
quently our spirits good, we are easily reconciled to these kinds
of hardships. . . . The mildness of the climate obviates all in-
conveniences that might accrue from a total want of glass, or
even paper, in the windows; or of a door or shutter that can be
fastened close enough to keep wind or rain out.

'As soon as we arrive at one of these barns, called *Ventas*, our
first care is to set up our beds. The kitchen is generally at one
end; the mules stand in the back part, and our apartment is a
partition run up against the wall of the street, with a hole or two
for light, defended by three or four very useless iron bars, for
a pigmy could not squeeze through the window.

'Next, our cook takes his stand at the hearth, to warm our
broth which we carry, ready-made, in a kettle behind our
chaise; and if he can procure fuel and elbow-room, tosses up a
hash, or some such campaign dish. Sometimes we are lucky
enough to have an opportunity of setting our spit, or broiling a
chop upon our grid-iron; but these luxuries we are not to
expect above once or twice in the course of a week.'

Nor do I regret the mid-nineteenth century, when Théophile
Gautier remarked:

'Not far from this *venta*, to the right of the road, stood some
pillars on which the heads of three or four malefactors were
exposed to view: this is always a reassuring sight, and proves
that one is in a civilized country.'

At the same period Richard Ford recorded the muleteers'
opposition to the railways:

'The muleteer constitutes one of the most numerous and
finest classes in Spain, and is the legitimate channel of the semi-
Oriental caravan system. He will never permit the bread to be
taken out of his mouth by the Lutheran locomotive; deprived
of means of earning his livelihood, he, like the smuggler, will take
to the road in another line, and both will become either robbers
or patriots. Many, long, and lonely are the leagues which
separate town from town in the wide deserts of thinly-populated
Spain, nor will any preventive service be sufficient to guard the
rail against the *guerilla* warfare that may then be waged. A

handful of opponents in any cistus-overgrown waste may, at any time, in five minutes, break up the rail road, stop the train, stick the stoker, and burn the engineers in their own fire, particularly smashing the luggage-van.'

By the way, my grandfather, in 1849, was travelling in a train thus attacked. Opposite him sat an English colonel (a Peninsular War veteran, come to re-visit Spain) who continued to read *The Times* until the hubbub ended.

Spain is at last admitted to be both safe for foreigners to visit and well equipped to receive those in need of ease and comfort. Moreover, she cannot complete her economic recovery without tourism; which has become a major industry. Yet the emotional fervour of this country even at its most passionate, should never be sacrificed for the benefit of tourists.

The individual tourist should be encouraged to move about freely in the real Spain and treated as a honoured visitor, so long as he behaves with the same courtesy that Spaniards expect of one another. And not too much attention should be paid to his criticisms, which are often astonishingly stupid. An educated American whom I met had two main complaints against Spanish custom: one was the pouring out of wine from old dusty bottles. . . . The other was the disgusting practice of child marriage. This charge puzzled me until I discovered that he had visited Spain in the Easter vacations when the streets were filled with little girls in bridal costumes and little boys in sailor suits on their way to the First Communion.

Germans are by far the most assiduous travellers: no less than one in every three goes abroad. They prefer Italy and Austria to Spain; but even so they will outnumber the British here by five to one. They come south not only for the sun but for self-improvement, and their agencies undertake to supply them with mass-culture as well as the necessary tan. This creates a serious problem. Only a very few of each mass-tourist group, of whatever nationality, has sufficient historical or artistic background to appreciate what he is shown; and the groups surge into the show places like a football crowd, with their guides using megaphones, and making it impossible for the educated individual to approach, much less concentrate on, the works of art in question. These groups should, at least, compulsorily adopt the device now common in America: which is to forbid loudspeakers and shouted explanations by

professional guides, and oblige group members to wear small ear-
phones which will give them, unheard by anyone else, an official
account of what they are seeing, over a short-range electronic
circuit.

The American writer Anthony Kerrigan now many years
resident in Spain has (far too late) published the following appeal
for the preservation of El Terreno:

'El barrio de El Terreno está en la agonía. Este gran barrio,
con su original sabor y gracia, su aire único, va desapareciendo
bajo los martillazos de especuladores. Toda la gracia isabelina,
todo el característico estilo de este caserío construído por
hombres de amplia imaginacíon y generoso gusto, se está
sacrificando en nombre del estranjero, que cuando la destruc-
cíon está terminada, se irá a otro sitio, donde no haya llegado la
peste de la usura.

'Los patios de las grandes casas se llenan de viviendas
apretadas, las torres se derrumban para dar lugar a más cuar-
tuchos, las vistas desaparecen para todo el mundo, y en su sitio
aparecen las consabidas cajas de zapatos peculiares de los
barrios de masas industriales en Johannisburg o en Lenin-
grado. Lo característico del momento es una vivienda o un
piso que se alza a base de los materiales más bastos, y sin la
distinción de la más minima traza del arte que se llama arquitec-
tura.

'Todo el triste juego se descubre en el momento en que se
cuelga el rótulo de alquiler: ni una palabra de español suele
aparecer allí. Salvo algunos que leen *A LOUER*; todos dicen
TO LET. Aquí no se quiere españoles. Todo menos eso. Estas
casa son para sacar cuartos al forastero rápidamente, no para dar
comodidad al residente, ni mucho menos para añadir tono al
país.

'El estilo, el tono, la gracia del barrio desvanecen.

'Encima de lo triste está lo equivocado. ¿Por qué? como
pueden pensar los especuladores que van a llenar estas casas
(muchas de ellas sin agua y ninguna de ellas propicias para
calles tan estrechas) con forasteros que están precisamente
en busca de todo lo contrario? ¿No llegará el día en que El
Terreno . . . y quizá también otras zonas de la isla . . . se habrá
convertido en un desierto de rascacielos abortados, totalmente
vacíos?

'Mientras tanto ¿no hay ninguna autoridad competente que tenga el más mínimo interés en evitar el desastre?'

Yes: what can one do against the so-called Spirit of Progress? Since Kerrigan wrote, an early eighteenth century convent with remarkable baroque architectural features has been offered for sale in the centre of Palma. The inmates, a Mother Superior and five nuns, were obliged to make this sacrifice by sheer starvation; they had been living mainly on potatoes grown in the convent garden on soil now worth some 15,000 pesetas a square metre. A new convent with all modern conveniences has been promised them outside the city limits; and it is thought unlikely that the old one will be spared as a National Monument. Yet a good Old City still remains untouched, and one can wander around the old narrow streets on the further side of the Cathedral and never meet a tourist; a quarter of a mile away they are so thick in the streets that they might be watching a procession.

It seems to be a rule in every European country that not only different Ministries but their various departments tend to regard themselves as mutually independent—with a mixed feeling of deference and hostility reserved only for the Minister of Finance whom they cannot afford to antagonize. The patriotic Minister of Defence naturally put his needs beyond all others: if he wants a fertile plain for use as an artillery range, the Ministry of Agriculture is not expected to raise a protest; and if the noise disturbs a sanctuary for wild birds, well, the poor creatures had better put their country first and get used to it. In England departmental exclusiveness has reached a very fine point. When recently it was discovered that a valuable mediaeval document got torn down the middle, one half being lodged in the British Museum and the other in the British Record Office, the lawyers who attempted to reunite them agreed that this would be impossible without a special Act of Parliament. Such matters are more easily arranged in Spain. Palma, for example, has no less than five museums, none of them worthy of so ancient and rich a city. Their contents are now to be united in a single, large well-constructed building under Municipal direction.

An important result of individual tourism is that at least one in every hundred becomes so enchanted by Spain that he decides to stay here as a resident. Here, I must emphasize, from my own experience, that any district favoured in this way should be kept

Spanish, and unspoilt by cheap or haphazard building. Most of these would-be residents have chosen Spain as a home for their old age and if treated courteously will react in the same way, bring in capital and create work for the local people. They should not be discouraged from building houses around a village centre; so long as the architecture is solid and in harmony with the existing buildings, for one large ugly house in a bizarre style or a collection of cheap little chalets and villas can ruin the *báraka* of an entire neighbourhood. We have had trouble with this sort of thing in our village, and two years ago when a few of us residents appealed to the Fomento de Turismo at Palma asking them to enforce the old rule by which every new house must be built in the local style—of limestone, with hewn corner-stones and a tiled roof—we were informed regrettably that they had the power only to guide taste, not to enforce it.

The sacred relation between hosts and guests, well understood in Spain, can be taught only by example, and new residents should therefore never be allowed to form tight self-sufficient social groups by buying up a large country estate, building twenty or thirty houses on it, and making it a little Germany, a little England, a little Holland, a little Sweden. Small national colonies are being planted all over Europe. The leaders choose the most romantic sites and show no desire to be integrated into the local life. My view is that nationalities should be mixed in all new housing estates and their occupants obliged in self-defence to use Spanish as a common language. It is perhaps too much to expect an illiteracy tax put on all residents who cannot, after two years' grace, satisfy the local schoolmaster, mayor and doctor that they can carry on a simple conversation in Spanish.

Now that the Ministry of Tourism has been given wider powers, beautiful small towns and villages threatened by mass-tourism will, I hope, be preserved as cultural reserves: as has been done in Italy. For example at Portofino near Genoa (where my daughter has a *castiletto*) nobody may erect a new building or alter the façade of an old one. A Milanese textile millionaire bought a site there and began to build a summer palace, assured that bribery could make the local authorities turn a blind eye. They let him get the roof on and then dynamited the building. The French have also begun to control architectural modernism in the older parts of Paris. I agree that the Spanish temperament makes such policies difficult to enforce. Local authorities are notoriously shortsighted. But it is essential that the cities which have not yet been 'discovered' should be restrained from sacrificing their natural beauties to the machinery of tourist propaganda; which starts at the centre and spreads like a cancer until the main streets become as soulless and anonymous as airports. What if Alicante or Burgos were to suffer the fate of El Terreno?

Queen Salote of Tonga made herself the most popular woman in England—next of course to Queen Elizabeth—when she drove through pouring rain in the 1953 Coronation procession with the hood of her carriage down. This was not done from pride, obstinacy, or the pleasure of getting wet, but simply because she wanted to get a good view of the English people—the perfect visitor in fact. Lately she has risen still higher in my estimation by a letter that she wrote to an American company that plants immense, functional well-furnished well-run expensive hotels in the capitals and sub-capitals of the world, and that wished to include Tonga in their chain. Queen Salote informed them that a careful scrutiny of the island map did not reveal a single spot worthy of their kind attention. Before they could write back offering to assist her in this matter, she asked her Minister of Finance to find out what was the smallest sized *pensión* that would pay expenses for housing casual visitors to Tonga, and so relieve her subjects of having to offer unlimited private hospitality. He told her 'Twenty rooms', and she fixed this by decree as the maximum size, forbidding more than one such *pensión* to be built in the same locality.

If only Queen Salote's golden rule could be applied to the yet unspoilt towns and villages of Spain! With the further proviso that only individual tourists would be accepted at the *pensións*! But Queen Salote was an idealist, and in Tonga her wish was her command. Since her death, I understand, this decree has become a dead letter. If my village cannot be protected from further exploitation, I may yet find myself retreating to some sheep hut a few hundred feet above my house in the prickly oak belt—this was once used for charcoal burning, but now the charcoal burners have become barmen and their daughters chambermaids in the big Palma hotels—there to end my days. The prickly oak belt lies above the olive terraces which rise to about a thousand feet; and the olive harvest is also being neglected because of tourism. Where in 1900 there were thirty terrace-builders and repairers only one is now left; so that the terraces tumble down in times of heavy rain and the sea turns red with the soil. Nevertheless the tourists are invited by their guides to admire the olive trees. In a cartoon recently published by the *Baleares* a peasant asks: 'But when the trees are all cut down and the wood has been used to make salad-bowls and boxes and such-like for the tourists what will we do?' His friend answers: 'Don't worry: the tourist agents will import plastic ones.'

21

The idiom of the people

(1958)

The Idiom of the People is a book about our English folk-songs—not the tinkly, gentle, schoolroom-piano pieces—but the real, strong unexpurgated folk-songs, as resurrected by James Reeves, after nearly forty years, from the unpublished note-books of Cecil Sharp. The English Folk Song Society was founded in 1899 by a number of highly respectable musical knights and professors, including Sir Hubert Parry, Sir John Stainer, and C. V. Stanford, none of whom happened to be eminent in literature. Their self-imposed task was to co-ordinate the efforts of such private folk-song collectors as Frank Kidson, Lucy Broadwood and the Rev. Sabine Baring Gould, and rescue as many unrecorded songs as possible before they were forgotten. Yet, as Kidson wrote (and his judgment was generally supported by his associates):

'It must be conceded that the rustic muse produced better melody than it did poetry, or even rhyme.'

Baring Gould wrote in the same strain:

'My own estimate is that the tunes are of the utmost value, but that the words are of less account.'

The tunes, as they survived in the memory of country people, had no accompaniment and were usually sung in bold, uncompromising style, without pathos or sweetness, but with compelling rhythmic eccentricities. Dr. Ralph Vaughan Williams, who joined

the Society in 1904, found in English folk-song his main inspiration. Until his day, English music had fallen so far under German
influence that it presupposed the German *Volkslied*, melodically
far less interesting. He made it English again. Vaughan Williams
recently came here to visit me in Majorca; he reminded me that the
time we had met, in 1912, I had sung him a ballad of Napoleonic
times that my sister and I had just collected (on a phonograph)
from an old busker, or mendicant singer—one of the last of his
line. I should explain that Dr. Vaughan Williams was very friendly
with my father, Alfred Perceval Graves, an early member of the
English Folk Song Society, who helped to found their Irish and
Welsh counterparts. What is more, as adviser to the old Board of
Education, he first introduced folk-songs into the curriculum of
British elementary schools. I had forgotten the name of the ballad
in question, but Vaughan Williams remembered it well. It was
called 'The Bonny Bunch of Roses, Oh!', and he had honoured it
with a musical setting. 'This was how the busker sang it,' I said:

> Then up spake brave *Napolegon*,
>   And he took his mother by the hand,
> 'O mother, pray have patience
>   Till I have the power to command.
> I'll take ten thousand soldiers
>   And go to fight the foe, the foe
> Then, Mother, pray have patience
>   Concerning the bonny bunch of roses o!'
>
> And then he went to Morocco
>   And the snow was in the land, the land.
> Where those ten thousand soldiers
>   Did march till they could not stand, not stand!

(For 'Morocco', read 'Moscow'). Now, 'The Bonny Bunch of
Roses, Oh!' is not a true folk-song, but a composed ballad for
singing in taverns or fo'c'sles, or Caves of Melody and was
probably first published as a broadside. Yet it has certain obvious
folk-song qualities, so Vaughan Williams gave it the benefit of the
doubt. 'What is a folk-song?' was the subject of a fierce dispute
fifty years ago. A Board of Education hand-book published in
1905, sponsored and in part written by my father, laid it down
that:

'National or folk songs . . . are the expression in the *idiom of the people* of their joys and sorrows, their unaffected patriotism, their zest for sport and the simple pleasures of a country life. Such music is the early and spontaneous uprising of artistic power in a nation, and the ground on which all national music is built up; folk songs are the true classics of a people. And their survival, so often by tradition alone, proves that their appeal is direct and lasting. . . .'

Well, the first active member of the Folk Song Society to differentiate between the true folk-song and such composed songs as 'Rule Britannia!', 'John Peel', or 'Here's a Health Unto his Majesty!' was Cecil Sharp—a radical-minded and asthmatic genius, then Principal of the Hampstead Conservatoire of Music. Sharp welcomed this passage in the Board of Education hand-book and pointed out that true folk-song had little concern with patriotism or sport: the outlaw and the poacher were its heroes—not Marlborough or Nelson. Sharp became the most assiduous, accurate and knowledgeable of all folk-song collectors—in fact, his name is as closely associated with English folk-song as Professor Child's is with the Old English Ballad. Also, his revival of morris dancing, with Playford's 'Dancing Master' as the hornbook, and the rediscovery of English folk-songs in the Hillbilly country of Virginia and Tennessee has given him two more crowns of glory. He died in 1924.

One great difficulty with which Sharp had to contend was folk-song morality: it remained true to sixteenth and seventeenth century standards; its humour was broad and its references to the delights of sexuality were uninhibited: not obscene, but innocently direct. Baring Gould spent his life in collecting fine West Country folk-songs and expurgating the words. His notes abound with such phrases as: 'Objectionable'; 'not my choice'; 'impossible to print'; 'very indelicate'; 'very gross'; and 'The coarseness of the original words obliged me to re-write the song.' It is not generally realized that many old favourites of the Victorian drawing-room and concert hall, including 'John Anderson my jo, John' are artistically incomplete without certain 'objectionable', 'not my choice', and even 'very gross' stanzas. Sharp came up against the same taboo, but salved his historical conscience by keeping note-book records of the originals (now at Clare College, Cambridge), to which Mr. Reeves has had access. *The Idiom of the People* is a study of how the songs really sounded, before being altered for drawing-room or Church Hall performance with piano accompaniment. It was a paradox (he notes) that although the musicians who founded the Society could not bother too much with the words of a folk-song, yet for the singer himself the words were all that really mattered— he took the melody for granted. What is more, the melody, as instanced by the first stanza, seldom gave a true guide to what followed: almost every stanza has its rhythmic and musical variations.

A great many true folk-songs faithfully report pre-marital seductions of young women—'not very delicate', 'impossible to print'—followed as a rule by the marriage and happy births of boy children. Sharp was obliged, for instance, to print 'Oh no John, no John, no!' in a blamelessly coy version. The girl in the song had promised her husband, a Spanish captain, always to say 'no' to young men; but the lover cleverly framed the questions to his own convenience. In the original the following dialogue occurs:

> Madam, may I tie your garter,
> May I tie it above your knee?
> And *if* by chance my hand should *slip* a little farther,
> Should you think it amiss of me?
> O no John, no John, no John, no!
>
> My love and I, we went to bed together,
> There we lay till the cocks did crow.
> Unclose your arms, my dearest jewel,
> Unclose your arms and let me go—
> O no John, no John, no John, no!

In Sharp's published version the girl yielded to her lover only when their wedding bells rang.

There are certain conventional folk-song metaphors for sexual pleasure, such as 'plucking flowers'; and for pregnancy, such as 'wearing my apron up to my chin'. So in 'The Brisk Young Lover':

> A brisk young lover courted me,
> He stole away my liberty,
> He stole it away with a free good will
> Although he's false I love him still.

All down in the meadows as she did run
A-gathering flowers as they sprung,
Of every sort she plucked, she pulled
Until that she had her apron full

When I wore my apron low
My love followed me through frost and snow
But when I wore it up to my chin
My love passed by and never looked in.

There is a bird on yonder tree
Some say he's blind and he cannot see,
I wish it had been the same by me
Before that I gained my love's company.

One of the commonest metaphors is 'morning dew' for 'virginity':

O love is handsome and love is kind,
    And love's a jewel while it is new,
But when it is old it waxes cold
    And fades away like morning dew.

In 'Blowing Away the Morning Dew', the lady says to the man who saved her from drowning:

O take me to my father's house
    And you may lay me down,
And you shall have my maidenhead
    And fifteen hundred pound.
Then blow away the morning dew,
    The dew, o the dew,
Blow away the morning dew
    How sweet the winds do blow!

Mr. Reeves has made a long study of the well-known song 'The Foggy Dew', best known from Benjamin Britten's and Peter Pear's gramophone version, in which a weaver takes a wildly hysterical girl into his bed for fear of the foggy dew—the only thing he ever did wrong—and does not afterwards marry her, though he has a bastard son who closely resembles her, and who follows the same trade as himself. Mr. Reeves believes that this now reigning version is a late falsification of a far simpler original,

collected by Sharp in several variants. In Sharp's version, the girl
spends the night with the weaver, is afflicted by remorse, until
calmed with the assurance that 'the foggy dew is gone'. They are
married 'the very next day', and discuss the probable future
arrival of a large family. Now: the girl's agitation in this story,
Mr. Reeves reasons, was fear of becoming an old maid: 'dew' is
'virginity' and, according to the *English Dialect Dictionary*,
'foggy dew' is the dew which collects on spiders' webs across the
fields in summer: that is to say an emblem of enforced spinster-
hood, not the pure virgin 'dew of Aprill that falleth on the grass'.
Yet Mr. Reeves is still a little puzzled by the mysterious development of the story in the Britten–Pears version; but it may, of
course, be that this version in which the fair *young* maid—note
the *young* maid—not the woman of fading charms, comes des-
perately into the weaver's bed for fear of the foggy dew, *is* the
original one; and that Sharp's is the debased form. I suggest, in
fact, that its provenience is Ireland, where 'foggy dew' has an
altogether different connotation. The tune sounds eighteenth
century Irish to me; and the name of the song is first recorded in
Ireland: 'to the tune of the Foggy Dew', in the same song collection
(I think I am right in saying) which contains 'to the tune of the
Cool Cellure'. 'Cool Cellure' is Irish for 'the White Breasted Boy',
and my guess is that 'Foggy Dew' is really *Foga Dhu*. This would
never have occurred to me, had an Irishman not told me once that,
in the Irish version with which he was brought up, the girl took
the desperate step of seducing the weaver—presumably a Protestant Ulsterman—to escape the *Foga Dhu*, 'the Black Instruction,
or Education—black in the sense of sinister and joyless—at the
Catholic convent to which her parents were sending her as a
novice nun. If this is so, the song must have been brought to
England, rewritten and printed as the broadside reproduced in
'Pinto and Rodways' *Common Muse*', apparently the ancestor of all
Sharp's variants. The novice nun's desire to escape the *Foga Dhu*
made no sense in England; but an unmarried woman's fear of the
'Foggy Dew' did.

There are lovely stanzas in most of the songs quoted here:

> He gazed high, he gazed low,
>   He gave an underlook,
> And there he saw a fair pretty maid
>   A-bathing in the brook.

> It's better for young ladies,
>   To be sewing a silken seam
> Than it is to be, on a May morning,
>   A-swimming against the stream.

And these two stanzas suppressed from the well-known 'Billy Boy':

> Did she light you up to bed, Billy Boy,
>   Billy Boy?
> Did she light you up to bed, my Billy Boy?
> Yes she lit me up to bed,
> With the bowing of her head,
> She's my Nancy, please-my-fancy
> I'm her charming Billy Boy.

> Did she lay so close to you, Billy Boy,
>   Billy Boy?
> Did she lay so close to you, my Billy Boy?
> Yes she lay so close to me
> As the rind unto the tree
> She's my Nancy, please-my-fancy
> I'm her charming Billy Boy!

22

My best Christmas

'Queen Victoria was still alive that Christmas, and I was four and a half years old.'

'Who was she exactly? Queen Elizabeth's grandmother?'

'No: great-great-grandmother.'

'Wow! Do you remember her?'

'Yes: a fat little lady in black riding through the Park with an escort of Lifeguardsmen—her open barouche drawn by two splendid high-stepping grey horses, and the band playing: "Make way, make way, for the rowdy-dowdy boys".'

'Barouche?'

'Yes: no cars in those days. The streets cobbled, and so filthy with horse-droppings and mud that everyone wore boots. Ragged boys with dirty faces used to sweep the crossings with brooms, and beg for halfpennies. Sometimes they turned cartwheels to attract attention.'

'Wow! How ancient you are! Where did you spend that Christmas?'

'At home, near Wimbledon Common. A big house with twenty-five rooms and a coal cellar. But no electric light or lift, or vacuum cleaner, or refrigerator, or radio, or telly. Only rather dim gaslamps, and coal fires, and a grand piano.'

'Were Christmas trees invented then?'

'Yes, Queen Victoria's husband, Prince Albert the Good, brought them in from Germany. . . . We always had a big one in the drawing room. The same coloured glass decorations lasted year after year—never got broken. Things were made to last in those days and people treated them more carefully. . . . We children always waited outside in the dark, cold hall for an hour or so, telling ghost stories, while Mother and Father dressed the tree and sorted out the presents.'

'Were they hung on the tree?'

'No: each of us had a chair or a sofa or small table, covered with a white linen cloth, and the presents laid out on it. But when at last the door opened and we rushed in and the tree blazed out at us like the Jewelled Garden of Paradise, we had to join hands first and sing: "O Come All Ye Faithful". Mother accompanied us on the piano with the loud pedal pressed hard down. At the foot of the tree was a Crypt—with St. Joseph and the Virgin and the Christ Child and the ox and ass, and the Three Wise Men. Then Father Christmas knocked at the french window leading to the garden, and came in. He waved his hand at us and told us his reindeer were stabled at the "Swan" just across the road and wished us a happy Christmas. He complained of the cold so much that my father poured him a glass of cherry brandy. He drank it noisily and went out again into the thick fog, shouting: "See you again next century!" That's how I can fix the date: 1899!'

'Tell me about your presents.'

'I got a musical box that played "Home Sweet Home", and two boxes of soldiers—the Royal Fusiliers and the Egyptian Camel Corps—and a toy helmet and a toy drum, and a prayer-book in red morocco leather, and a painting book, and a clockwork horse.'

'You're making it up, aren't you?'

'No; I remember the list because soon afterwards I was taken away to a scarlet-fever hospital and my mother had most of my toys burned. The doctor said they were infectious for the baby. But my favourite sister hid the helmet and drum in the tool shed, and used to play with them sadly when her nurse wasn't about.'

'Did you believe in Father Christmas?'

'Yes, until the Mix-up Christmas (I'll tell you about that later), although he wore the same boots as Uncle Charles. But he hadn't such importance in those days as the advertisements have built up now. Christmas wasn't just fun and games. It was *Jesus's Birthday*, on which we gave one another birthday presents—a day of thanking God and being especially kind to everyone. We emptied out our money-boxes for the presents. I remember we always used to give the cook and the parlour-maid scented soap, at 2d. a cake. . . . We got a penny a week in those days, and occasional tips from uncles and aunts.'

'A penny a *week*; sounds sort of stingy. . . . Did you hang up your stockings?'

'We did, and anyone who had been naughty that winter got coal instead of almonds, raisins, apples, tangerines, a negro-teeth puzzle, and white sugar mice with pink eyes and string tails.'

'Wow! Did you often get coal?'

'Never. I was always as good as Prince Albert.'

'Ha, ha! What happened on Christmas Day?'

'We dressed up and went to church, which was decorated with chrysanthemums and holly. But the vicar wouldn't allow mistle-toe; he said it was frivolous. Then back to Christmas dinner. The whole family was there: five boys (counting the baby), four girls, and Uncle Charles who couldn't spend Christmas at home because Aunt Alice had left him. Yes, turkey, plum-pudding and mince pies *had* been invented. In fact our cook had once been cook to General Gordon and used a plum-pudding recipe in his own hand-writing.'

'Who was General Gordon?'

'The Dervishes killed him at Khartoum. I once showed you the scene at Madame Tussaud's.'

'Did you? I don't remember. Go on with the story.'

'Then we pulled crackers, and put on coloured caps and asked one another riddles. . . .'

'Such as?'

'Such as: "Why did Kruger wear thick boots?" '

'Who was Kruger?'

'President of the South African Republic. The Boer War had been on for two years that Christmas and every streetboy was whistling the song:

> Good bye, Dolly, I must leave you
> Though it breaks my heart to go—
> Something tells me I am needed,
> At the Front to fight the foe.

But nobody got called up; and it wasn't much of a war. Life went on as usual. Bombs and tanks and planes hadn't been invented yet.'

'But why *did* Kruger wear thick boots?'

'To keep De Wet off defeat.'

'I don't dig you.'

'De Wet was one of Kruger's generals.'

'Anyhow, what did you do that evening?'

'We went to a special children's service at the Parish Church: cinemas hadn't been invented, you see.'

'Then why was it your *best* Christmas?'

'Because it was the reallest.'

'Oh! . . . What's happened to the Wimbledon house?'

'Sold and cut up into six flats. . . . I suppose six small families live in them now, and on Christmas Eve there'll be six tiny Christmas trees lighted—probably the artificial wire- and grocer's-grass sort that fold up, with a little string of coloured electric light bulbs tied on. . . . And a couple of elderly baby-sitters will be drinking sherry there and listening to the carol-singers on TV, while the young folk go off somewhere to dance.'

'Well, I daresay that's a bit more fun than singing hymns to a grand piano and asking riddles. By the way: if I'm still on your Santa list what I *want* is a really good set of bongo-drums. . . . Oh, and you had something to say about a Mix-up?'

'Yes, two years later—when Uncle Charles came in by one door and said he was Father Christmas, and Uncle Bob came in by the other, just after Uncle Charles had gone, and said he was Santa Claus.'

'Wow!'

23

Charterhouse flourishes

This curiously outspoken book, *Charterhouse: an open examination*
—the jacket of which suggests a Butlin Holiday Camp brochure—
has been written by fifteen contemporary Charterhouse boys on
mass-observation principles, under the guidance of an intelligent
master. The sole topic of major importance that has been left out,
most understandably, is the complicated and engrossing local
sociology of 'cases', or romantic homosexual attachments, about
which—at least in my time—a book of much the same size as this
could easily have been written.

Charterhouse began in 1611 as a London charity school for forty
poor scholars, and has ended as an outsize academy for young
gentlemen. In 1872, it moved from Smithfield to a windy hill
overlooking the Wey near Godalming. Our young authors call
this choice 'a touch of genius', because the landscape was
beautiful and the site included a quarry capable of translating
into grim stonework F. C. Harwick's austere Victorian-Gothic
ideals.

But fresh air is not everything, and I doubt whether Westminster
School has lost much by staying in London. The new Charterhouse would have been more happily built into some small market-
town where, as at Eton or Oundle, the boys could walk from dor-
mitory house to classroom along public streets, with shops and
pubs and bustle, inhabited by ordinary people of all classes and
both sexes. Most of the less attractive aspects of school life
recorded in this book are due to its monastic isolation from the lay
world: the boys have to depend too much on one another's company and resources. Yet these are hopelessly limited by a strange

tradition forbidding boys of one house to enter any of the other ten, except on a fagging errand; or different age groups in the same house to become intimate.

Incidentally, Thomas Sutton, the founder, an able merchant prince, must have turned in his grave when Old Charterhouse was sold to the Merchant Tailors' Guild at so modest a price that, by resale of half the playing fields, they got the school itself almost gratis.

Charterhouse plays soccer, the ground being too hard for rugger. 'A head of extreme nervous tension builds up in these unnaturally segregated establishments'—so psychologists say—'and needs constant violent abreaction.' In rugger, a boy can go all out, shoving in the scrum, tackling hard, fighting like mad to grab the ball, and feels glorious as he staggers off the field; in soccer, where he may use only feet and head, the abreaction is no more than partial. As a result, idle 'mobbing' of some simple-souled individualist by a faceless crowd who, time after time, wreck his study or cubicle, occurs far more often at soccer than at rugger schools.

A curious feature of mobbing at Charterhouse, for the unchecked persistence of which (since I was a poor scholar there fifty years ago) this book provides detailed evidence, is that local opinion countenances it as a salutary correction of un-Carthusian activities; yet regards 'buck-ups', meaning honest stand-up fist fights, as bad form.

Many notable personages have been through the mill at Charterhouse: Archbishops, Law Lords, Governors-General, Field-Marshals—and the great Baden-Powell himself, founder of the Boy Scouts. They all seem to have proudly undergone its unvarying discipline: the Classics, the Scriptures—two hours of Scripture a week and daily Chapel are still compulsory—the boot, the birch and the monitorial single-stick. Masters play a small part in this educative process: elder boys toughen the younger by means of a disdainful and brutal insistence on numerous taboos, graded according to seniority and proficiency at games, called *post-te's*—a system which the authors of *Charterhouse* record in faithful detail.

Ordinary boys thrive under their ordeals; others either have nervous breakdowns—a brilliant fifteen-year-old scholar came to me for a long rest cure last year—or survive gloriously: such as Thackeray, whose letter to his mother from Old Charterhouse

(now in the local Museum) is one of the most anguished I have
ever read—and my old friends Sir Max Beerbohm and Sir Ralph
Vaughan Williams who, though in the same form, could never
grow intimate, since they belonged to different houses.

Max wrote a Latin poem about Charterhouse, reproduced in
J. G. Riewald's *Max in Verse* (just published by Heinemann).

Floruit innumeros schola Carthusiana per annos
   Olim Londinii pessima pernicies, etc. . . .

Charterhouse School has flourished for countless years.
   Once it was the worst plague-spot in London;
Now it flourishes high on a windy hill
   And teaches misery to five hundred boys,
It will continue to flourish, and so will the Kingdom of
                                   Pluto—
   Though I may experience the latter hell, I shall never
                                 forget the former.

In old age, Max apologized for this: 'I thought Charterhouse a
very fine school, really; but I am not a Carthusian of the strictest
sect. My delight at having been there was (don't you know?) far
greater than had been my delight in being there.' He added that
Charterhouse in the 1880s did not tend to repress individuality
even in 'an odd child like myself, who liked Latin verse and Latin
prose, and did not care a brass farthing for games.' What Max
meant was that true individuality cannot be repressed, though
Charterhouse had tried very hard in his case.

The word *hashy* survives from my time and is here defined as
'a repulsive addiction to school-work', the authors admitting that,
of course, games are expected to occupy first place in their lives.
Since it was, I recall, *post-te* to show the least interest in school-
work, cheating became laudable. Whether this tradition, too, survives, the book does not reveal. A 'points' system of compulsory
games is still maintained: boys must score so many a week under
pain of a beating—football and cricket counting for twice as many
points as tennis, squash or boxing.

The authors agree that the staff are able and progressive-
minded, but that 'with obvious exceptions, Carthusians are mentally lethargic. . . . This is a fault of tradition, not of the authorities
. . . who provide numerous lectures and entertainments of the

highest quality'—to which, however, little attention is paid. One
boy shrewdly notes:

> The sons of ambitious, ruthless, cautious businessmen now
> account for two-thirds of the public school population every-
> where but at Eton; these cannot afford to possess a dynamic
> character, and that is why the schools are becoming stagnant and
> cheapened by materialism.

Thus the main beneficiaries of this character-building education,
designed for rugged and phlegmatic rulers of a far-flung Empire—
which has long ago disappeared—are, paradoxically, the few
misfits who actually *like Latin*, as Max and I did, or who dedicate
themselves passionately to some spiritual or artistic obsession.
A few seem to be still about. Here is one of them:

> . . . The rest of that morning was a relapse into sleep. First there
> was a hash in which the beak droned on, as if he were talking to
> himself, while some drew doodles on scraps of paper, some ate
> sweets, some read books under their desks, and I dozed. The
> school is enlightened about maths now, so that in the next hash,
> instead of learning compound interest we saw a programme
> about relativity on television. . . .
> It was a half-holiday and I played for my house in Colts. We
> were two-nil down at half-time, when our opponents stood
> together in a bunch discussing the game, with everyone pro-
> posing his own pet movements and attacks. The second half
> dragged on from goal to goal. Their centre-forward was thor-
> oughly crooked—elbowing, shoving and hacking. A bad-
> tempered game; I was only too glad to get back for a shower.
> When two football teams converge on five showers, the late-
> comers have to wait a quarter of an hour, but I ran back and
> arrived first. Afterwards I found the balm I wanted in two hours
> quiet painting at Studio. When a picture goes well my spirits are
> raised. I walked back as the sun was setting, looked at the gold
> and copper leaves in the magic twilight, and felt truly thank-
> ful.

A minority view, however, suggests that *post-te's* may be on the
wane. Although the central core of traditionalism, the 'block
houses', remains proudly conservative, insidious signs of modern-

ism are reported from one or two small outlying houses. For 'Pageites,' the worst offenders, 'who display a total inability at games, nothing is sacred.' Their house is cosy, they are addicted to art, drama and even jazz; worse, 'their head-monitor will help the most junior boy to carry his trunk upstairs'.

24

Miss Briton's lady-companion

Not every man remembers his mother with deep affection. A good many have had little cause to do so. Yet of this unfortunate minority some take one road, some another. Weaklings blame their moral lapses or their ill success in life on neglectful, selfish or tyrannical mothers. Others, the noble hearted, learn to bear them no rancour, to stand on their own feet and find love elsewhere. I remember being puzzled as a child by a verse in *Hymns Ancient and Modern*.

> Can a woman's tender care
> Cease towards the child she bare?
> Yea, she may forgetful be—
> Yet will I remember Thee.

The idea that any mother could possibly behave unkindly to her own child surprised me—I was one of the luckier ones.

My respect for Winston Churchill, whom I first met in 1915 and with whom I exchanged occasional letters until the 'Forties, rose enormously after his death. I then read for the first time of the almost brutal contempt shown him, as a mentally retarded boy with a cleft palate, by his beautiful Jerome mother. And the *Encyclopaedia* supplied the reason both for his physical abnormality and for her unmaternal attitude. His father, Lord Randolph Churchill, had died from general paralysis of the insane. Every doctor now knows what disease causes this fearful condition, and what effect it often has on the patient's children; one can feel only the utmost sympathy with an innocent wife and mother who suffered so much.

And although Winston had many faults and, when younger, often acted with great irresponsibility, who can fail to admire the strength of his resolve never to brood revengefully, always to champion the deprived and oppressed? It was not, indeed, until his middle thirties that a chance medical discovery cleared his blood of the inherited taint, and set him at last on an even keel.

One can never tell. Who has not seen splendid talented children born from base soulless stock, and splendid parents cursed with worthless and evil children? Psychologists are baffled by the paradox. In the case of evil children, they usually accuse the mothers either of weaning them too early, or of weaning them too late, or of bottle-feeding them, or of beating them for their faults, or of not beating them at all. Or even of pre-natal misconduct. But it is never quite so simple. Heredity, which is as powerful a factor as environment, has become far too complex a subject for even a gifted psychologist to lay down the law about. I prefer to think that a child is born either with or without nobility of heart; and that although a mother may either foster or discourage this gift, she cannot be held responsible for its absence. And that goes for fathers as well. I write as a father of eight wholly dissimilar children. And as the eighth of a family of ten, also wholly dissimilar. But I give my mother full marks for nobility of heart and although, being extremely puritanical, she often disapproved deeply of my actions, I never resented her attitude in the least—nor, for that matter, felt that I deserved it.

This is her story. In 1848, a year of revolution throughout Europe, which sent independent-minded citizens, especially Germans, flocking for refuge to the United States, my grandfather, a Bavarian medical student, was expelled from his Prussian university for protesting against the trial for high treason of a young Jewish socialist named Karl Marx who had married into the Prussian aristocracy. My grandfather thereupon left Germany and travelled all around the Mediterranean. According to my mother, he bathed on one occasion in the Dead Sea where the salty slime on his skin so disgusted him that he mounted his horse and rode fifty miles north to the Jordan valley where he washed himself clean. In Spain he was one of the first passengers in the newly-constructed railway from Madrid to Toledo; it had caused great resentment among the muleteers. Finding their livelihood threatened they would lay tree trunks across the track by night and having forced the train to stop, would rob and terrorize the passengers.

My grandfather was seated in a compartment opposite an English colonel come to visit the battlefields of the Peninsular War, throughout which he had fought as a young subaltern. Suddenly the train stopped with a bump, shots rang out, followed by curses, screams, prayers and a general hullabaloo. The colonel slowly laid down his copy of *The Times*, reached for his pistol, primed and cocked it and then returned impassively to his reading. My grandfather, much impressed, thought: 'What a wonderful race! I must go to England and complete my medical education there.'

This he did, I believe at St. Thomas's Hospital, and presently volunteered as a surgeon for the Crimean War, where he worked for some months with Florence Nightingale in a nightmare hospital at Scutari.

Just before sailing he had married a Danish girl, the orphan daughter of Tiarks, the Greenwich astronomer, but my mother, his first child, was not born until the war had ended. They returned together to Germany, where he presently became Professor of Medicine at Munich University and, so far as I know, the first doctor in Europe to supply his hospital with tubercle-free milk; which he did by buying a farm and personally testing his herd of sixty cows. He had learned about infected food and drink at Scutari.

My mother, born in London at the house of a Miss Briton, my grandmother's guardian, was soon the most responsible member of a huge family of boys and girls, and appointed by her father to keep them clean and in good order—which the scared, gentle little Dane, her mother, was incapable of doing. She took the job seriously and soon earned the nickname of 'Scrubbing-brush'. My uncles and aunts all turned out good citizens but, though later expressing their gratitude to her, were not altogether sorry when she was suddenly whisked off to London. That was the year 1873.

The reason given was that Miss Briton, now decrepit and lonely, needed a cheerful lady-companion; but in effect my mother had been banished from Munich for her own good. The then Bavarian Prime Minister—or so I later heard from an aunt—had fallen in love with her at a ball. Though rich, handsome, noble, virtuous and popular, he had two great disadvantages: he was far too old for her, and he was a Roman Catholic. My impression is that her heart responded, but that the match could not possibly be accepted by so Protestant a family as hers. Marriage would mean Catholic grandchildren, which in turn would mean that the religious unity of the family would be broken. The Prime Minister could not very well pursue her to London; nor would Miss Briton have admitted him across her threshold had he done so.

Here the story grows rather grim. My mother knew where her duty lay and always followed it, by however thorny a path. She felt bound to obey her experienced and powerful father, and at the same time to pay the debt of love that her mother owed Miss Briton. So she became not only lady-companion but cook-house-keeper, secretary and nurse to an old recluse living in a tall, cold, inconvenient late-Georgian house in Kensington. Miss Briton, of whose family I know nothing except that they manufactured lead soldiers, suffered from a delusion of extreme poverty. My mother had to sleep on a straw mattress in an iron bed next door to her, and all other rooms but kitchen, toilet, cellar and living room were kept locked up. She was given so minute a house-keeping allowance that she always had to buy the poorest cuts of meat and the cheapest fruit and vegetables; and to practise the most rigid economy with coal. She learned never to throw away a crust, always to scrub potatoes rather than peel them, to deny herself all finery and never even indulge in scented soap. Nor had she any friends of her own age, if only because she could not offer a fair exchange of hospitality with them. Her one solace was a piano.

Her brothers and sisters in Bavaria grew up, ate well, drank well, made scores of friends, were taken on tours to the picture galleries of Italy, and to Vienna for the Opera, attended the best concerts, married, had children. But she missed everything and spent her evenings playing bezique with Miss Briton, who got so upset when she lost that my mother had to bend her conscience, just a little, by cheating herself and allowing Miss Briton the victory. Apart from reading 'improving' books from a library—I don't think she ever read a novel in her life, except in old age to please my father—and occasionally visiting the museums in the neighbourhood, she had no real life at all. She soon lost all traces of her German accent, though Miss Briton, who had been born in the reign of George III taught her a very old-fashioned form of English; so that she used, I remember, to pronounce 'gas' as 'gahs' and 'soot' as 'sutt'.

If she had been sacrificed in this way at the age of twenty-five or so, when she knew more about the world, she would doubtless have taken a more independent line, asking to be relieved at her post, occasionally at least, by one of her four sisters. She would also have insisted on more help in the house and a higher standard of living. But no friend appeared to fight her battles for her, and at least she was not a nun. So she prayed, suffered, hoped and did her duty cheerfully.

One morning, many years later, in the eighteen-eighties, Miss Briton, who liked to be called 'Granny', sighed: 'Dear Amy, I fear that I may have no more money left in the bank after this grievous expense of mending the broken water-pipes. Pray, my dear, set my mind at rest! I do not, as you know, like to trouble you with money matters but today, I beg you, go to my room— here is the key of my writing desk—for I wish you to see what money we have left, if any. It would be a great inconvenience if we had to dismiss the scrubbing-woman.'

Half an hour later, after going through piles of quarterly and annual bank-statements, my mother came down in a daze, saying: 'Granny, only imagine! You are RICH! Read these!'

Yes, she was worth over one hundred thousand pounds, which today would have the purchasing value of perhaps five million dollars.

'This is indeed most welcome news, Amy. If the bank has made no error, we can now retain the scrubbing-woman. And, as you know, you are my sole heiress when I come to die.'

So my mother bought herself another blanket and no longer lived wholly on porridge, parsnips and scrag-end of mutton as heretofore, and a year later Miss Briton died in her sleep. That was the year 1890, when a woman was reckoned a 'wall-flower' at the age of twenty-seven and an 'old maid' by thirty-two. Being now nearly thirty-six, my mother decided to go to India as a medical missionary. She did her training and was on the point of booking a one-way passage by the P & O when—

I should have mentioned that as inheritrix of this huge fortune my mother had decided that she might prove a better missionary if she disburdened herself a little—like the loaded camel in the Gospel parable which could not be led through the Needle's Eye gate at Jerusalem without removal of its panniers. But she was not altogether imprudent. Though dividing her inheritance in five equal parts, one of which she gave to each of her four married sisters, she kept one for an emergency.

The emergency came almost at once. My mother's family, the

von Rankes, were already connected with the Anglo-Irish Graves family. Her learned grand-uncle, Leopold von Ranke, since famous as the 'Father of Modern History' because the first historian to insist 'on what had actually happened, rather than what he would have liked to have happened'—as my mother put it to me very clearly—had to the surprise of both nations married the beautiful Clarissa Graves, a Reigning Toast of Dublin. So it was natural enough for my mother to meet Clarissa's nephew, Alfred Perceval Graves, already well known as a song writer. He had written 'Father O'Flynn', 'Trotting to the Fair', 'The Jug of Punch' and many other late Victorian favourites—now too often regarded as folk-songs, though the copyright will remain in our family until the year 1985—but, being a bad business man, made no money from them. His wife had recently died and he was now a struggling Government Inspector of Schools in the West of England.

I do not know whether her family and his arranged the marriage in contemporary style, but certainly both my mother and my father agreed to its convenience. He was active, sprightly, good-looking and the son of an Irish bishop. She was tall, strong, beautiful, with an unlined face and black hair that did not turn grey for another half-century. And had a great many wifely talents. So she consulted her conscience, which told her that God had protected her against a previous unwise and irreligious marriage, and that the Indians were less deserving than this sad, charming, talented *Protestant* widower—only nine years older than herself—with five high-spirited quarrelsome children in need of a new mother's care. So the wedding took place soon afterwards.

At first, to judge from a diary which has survived, life was astonishing and difficult. Too many things happened, too many people came calling. My mother who did not expect at so advanced an age—she was now thirty-six—to have children, had never in her life shared a double bed with anyone or even, it seems, been taught the facts of life. The five orphans naturally resented her taking the place of their wonderful, joking Irish mother, and her German Scrubbing-brush methods were far from suitable for Irish children, two of them red-haired. Moreover my father, for all his respect and affection for my mother, was still in love with Janey Cooper, his first wife about whom he used to talk in his sleep. Which gave my mother nightmare dreams about meeting Janey in Heaven where although there is 'no marrying or giving in marriage' such encounters could not help being awkward for wives unable to forget earthly monogamic principles.

And Janey had always kept him in order by constant playful teasing, which was a technique wholly beyond my mother's knowledge or powers. She had been trained to obey the Head of the House, without question or evasion; which was not the best thing for his character. They never bickered but mainly because, though my father was a hot-tempered man, it takes two to make a quarrel and at worst she looked pained and disappointed.

For awhile she still had nothing of her own, except responsibilities and the small fortune which she now allowed him to draw on for his children's education. She soon won their gratitude by helping them with homework and inviting their friends to stay. And then at the age of thirty-seven she had a child! A girl.

I am sorry to say that my mother did not greatly value daughters, having been one herself. Her view was: 'girl babies are quite useful to practise on' as her mother had told her. Boys were all that really counted in God's eyes—could she hope for another child? She could. But it was another girl—to practise on!

And then the most wonderful possible thing happened to her. She had a boy. Which incidentally was the most wonderful thing that ever happened to me. I unashamedly adore life. Nor was this the end of her triumphs. She seemed to get younger and younger, happier and happier, and bore my father two more sons, the last when she was forty-nine. And no more daughters, since practice had by now made her perfect.

They built a big house near London, where my father was now working, and another in North Wales where he had once taken her for a holiday by the sea. Stumbling on a peculiarly romantic spot near Harlech Castle she told my father: 'Alfred, this is beautiful beyond expression. I should like to die here.'

'Why not live here instead?' he countered impulsively in her own practical language.

So they bought the site and built a big house on it, and when my father retired, sold the London house and went to live there. It was our holiday heaven, with a sandy beach, wild hills, blackberries, raspberries, blueberries, flowers, mushrooms, adventures. For as we grew older, she allowed us more liberty, though continuing as religious as ever and pleading with us to take no risks in rock-climbing. 'I do not like broken children any more than you like broken toys.'

On a picnic one day she began singing a German song, to the effect that the person whom God wishes especially to bless He sends out into the wide, wide world. And afterwards, looking around us in pure joy, she said, 'You can't think how *fortunate* I feel, my darling children. . . . There was a man once, a Frenchman, who died of grief because he could never become a mother.'

We had family prayers every morning, and as a rule went to church twice every Sunday, which was the day when we were forbidden to play cards or other games of chance. I remember persuading her to let us play charades on Sunday evenings provided that the scenes were wholly Biblical. None of us drank or smoked or had friends of the opposite sex until we were grown up. Yet somehow we never felt deprived, which is surprising when I look around me today. She trusted that eventually we should all meet together in God's glorious heaven, long after her own death. As an equally sincere salvationist, I asked her innocently once: 'Mother, when you die, will you leave me any money?' 'Yes, of course, darling.' 'Enough to buy a bicycle?' 'Yes, I hope so, but surely you would prefer having me to having a bicycle?' 'Well, but you'll be having a marvellous time in God's glorious Heaven, and I could ride the bicycle to put flowers on your grave.'

My mother (and this is no criticism of her) did not know how to dress, having been warned as a girl never to indulge female vanity and as a young woman having been unable, under Miss Briton, to experiment in fancy clothes. I only once remember her buying herself a present, and that was when I was about twelve and she showed me an antique shop where I could spend some birthday money on coins for my coin collection. There she found a gold Irish 'Tara' brooch, which she bought 'to please your father'. It was a bargain at only a trifle more than its intrinsic value in metal, and she wore it for the rest of her life almost every day. In those years only royalty, actresses or prostitutes 'made up their faces'; 'rouge' was a dirty word; and my mother actually spoilt her complexion by constant washing with carbolic soap. She also lacked any sense of humour except the simplest and most innocuous kind; but again this is no criticism of her. True humour is based on multiple meanings, and on a recognition that often only a hair's breadth of truth separates complete opposites. To her white was white, black was black and every word, except parables and metaphors, must be taken literally. She did not understand irony, sarcasm, or jokes about other people's misfortunes.

o

She was, however, a heroine in times of emergency. One day when we asked her whether she had ever ridden in a railway truck, she admitted that, yes, once after a severe railway accident she had helped in the rescue work, had administered first-aid, and taken the injured to hospital in a coal-truck. But our most splendid recollection was when we were very young, in the days before domestic electric light. At supper one evening, the kerosene table-lamp suddenly flared up. The screw that worked the wick had failed and a black pillar of smoke soon clouded the room. My father and elder brothers watched aghast, but my mother rose and said simply to my half-sister Susan: 'Susan, open that door if you please, and then the door into the drawing-room, and then the drawing-room door into the garden. Make haste!' She took up the flaming lamp, protecting her hands with a table napkin, and followed Susan through the hall, through the drawing-room, and into the garden where she set the lamp down on a path. Five seconds later it exploded. Not long afterwards she went to stay with a sister at Zurich, but in fact for a newly-invented throat operation there, with old-fashioned anaesthetics, insufficient analgesics, and only one chance in four of recovery. Yet she did not allow us to guess her anguish when she cheerfully kissed us goodbye. Later we learned that she had sustained herself with the hymn:

> Faint not nor fear; His arms are near,
> He faileth not, and thou art dear.

After that, all went well with her and us until, soon after my nineteenth birthday, the First World War broke out. The news dismayed my mother. She could not at first believe that the Germans could really have invaded Belgium in breach of a sacred treaty. 'My people must have gone mad,' she cried. I had just left school and would have gone on to Oxford University that autumn, but instead volunteered for the Royal Welch Fusiliers, our local regiment. Within a few months I found myself a young officer in trenches that faced Bavarian troops. Were my uncles and cousins among them? This fratricidal situation was so horrible that for awhile my mother broke down and lost her faith in God. How could He allow her to suffer so? For which, a year later, her punishment was a letter from my Colonel, after our battalion had lost over two-thirds of its strength at High Wood, to the effect that I had fought very gallantly but had died of wounds, and that the doctor believed me to have suffered very little pain.

So she opened her heart to God with the Biblical: 'The Lord hath given, the Lord hath taken away. Blessed be the name of the Lord.' And the next thing was a letter from my Aunt Susan—Janey's sister, who lived in France and had noticed my name on a list pinned to a hospital ward door; she was visiting her son who had lost a leg in the same battle. I had been left for dead and escaped burial only because everyone was too busy fighting, or looking after the wounded, to spare the time. My mother's faith returned, and after another spell in the trenches, I got pneumonia, was forbidden further active service, married and had a child—'a daughter to practise on' as she told my wife. Eventually the war ended and all again was well. But my mother's four sisters, with whom she had shared her inheritance, had been ruined by patriotically investing it in German Defence Bonds. So of course she helped them as far as she could, all but one of her own brood being by now more or less independent. And when my father died at eighty-six, she became the most respected woman at Harlech, with nobody to obey except God: meaning her noble conscience. At the age of eighty-eight she was found to have cancer, but since at that age it is seldom fatal, she continued unperturbed to practise her good works, which were many.

Her death was sad. One of her many descendants—though married at thirty-six, she was already a great-grandmother—got involved in a libel action which threatened crippling damages, and came to her for help. The worry caused a nervous breakdown, the local doctor could not deal with the case, and my once 'practised-on' elder sister, who had become a very good doctor, happened to be holidaying in Austria and got back too late to save her life.

What lessons I learned from my mother can be told in very few words. She taught me to despise fame and riches, not to be deceived by appearances, to tell the truth on all possible occasions—I regret having taken her too literally at times—and to keep my head in time of danger. I have inherited her conscience, her disinterest in sartorial fashions, her joy in making marmalades and jams, and her frugality (I hate throwing away crusts) though it often conflicts with a spendthrift extravagance learned from my father. I have not inherited her dogma, which was the cause of her sadly cutting me from her will when my wife and I separated—but she remembered the children instead, and eventually welcomed my remarriage. One word of wisdom, which she whispered to me when I was seven years old, has always stuck in my mind, and I pass it on to my children and grandchildren—by the way I became a great-grandparent last year.

'Robert,' she said, 'this is a great secret, never forget it! *Work is far more interesting than play.*'

Hence my obsession with work, which is also my play.

After her death I was sent that gold Tara brooch, which arrived in the mail with its pin missing. I took it to a Spanish jeweller to have a new gold pin fitted, but he assured me that a gold one would be unnecessary, since the brooch itself was not gold but pinchbeck. That surprised me. My mother had always worn it for gold, we had always accepted it as gold, and so gold it had remained until her death. It would have distressed her to know that she had not merely been cheated by the dealer but made party to a fraud on the public. . . . Or would she have taken this as an instance of God's just punishment on her for indulging female vanity?

*   *   *   *   *

There are, I find, variant traditions in our large family about my mother's life with Miss Briton. Some say that the old lady got justly scared about money when defrauded of £5,000 by a wicked solicitor, but that life with her was by no means so dreary as in my account. There is even talk of musical evenings: my mother, at the piano, delighting a wide circle of friends with her powerful contralto singing. It is said, too, that my mother cancelled her voyage to India not for my father's sake, but because of a peremptory letter from my grandfather at Munich: 'If you take this foolish step, my dear Amalia, we, your loving family, are resolved to forget you.' And that Miss Briton herself, though perhaps at my mother's insistence, divided her inheritance among all five sisters. They even give the house a different address and disregarding the evidence of a photograph dated 1857, which shows her at the age of two, knock a couple of years off her age.

Let them say what they like! She was my mother as well as theirs, and every legend of this sort has many variants.

25

The uses of superstition

(Talk at Massachusetts Institute of Technology, 1963)

I am interested to know how far superstition has survived here at the Institute of Technology; and will welcome any evidence that it has not been successfully banished even from the Laboratories. Meanwhile, let me discuss the phenomenon from a British angle.

Superstition means, properly, those ancient rites, taboos, or impulses that have survived a change of religious doctrine. Superstition has long been a charge levelled by the Protestant churches against the Church of Rome: meaning that Roman ritual incorporates a great deal of pre-Christian belief—worship of images, use of incense, attribution to saints of powers possessed by pagan gods, retention of pagan feasts, and so on. Yet Protestantism itself is stiff with superstitions that escaped the Protestant reformation and the gross severity of the Commonwealth—which even for awhile suppressed the Christmas festivities—and that persist even in our own epoch of ninety per cent agnosticism.

Such are: belief in the magical power exercised by the moon, or by the spirits of the dead; or belief in ill-luck attached to certain objects, places or practices. It is easy enough to deny the validity of these beliefs on logical grounds. To point out that black cats, for example, are considered the worst possible bad luck in the southern states of America, though in Europe they bring good luck, and only the deaf white cat brings bad. Peacock feathers are bad luck in an English home; but lucky in India. Perhaps this is because the English hate rain, as the Indians do not; and because peacocks raise their screaming voices when rain is coming. If so, peacock feathers belong to the same category as umbrellas when opened indoors. Opals are said to be unlucky stones. This is a British superstition not recorded before the publication of a Victorian thriller, *The Unlucky Opal*, about a hundred years ago, and doubtless spread by the London jewellery trade to keep up the price of less romantic stones against Australian opal-dumpers; but the splitting of opals in changes of weather is held to presage sickness and death, and indeed they are very sensitive stones. In India, opals bring good luck. The notion that May marriages are unlucky can be logically discounted by the massive calendar changes made under the Emperor Augustus, and again in the seventeenth century, which upset the whole reckoning of months. Yet what power can logic have over superstition?

Two examples of bird superstitions stick in my mind; both from the First World War. The first was in 1918, when I lodged in a farmhouse near Rhuddlan in Flintshire. One Monday, washing day, a cock walked up to the front door and crowed. Mrs. Williams eyed it in disgust: 'Now I'll have to put off my washing until tomorrow morning—glory be to goodness, and clean up the old house.'

'Why, Mrs. Williams?'

'There's strangers coming to visit. Don't you hear the cock? A proper herald angel is that cock!'

By dinner-time the house was swept and garnished—kitchen, parlour and spare bedroom—and an extra large meal cooked. Then arrived the Liverpool cousins, unannounced except by the cock—and Mrs. Williams was there in her Sunday best to welcome them.

The other example was in France, two years before this: an Irish friend of mine named Cullen, an infantry captain, was marching up the *pavé* road with his company, from reserve billets to support billets, and saw a magpie in a field. He fell out, put the company in charge of a lieutenant, and waited for the other magpie to arrive—because of 'one for sorrow, two for mirth'. Now, in normal times, France is so stiff with magpies that one pays no attention to them; but this was 1915, and all birds were getting pretty rare in the fighting areas. Cullen waited until dark before he rejoined us, disappointed and hungry; and found a telegram waiting for him—his brother had been killed in the division to our left . . . I daresay the magpie's mate had been killed too.

The magpie, by the way, is about the only bird still generally regarded in Britain as bringing auguries. *Mag* may stand for 'magic'; its other name is Pie-Annet, the pie (two-coloured bird) of the goddess Annet, or Anatha, or Annis who is Milton's 'Blue-faced Hag'.

But the point of these two stories is that the absolute conviction with which the auguries were accepted—strong enough to make both Mrs. Williams and Captain Cullen interrupt their normal day's routine—suggests that both of them had precognition of the events portended. No logicality would have altered their conviction.

I was brought up as a Protestant but renounced my faith in the Christian doctrine at the age of fifteen, being no longer able to subscribe intellectually to the main tenets of the Apostles' Creed. I began to doubt that a Father God had created heaven and earth. If any God did (in the practical sense that a realization of the Universe's existence arose from a belief in an all-powerful anthropomorphic deity), this was more likely to have been a Mother-goddess, the oldest myths being unanimous on there having been a Creatrix before there was a Creator. So the Creed no longer makes much sense to me and I therefore give God only a *de jure*, not *de facto* recognition: when I swear on the Bible in Court, or stand to attention while 'God Save the Queen' is being played, or go to a church wedding, or bow my head at College Grace. Yet though determined against the validity of most Church doctrines, I should find it both needless and uncomfortable to abjure many superstitions which are part of my cultural heritage, chief of which is the idolatrous respect paid to a Bible. I could never (except to save life), bring myself to stand on a family Bible, or even lay another book on top of it. Yet I once knew a rebel Scot who had suffered so much from a godly upbringing that he made a practice of stropping his razor on a New Testament.

My family—the Anglo-Irish side—have always bowed nine times to the new moon; have hated seeing it through glass; have refused to allow blackthorn or hawthorn in the house; or to sit down thirteen at table, or to have candles lighted at the same time, or to pass the wine from right to left, or to walk under a ladder, or to put boots on a table, or to spill salt without throwing a pinch over the left shoulder, or to sail the seas on a Friday. If they break a mirror, they always throw the pieces into running water, if they find themselves boasting of their good luck or immunity to illness, they always touch wood, and always say 'God bless you!' if anyone sneezes. They also preserve taboos against eating horse flesh, frog legs, and all British mushrooms except the champignon.

They also are careful never to pass one another on a staircase. This is a fairly usual list.

The historical reasons for all the superstitions are plain enough. The moon was once a powerful goddess who assured, among other things, the fertility of the soil, rain in due season, and the security of our daily bread. My Majorcan gardener will sow only while the moon is new, unless he sows onions and garlic, which notoriously favour the waning moon. I would never dare offend him by insisting on his getting the potatoes in while the weather still held; he would only get his own back by one of the countless sly ways known to gardeners. Besides, I read somewhere in a scientific journal that when the rate of plant growth was tested in an underground chamber lighted by electricity a hundred feet down, it proved to be far speedier when the moon was young. I don't mind you laughing at me when I buttress my superstition with an alleged scientific experiment which I have not checked; but clearly if I didn't believe in my gardener and therefore in the new moon, who would take charge of my garden? Besides, again, the moon for me represents powers which I discuss in my *White Goddess*: of inspiration, magic, love, and so on. We bow nine times to her because three is a number associated with the moon—new, full and old; and nine is three times three. Three is also associated with woman: pre-nubile, nubile, and post-nubile—or girl, nymph and crone. Nine asserts the power of death in life, and of life in death: of the goddesses Hecate and Persephone. Among the most disgraceful aspects of technological civilization are its disrespect for the moon as merely a burnt-out satellite of the earth, useful as a nuclear missile target; for woman as the non-intellectual sex; for love as mere sexual behaviourism.

The fear of seeing the moon through glass is a death fear: in Celtic mythology, the dying hero is taken by the Moon-goddess to her glass castle at the back of the North Wind. Bringing mayflower into the house is to curse the marriage bed: because the old matriarchal goddess Maia, or Cardea, to whom the may-tree was sacred, hated patriarchal marriage and demanded propitiation at Roman weddings: she would otherwise produce miscarriages or deaths in childbirth. Blackthorn brings a different sort of bad luck: in Celtic mythology it is the tree of strife and will divide a household against itself. But such superstitions are on the wane in Britain. Since 1918, poppies are the flowers that one mustn't bring into the house: a commemoration of Earl Haig's destructive strategy at the Somme and Paschendaele. In hospitals it is lilies, of course, because of funerals. British hospitals are hot-beds of superstition: one of which is that all patients, whatever their condition or disease, must be woken up and washed at the crack of dawn. And another, invented by Florence Nightingale, that all flowers at patients' bedsides must be removed after dark because of the poisonous fumes of carbon dioxide which they exhale at night.

Three candles alight at the same time are a reminder of the three formally lighted at the head of a corpse in honour of the Trinity. From this superstition, perhaps, derives the one against lighting three cigarettes with a single match, which was first formalized during the Boer War. Boer snipers at night needed the time it took to light three cigarettes before they could aim accurately at a British outpost. The number thirteen is also connected with death. Thirteen men sat down to the Last Supper. One was crucified, and one hanged himself soon afterwards. Yet thirteen had been a death number many centuries before that, because of the thirteen months in the Common-Law year.

And, by the way, it has always been unlucky in my family to see a parson mounted on a white horse: this is because of Death in the Apocalypse, whom the parson represents when he officiates at funerals. The parsons in my family always rode a horse coated in clerical black, and with not a white hair on it. Come to think of it, I've not seen a parson on a white horse for ages; and white motorcycles don't count.

Wine must not pass left-handedly; that is, against the course of the sun which is regarded in patriarchal society as the way of righteousness: the right hand is always the lucky and honourable one. *Droit*, *derecho*, *rechts*, *right* and *rectus* all have the same connotation. The left is *sinister*. Nevertheless, when I am host at a dinner and set the wine in motion, I always take advantage of my ancient privilege and give the glass of my right-hand guest a back-hand filling. This is a covert reminder that the motion from left to right (called in Ireland 'widdershins') is lunar and of more ancient sanctity. Even the Moslems, though avowed patriarchalists and reserving the left hand for the dirtiest offices, superstitiously commemorate their ancient moon-worship at Mecca by a left-to-right procession around the Kaaba.

Walking under a ladder is unlucky, not because the paint pot may fall on you, but because that is the way to the scaffold, and in the old days nobody felt safe from injustice, however nobly born.

Boots are unlucky on the table because when a miner or quarry-man or steeplejack is killed in an accident he gets laid on the kitchen table with his boots on. . . . Salt is an emblem of hos-pitality, and to spill it invites quarrels; so you throw a pinch over your left shoulder to blind the Devil before he notices the acci-dent. To break a mirror is unlucky because it has reflected your face, and in primitive belief your soul has entered into it. Run-ning water, sovereign against most witchcraft, washes away the ill-luck.

An unwillingness to sail on a Friday is comparable to the Jewish respect for the Sabbath. Friday was sacred to the Love-and-Sea-goddess Aphrodite, whom one honoured by sacrificing to her ashore; Saturday was sacred to the god Saturn, whose reposeful Golden Age preceded agriculture.

One touches wood—it should really be ash, not just any wood—in honour of the god Woden, whose sacred tree it was; because Woden claimed control of the nine fatal Norns who punished boasters. . . . 'God bless you!' greets a sneeze, because a sneezing fit was an early symptom of the Black Death. The reluctance to eat horseflesh derives from a taboo which reserved it for the well-born members of a totemistic fraternity at the pagan Feast of the October Horse. When the feast was suppressed by the Church, the taboo became total, and what had been holy changed to an abomination. In fact, though Denmark had been famous for its pagan horse feasts, in the early nineteenth century crime was discouraged there by the knowledge that only horse-beef was provided in the State prisons.

The mushroom taboo seems to have been similarly instituted to protect certain hallucinogenic mushrooms which were reserved for sacred mysteries. Frogs got included in the same taboo because of their kinship with toads. The toxin from toads' sweat glands, *bufonenin*, is identical with that from the white spots on the fly-cap, one of these hallucinogenic mushrooms. The horror of eating human flesh is not a natural instinct, but dates from a time when cannibalism was reserved for royalty and priests. Incest, similarly, was a royal prerogative, to which commoners dared not aspire. There can be few members of my audience who would not rather do a spell in prison than commit either cannibalism or incest—

though these practices are physically harmless and not even illegal, unless aggravated by murder, rape, or some extraneous crime. I remember once being approached by a South Wales mountain-boy for an Army 'separation allowance': paid to any serving soldier for the mother of an illegitimate, but acknowledged, child. The woman he named, the child's mother, was also his own. Nothing in King's Regulations prevented the award. . . .

Ancient superstitions in Britain are dying out under industrialism. I regret this trend. The man who stops in a crowded street and bows to the moon is not one who would wilfully destroy an Elizabethan house and replace it with a petrol station, or who would behave unchivalrously to women. Most superstitions do no harm, and are to urban life what grace notes are to a folk-song: they give it character. I would go further, and say that strongly held superstitions are necessary counter-weights to the unfettered intellect.

I regret only the commercialization of public superstitions. The two worst examples are Christmas and funerals. Christmas was chosen to celebrate the nativity of Jesus as arbitrarily as British sovereigns now choose their official birthday; the Church Fathers didn't care about the original date. They merely wanted to distract attention from their cult by taking advantage of a somewhat similar pagan holiday—the sun's victory over darkness on the day after the Winter Solstice, when the nights at last begin to shorten. Thus Christmas became a charming mixture of several pagan rites, including the Roman Saturnalia, the German fir-tree festival, the Mithraic feast of the Unconquered Sun, various Greek advents of the Divine Child, the Celtic victory of the Robin over the Wren, Druidic mistletoe rites, and so on. Look at Christmas now! It has become one more cleverly advertised fiction (like the bomb scare and the Cold War) for unnecessary expenditure serving to keep up full employment. That the expenditure is disguised as good-will gifts, rather than weapons of defence or fall-out shelters, makes no odds: the ancient superstition still persists that although we could get along perfectly well on half the effort taken to produce the present shoddy results, it would be immoral if only half of us worked in happier conditions and produced better and longer-lasting goods. The rest would be parasites; besides, Jesus said: 'The poor will always be with us.'

The other most grossly exploited superstition is that of funerals.

In a society as irreligious and aimless as ours, fear of death is one of the few strong surviving emotions. Marriage used to be a solemn family affair in the days before divorce and registry office weddings; now it is casual and easily dissolved, and a great mass of wedding superstitions have fallen away. But death, unlike marriage, is ineluctable, and in Britain it has become increasingly difficult to die and be disposed of without an expensive religious ceremony. Ideally, once death has been certified, the body should be whisked out of sight and reduced to fertilizer for some reafforestation scheme. Trees are sacred things. As it is, our Welfare State rewards the Church for its support of law and order by pledging itself to gigantic funeral expenditures on behalf of its insured employees, deducted of course from their wages. They pay something like thirty pounds a head for tidily storing up their mortal remains in vast, charmless necropoles, against a hypothetical Day of Judgment. Happy Christmas to them all. And happy funerals to them all: with hearses, coffins, head stones, undertakers, mourning and funeral feasts. . . . Mourning, though not taken so seriously as when I was young, still tyrannizes over hapless widows and orphans. Funerals should really be ceremonies not of grief, but of triumph, if one believes that God has called the soul to its everlasting habitation—which, unless the corpse had a criminal record, is usually assumed to be Heaven. And even in the exceptional case of a real s.o.b. dying—for the break-down of religion has been accompanied in Britain by a notable rise in sportsmanship and courtesy— surely one should rejoice at his disappearance from our midst and in God's deterrent use of hellfire?

What is mourning *for*? Mourning is a genuine old superstition, dating from times when one was afraid of ghosts paying off old scores. What if they suspected their relatives of murdering them? Some ancient European tribes used to immobilize the ghost by cutting off the feet, hands, tongue and genitals of its corpse. The ancient Majorcans were more thorough: they jointed every limb, cracked the skull, and threw heavy stones on top of the remains. Cremation was elsewhere instituted as an even surer means of sending the ghost safely to another world. With inhumation the ghost is still left hanging about, and often demands food and drink offerings. But the point is that, before the corpse can be safely disposed of, ghost and all, it is safest not only to simulate an extravagant grief for its death, but to disguise oneself against its vicious haunting. You pour dust on your head, scratch your cheeks, rend your clothes, and throw sackcloth over you, in the hope that the ghost will not recognize you any longer. Victorian mourning was a splendid disguise; but at that epoch, a ghost's suspicion of his surviving relatives, and his jealousy at seeing them devour his substance, was supposed to flag gradually after the first year. Widows then went into half-mourning, which meant that they could relieve the black with a touch of purple, a colour then otherwise avoided, and prepare for re-marriage after another decent interval.

War is a strange phenomenon: it modifies so many superstitions. The ban on murder is suddenly lifted. Indeed, the old proviso that the victim should be a soldier in recognizable uniform has been dropped, since air bombardment came into fashion. Robbery has, also, always been permitted under the name of plunder; and rape of enemy women condoned in a city taken by storm. . . . Total war spells total shamelessness. I knew a nice, clean-minded girl, who volunteered for British Secret Service work around 1941. She was an artist, and her first job proved to be designing obscene postcards, showing Hitler in various compromising or ridiculous positions, for dropping on German camps; from this she graduated to producing large quantities of forged German ration-cards, for dropping on industrial suburbs. . . . As for funerals, in the First World War, if one of our blokes was lucky enough to have his corpse recovered intact, a padre was sometimes found to give him an individual burial—but oftener not. I officiated once or twice myself without fee; and with no allowance for funeral bake-meats, or for a coffin, or for a weeping marble angel. . . .

The unluckiness of Friday for sea travel has been extended to its unluckiness for any journey or enterprise, especially when combined with the number thirteen. One reason for this seems to be that Friday is a blessed day in Islam, full of stored-up blessedness. A Moslem says: 'I will prepare myself for Friday and then, please God, you will see what you will see.' As a result, the unfortunate Crusaders always got it in the neck on Fridays. Their priests tried to restore morale by insisting that, so far from being an unlucky day, Friday was the best in the whole week: on Friday, mankind had been ransomed from eternal damnation. This view was adopted officially in the later Middle Ages, when Philip II of Spain made a practice of sending out his expeditions on a Friday. I must check on the Spanish Armada; but my bet is that it sailed both from Spain and from the Low Countries on Fridays. What is more, the Spaniards artificially fixed Tuesday the Thirteenth as an unlucky day, which it still is. I suppose Tuesday was chosen because *Martes* (Tuesday) is sacred to Mars—the bloody planet.

Theophrastus the Hellenist has a good picture of the superstitious man who tortures himself by a thousand fears and caveats: I can't remember all the details, but he would rather have died than eaten bean soup—a Pythagorean superstition, which held that the souls of one's ancestors got into beans, and if a woman ate them they had a hope of re-birth. But to be eaten by a man would destroy their hopes. It seems that the belief began from a confusion between the word *pneuma*, which means 'the breath of life'—but also any involuntary eruption of air. Beans are notorious for causing flatulence.

I find myself far more at home with mildly superstitious people —sailors and miners, for instance—than with stark rationalists. They have more humanity. Particularly, I like theatre people, who are riddled with superstition. The *Macbeth* superstition is a curious one; the very fact that the three witches utter a convincing curse had always made such an impression on the cast and the stage-hands that nobody can recall a production of *Macbeth* in which somebody did not suffer a spectacular loss or accident, even if the bell tolled only for the double-bass or the prompter's assistant. The superstition has extended itself to a total ban on any quotation from *Macbeth* in any part of any theatre. No live flowers are allowed on the stage, a superstition explained practically as due to the danger of their falling and of people slipping on them; but more plausibly as a warning against the unwarranted and therefore unlucky anticipation of bouquets. This 'touch wood' warning against over-confidence, which has the effect of keying the cast up to doing their very best, appears also in the superstition, now waning, against saying the last line of a play at a rehearsal. That last line should be reserved for the roars of applause on the first night.

Whistling in the dressing-rooms is another breach of etiquette. Anyone who whistles must turn around three times, go out, knock for re-admittance, and be greeted as if entering for the first time. Whistling brings wind, wind brings bad weather, bad weather used to empty the theatres—though now it is the other way around. Theatre people hate heat waves. They are uninsured against lean times, and cannot afford to make the least false step. As a rule, the more dangerous the trade, the more mentally and emotionally alert, and therefore the more superstitious the worker. I remember, by the way, a dirty trick played on a boxer who believed in the superstition 'See a pin, pick it up, all the day you'll have good luck'; a betting man who stood to make a packet by this boxer's defeat, dropped a handful of pins by the ringside just as he was climbing into the ring and prevented by his gloves from picking up even a token pin. . . . What he should have done was to spit on his own chest and say '*absit omen*'; but unfortunately he knew no Latin, and so got knocked out in the first round.

The historical reason for some superstitions is often hard to find. I puzzled the other day when a Scottish woman told me that if a sheet, in folding, has acquired a diamond shape at the junction of its creases, one should never spread it on a bed. The only sense I can find in this is a reference to the nine of diamonds as the 'curse of Scotland'—the card which, when it was played, was the signal for the Campbells' treacherous massacre of the Macdonalds at Glencoe. The 'curse of Scotland' has a row of four diamonds on either side, like bed rails, and another in the centre. . . . Or has anyone a better solution?

Ancient Greek superstitions, taken over by the Jews and Arabs, have persisted with us on a personal, rather than a public, way. Most people have a lucky number: usually associated with their birthdays, but not always. Mine, for example, is 23; but I refuse to disclose the historical reasons for my choice—by the way, my birth date is 24, not 23—or even the magical reasons. Most speculative financiers keep a close watch on numbers, and their decisions are often taken by numerical omens. A close friend of mine, a Spaniard (whom I once helped when he was living on ten shillings a week and who is now a millionaire) told me recently: 'I had to make a decision yesterday which meant £25,000 if it came off. The margin of doubt was wider than I usually risk. On the way to my office I happened to look at my speedometer. It marked 72227, which is *capicua*. (The English word is 'palindrome', a number or word which reads the same backwards as forwards.) So I knew I was all right.'

I saw what he meant: he belongs to the masterful type that favours 7 (not to the reflective type that favours 5; nor to the fateful type that favours 3); and the triple 2 in the 72227 number spelled 'gain'. Of course, the deal came off. My considered view is that when calculating chances of a successful deal, only a limited amount of factors can be immediately apparent even to an astute and well-informed man; what he calls 'hunches' are provided by an inner voice that works from a deeper level of perception—from an awareness of tiny straws in the wind which, though real enough, cannot be logically framed. Often his intellect puts on the brake, asking: 'What evidence have you for this?' The inner voice does not talk the same language, but confirms the basic certainty of its hunch by a recognizable sign: here for example, it directs the eye's attention to a lucky number. It might just as well have been the registration plate of the car just ahead of my friend, or a telephone number in his note-book, as the speedometer—but his eye was caught and held by it.

These hunches, sometimes actually heard as inner voices, are foolproof only so long as one gives them immediate credence, and does not boast about them or try to control them intellectually. And the credence must be absolute, as in the stories I have told you of the lone magpie and the crowing cock. Most of you are too young to have heard the old story of the Russian kulak under the Czardom who, one Spring day, heard an inner voice cry: 'Ivan Ivanovitch, sow rye!' He sowed rye when every other kulak was sowing barley, and harvested the best crop for miles around. Next year, they all planted rye; but his voice warned him: 'Ivan Ivanovitch, sow barley!' He rented some derelict land and sowed barley to such purpose that, although everyone else was ruined, he made enough profit to emigrate with all his family. Arrived in New York, his voice gave him further instructions: 'Ivan Ivanovitch, buy scrap metal. . . . Ivan Ivanovitch, buy jute sacks. . . . Ivan Ivanovitch, buy . . .' He always sold at a hundred per cent profit. Soon he was pretty well off. The voice said: 'Ivan Ivanovitch, buy Bethlehem Steel. . . . Ivan Ivanovitch, buy Cuban tobacco. . . .'

When he was worth some $30,000, he went down to Las Vegas and took his place at the gaming tables. The voice cried: 'Ivan Ivanovitch, play red, five times running; and double your stakes each time!' At a thousand dollars a fling, he was soon worth $32,000 more.

Then he went to the top table, where the smallest stake accepted was ten thousand dollars. The voice said: 'Ivan Ivanovitch, lay all your money on 7!' Seven turned up, and you can work out for yourselves what he was worth then. . . .

Enormous quantities of notes were thrust at him in bundles and sacks. Then Ivan Ivanovitch said to himself in Russian: 'I guess I ought to stop.' But the voice insisted: 'Lay it all on 23!' He did so, not noticing that he had not been addressed, as usual, by his name. And in the greatest hush ever reported at Las Vegas, the ball skidded around the bowl and came to a stop at 24. . . .

'Oh, SHIT!' cried the voice.

26

Witches today

(1963)

Witches have made the headlines lately both in Germany and England. Mob-violence is reported from Franconia, a Catholic province with a somewhat backward peasant population, against half-crazed old women accused of bewitching their neighbours. Farmer Sepp's best cow dies mysteriously, lice infest his house, his well dries up, his wife miscarries. Who is to blame? Old Mitzi, of course, who lives at the end of the lane and once mumbled something nasty when Farmer Sepp accused her of stealing his apples. Nobody likes Old Mitzi, and the cat is doubtless a demonic familiar.

Julius Streicher, Nazi editor of *Der Stürmer* and Gauleiter of Franconia, exploited these old-fashioned witch-hunting instincts when he blamed the Jews for all Germany's ills. Now that the Jews have gone, peasants vent their spite on witches again. But the Franconian witch is always a solitary sorceress or sorcerer; it must not be thought that the recent outbreaks were directed against what was left of General Ludendorff's organized revival of paganism. His grandiose May Eve fertility rites on the Brocken, in which Hitler's English protégée, the Hon. Unity Mitford, acted as the Walpurgisnacht Maiden, have long been forgotten.

The sudden spread of organized witch groups in modern Britain follows naturally from Dr. Margaret Murray's anthropological studies: *Witchcraft in Western Europe* and *The God of the Witches*, published a generation ago. She surprised her readers by presenting witches as members of an ancient British fertility cult—akin to those of Greece, Italy and Germany—whom the Christians persecuted for their stubborn traditionalism and who, despite all witness to the contrary, were harmless enough. Until then, the popular view of witches had been the semi-comic Victorian one of old crones in steeple hats riding through the moonlit air on brooms. Witch-hunts were ascribed to mass-hysteria, like the frequent reports of flying saucers a few years ago; and lawyers could smile at our famous legal authority, Blackstone of *The Commentaries*, who wrote:

'To deny the possibility, nay the actual existence of witch-craft, is to contradict the revealed word of God.'

Blackstone had in mind I *Samuel* xxviii. 7 –25, where the Witch of Endor raised up Samuel's ghost for Saul. But he can have placed little reliance in the confessions of supposed witches, ex-torted under the Witchcraft Act of 1546 by inquisitors armed with the official hand-book, *Malleus Maleficarum*, or 'Hammer of Witches'. Witch trials had been a public scandal at the time, although Elizabeth's inquisitors did not use the rack, hot tongs, tooth-drawing, or other crude Continental methods which violated English Common Law. The witch's alleged crimes—of blasting crops, producing abortions in women and impotence in men, causing murrain among cattle, raising gales to wreck ships, killing by use of wax images or more direct means—were all subsidiary to the greater sin of a pact with the Devil. Confession of this sin was readily obtained by an anticipation of modern brain-washing techniques.

The word *witch* derives from the Anglo-Saxon *wicca*, 'a magician who *weakens* the power of evil'; Catholics held that these 'powers of evil' could be identified and weakened only by a priest. A witch was taking too much on himself by his spells. Before the Norman Conquest, however, a proved witch had merely to do penance, though in some cases for as much as seven years; it was not until 1564, that he could be condemned to death. Many thousands of witches were then hanged; most charges being prompted by fear, malice, revenge, hope of gain, or sheer fanaticism—just as, in wartime, spies are seen everywhere.

King James I intervened personally at the trial of the North Berwick witches, who confessed that they had attempted to wreck his ship by throwing a christened cat into the sea. This offended his common sense, and he shouted out that they lied. But Agnes Sampson, a leader of the coven, answered quietly that she did not

wish him to think *her* a liar. Drawing James aside, she repeated
word for word the conversation which had passed between him and
his Danish queen in bed on their wedding night. Such manifest
proof of second sight filled him with fear; and the witches were
accordingly hanged.

Witch-hunting in England was largely the sport of Puritans.
They took to heart the Mosaic command in *Exodus* xxii. 18: 'Thou
shalt not suffer a witch to live!' Though a distinction had been
hitherto made between 'white witches' who did cures or told
fortunes in the name of the Virgin or the Saints, and 'black
witches' who followed their own dark devices, a witch's colour
made no odds to the Puritans. After the Reformation, their madness slowly cooled, but it was not until George II's reign that the
various Witchcraft Acts were replaced by one making the crime
punishable only if used for monetary fraud. In 1950, this was
superseded by the 'Fraudulent Mediums Act', when a confession
of witchcraft became no more dangerous than that of atheism.

Three or four covens seem somehow to have survived in England
when Dr. Murray's sympathetic reassessment of organized
witchcraft made a revival possible. This followed the revival of
folk-dancing and folk-singing, which had been equally moribund
until the Reverend Baring Gould and Cecil Sharp came on the
scene. It was helped by Britain's rapid de-Christianization, which
did not imply a moral decline, but rather a criticism of church-
going as inadequate to spiritual needs and out-of-step with history
and science. Some of the younger generation took to psycho-
analysis instead. Some to ideal Communism. Some to the Conquest
of Space. Some to Nuclear Disarmament. Some to the baffling
precepts of Zen. Some to the adoration of sportsmen, movie
personalities or television stars. But the witch cult, presented by
Dr. Murray as a more ancient form of worship than Christianity,
attracted the dare-devils.

Its revival allowed full play to the stronger human emotions.
Witches met secretly in wooded country, not in cold Gothic
cathedrals or rural cemeteries. Women took as important a part
in the dancing, singing and feasting, as men. Each 'coven' consisted of six pairs, either husbands and wives, or engaged couples;
and an officiating priestess. All went naked. Tests of fortitude
under flagellation and horrific danger, the raising of spirits,
cauldron stirrings, incense-burnings, love feasts, round-dances
performed back to back, served one main purpose: that of reaching

an ecstatic state in which the magnetic force of the whole coven was focused on some unanimously chosen object. Strange phenomena were then experienced—among them, it was said, visions of past and future. To concentrate this force, the rites were performed in a magic circle cut on turf with the black-handled 'athame', or witch's knife.

I am not a witch myself and have never assisted at any Sabbath. Although most English witches of my acquaintance are honest idealists, the craft attracts hysterical or perverted characters and, there being no longer a Grand Master or Chief Devil to discipline them, schisms and dissolutions are frequent.

The main architect of this revival has been an elderly Scottish anthropologist, Dr. Gerald Gardner, curator of a Witchcraft Museum in the Isle of Man, and author of *Witchcraft Today*, a popular apology for his fellow-witches. He once studied East Indian magic, and published a scholarly monograph on Malayan weapons; but his doctorate came from no university award. Dr. Gardner was first initiated into a Hertfordshire coven whose traditions had, it seems, been reinterpreted by a group of theosophists before being aligned with his own views of what young witches need in the way of fun and games. A female deity, whom Dr. Gardner identifies with the ancient European Moon-goddess, was preferred to Dr. Murray's Horned God. He quotes a modern witch chant sung at a cauldron ceremony, known as *The Drawing Down of the Moon*:

> Queen of the Moon, Queen of the Sun,
> Queen of the Heavens, Queen of the Stars,
> Queen of the Waters, Queen of the Earth,
> Bring to us the Child of Promise!
>
> It is the Great Mother who giveth birth to him,
> It is the Lord of Life who is born again.
> Darkness and tears are set aside
> When the Sun shall come up early. . . .

Witchcraft Today, with a foreword by Dr. Murray, excited immediate attention. Sensational attacks made on Dr. Gardner by the British Press as 'a devil worshipper who puts around the dangerous idea that witchraft is not evil', seem to have been based on Montague Summers's highly coloured accounts of diabolism and blood sacrifice in his *Witchcraft and Black Magic*. Dr. Gardner, who believes in neither the Devil nor in blood sacrifice, received hundreds of fan-letters and applications for admittance to witch covens. Though travelling about, spreading his genial gospel and bestowing witch blessings, he claims to be no more than a humble member of a coven. Dr. Murray had given him her own blessing:

'Dr. Gardner has shown in his book how much of the so-called "witchcraft" is descended from ancient rituals, and has nothing to do with spell-casting and other evil practices, but is the sincere expression of that feeling towards God which is expressed, perhaps more decorously though not more sincerely, by modern Christianity in church services. But the professional dances of the drunken Bacchantes, the wild prancings round the Holy Sepulchre as recorded by Maundrell at the end of the seventeenth century, the jumping dance of the mediaeval "witches", the solemn *zikr* of the Egyptian peasant, the whirling of the dancing dervishes, all have their origin in the desire to be "Nearer, my God, to Thee", and to show by their actions that intense gratitude which the worshippers find themselves incapable of expressing in words.'

Apparently the equal division of the sexes in modern covens was Dr. Gardner's contribution to the craft; for Dr. Murray shows that although every mediaeval coven had its 'Maiden' as assistant to the Chief, men were in the majority. Sixteenth century records reveal that not only were witches re-baptized and given new names, but new marriages were celebrated at the Sabbaths between men and women who already had legal spouses. This practice has now wisely been abolished.

That witches existed in Britain from early times is undeniable. Members of a surviving Somersetshire coven still carry small blue tattoos in woad pricked below a particular finger joint, which stands for a letter in the pre-Christian Celtic alphabet. They call themselves 'Druids', worship a neolithic British god, and meet at cross-quarterdays—Candlemas, May Eve, Lammas and Hallowe'en—in a Druidic stone circle. Nevertheless, their traditions will be based on reforms made by some late eighteenth century antiquarian of the Edward Davies school. Members are chosen, after puberty, for certain natural powers of intuition and diagnosis, second sight, and thought control. Their membership, though tending to run in local families, includes professional men and women from London and Bristol . . . Very different from the spell-casting, love-philtres, poisonings and blackmail of ancient Franconian, or indeed present-day Majorcan witches! There is a village carpenter, living not many miles from my home, whose wife hearing that he was in love with the baker's daughter, once put a spell on him. He could no longer cross the doorstep into the street without fainting; not for thirteen years. . . . Then his wife died, he followed her coffin across the threshold and is now happily married to the baker's daughter.

*   *   *   *   *

Dr. Murray, Miss Christina Hole, Mr. Mervyn Peake, the late Charles Williams, and other investigators, seem to have ignored one important fact about the mediaeval witch cult: that it was brought to Europe by the Saracens, and grafted on a pagan Celtic stock. The Saracens had seized Spain in A.D. 711 (and were not expelled until 1492), controlled Southern France by 889, and soon added to it Savoy, Piedmont and part of Switzerland. Their witch groups, like the Dervishes, were devoted to ecstatic dancing, miraculous cures, and the pursuit of wisdom personified as a Divine Woman, from whom comes 'The Queen of Elphame', beloved by Thomas the Rhymer and other Scottish witch-men.

The God of the Witches is held by Dr. Murray to be a lineal descendant of a palaeolithic Goat or Stag-god who later became the Gaulish Cernunnus and Shakespeare's 'Herne the Hunter'. Yet the lighted candle which every Grand Master, disguised as a black he-goat, wore between his horns on the great Witches' Sabbath—whether in England or in France—points in a very different direction. Idries Shah Sayed, the Sufi historian, has shown that a candle set between two horns emblemized the ninth century Aniza school of mystics, founded by Abu-el-Ataahia. Abu came from the powerful Arabian Aniza ('Goat') tribe, to which our contemporaries, Ibn Saud's sons and the Sheikh of Kuwait both belong. The candle therefore meant 'illumination from the head of Aniza'.

A Grand Master always wore black, or blackened his face—to merge more easily with the shadows at nocturnal Sabbaths, it is said. For the Saracen mystics, however, 'black' symbolized 'wise' —the two Arabic words FFHM and FHHM being almost identical in sound. 'Robin, son of Art, an Ethiopian', the devil accused at a celebrated 1343 trial of appearing to the Irish noblewoman Dame Alice Kyteler, will have been merely her instructor in mystical secrets. 'Robin', the generic name for a Chief or Grand Master, represents the Persian *rah-bin* ('he who sees the road'). A Berber off-shoot of the Aniza school was known as 'the Two-Horned', and in Spain lived under the protection of the Aragonese Kings, who intermarried alike with the Prophet's royal descendants at Granada and with the English monarchy.

It is evidently this particular cult that reached the British Isles. An illustration on the cover of *Sadducismus Triumphatus*, a 1681 chap-book, shows Robin Goodfellow, horns on his head and candle in hand, capering among a coven of witches, who number thirteen like the Berber groups. A Two-Horned devotee wore his ritual knife, the *ad-dhamne* ('athame' to present-day witches) un-sheathed and, as a reminder of his mortality, danced in a *kafan*, or winding-sheet (which is the most probable derivation of *coven*), at a meeting known as *az zabat*, 'the Powerful Occasion'. Hence the 'Witches' Sabbath', or 'Esbat'. Two beautiful young French witches once told De Lancre, an Inquisitor at La Bourd, that their Sabbath was a paradise of inexpressible joy, a prelude to still greater glory, and far better than the Mass. The Two-Horned did, indeed, consider ecstasy no more than a prelude to divine wisdom. Some of them rode sticks, or brooms, like hobby-horses; cantering 'widdershins', against the course of the sun, as around the Kaaba at Mecca; which explains why English witches were accused of causing storms, mildew and blight by this means, and why it is unlucky for wine to circulate from left to right at table. Modern witches are careful to dance in the sun-wise direction.

It is not known at what period the Two-Horned cult entered Britain. The climate was favourable in 1208, when the Pope laid England under an Interdict for ten years, and King John sent an embassy to Morocco with secret promises that he would turn Moslem. And again, one hundred years later, when the entire Order of Knights Templar was accused of witchcraft and suppressed at the Pope's orders, but King Edward II rejected the evidence against his own subjects and pleaded for their lives. The Templars had been collaborationists with Islam during the Crusades: members of a mystical Saracen freemasonry. Former Templars may well have directed early fourteenth century covens, such as Dame Alice Kyteler's.

The original school of Aniza achieved a state of ecstasy by beating drums and cymbals, or rhythmic clapping in ever-increasing tempo; but in Europe hallucinogenic drugs seem to have been preferred at a later period, lest the noise of Two-Horned revels might come to the ears of Church officers.

The earliest accounts of broomstick rides say nothing of levitation; later ones suggest that an English witch, when initiated, was blindfolded, smeared with a toxic flying ointment, and set astride a broom. The ointment contained foxglove (digitalis) to accelerate the pulse, aconite to numb feet and hands, and belladonna, cowbane or hemlock to confuse the senses. Other witches fanned the novice's face and, after a while, she could no longer feel her feet on the ground. The cry went up:

> Horse and hattock,
> Horse and go,
> Horse and pellatis
> Ho, ho!

and she believed the Chief who told her that she was flying across land and sea. Other ingredients of this ointment were 'baby's fat' and 'bat's blood'. The bat was an emblem among Islamic mystics of unworldly wisdom—the power to see better by night than by day. 'Baby's fat' stands either for mandrake (*dodaim*, or 'little men' in Hebrew), or for hallucinogenic toadstools (*hombrecitos* in Spanish); and 'bat's blood' may have been soot.

Loathing of the crucifix is attributed alike to Templars and witches, the crucifix being a graven image of the kind which Moses (supported by Jesus himself, and by Mahomed) forbade to be worshipped. Both witches and Templars were in fact Christians, though heretical ones. Robin Hood ballads, sung at May Games around a pagan Maypole, suggest that the Two-Horned cult had been active in the reign of Edward II, who enlisted Robin and his merry men as Royal archers. Robin and Maid Marian belonged to a coven of thirteen; and the mediaeval art of archery was of Islamic origin. The story of how Wilhelm Tell shot an apple from his son's head, bears witness to the Saracenic occupation of Switzerland: it first appears in an Oriental poem written not long before the First Crusade. Witches, according to the *Malleus Maleficarum*, habitually aimed at crucifixes in the Devil's name; as Robin and his men aimed at the crosses on silver pennies.

But the Two-Horned did not dance naked; nor did any mediaeval

British witches. The modern cult has borrowed its nudism either from the Far East or from Germany—where souvenir shops in the Harz mountains have long been selling figurines of naked young Brocken *Hexen* astride brooms.

There is no need to worry about modern witches. In fact, they have a great many worries of their own: such as that of finding seclusion for their rites—difficult these days, except in private houses or at nudist camps. Also charges of obscenity and diabolism, still levelled at them by newspapers. The diabolic Black Masses described by Montague Summers are not witchcraft, but intellectual atheism: a revolt from within the Catholic Church against its prime mysteries.

In 1954, Dr. Gardner wrote gloomily about the future of witchcraft:

'. . . I think we must say goodbye to the witch. The cult is doomed, I am afraid, partly because of modern conditions, housing shortage, the smallness of modern families, and chiefly by education. The modern child is not interested. He knows witches are all bunk—and there is the great fear. I have heard it said: "I'd simply love to bring Diana in, she would adore it and she has the powers, I know; but suppose in some unguarded moment she let it out at school that I was a witch? They would bully and badger her, and the County Council or somebody would come round and take her away from me by these new laws nowadays. . . ." Diana will grow up and have love affairs, is not interested; or is interested but gets married to a husband who is not interested; and so the coven dies out or consists of old and dying people.'

Yet the craft seems healthy enough in 1963, and growing fast. It now only needs some gifted mystic to come forward, decently reclothe it, and restore its original hunger for wisdom. Fun and games are insufficient.

27

Translating the 'Rubaiyyat'

Omar Ali-Shah entrusted me, a year ago, with the task of translating Omar Khayaam's *Rubaiyyat* into English verse from the 'Jan Fishan Khan' manuscript, which has been in the possession of his princely Afghan family, senior in descent from the Prophet Mohammed, since a few years after Khayaam's death, when a contemporary Sultan presented it to them. That was in A.D. 1153. I had long enjoyed a close friendship with Omar Ali-Shah and his elder brother Idries, who is a 'Grand Sheikh of the Sufi Tariqa', meaning Chief Teacher of the Sufic Way of Thought—a Way exemplified in the poems of Hafiz, Rumi, Saadi, Khayaam—in fact of all the best-known classical Persian poets. I am, however, no Persian scholar and therefore followed closely an annotated English text with which Omar Ali-Shah had supplied me; and made the first draft of my verse-rendering in the corner bed of a large surgical ward at St. Thomas's Hospital, London, where the ghost of Florence Nightingale still walks, lamp in hand, and the quiet atmosphere encourages a careful reading of poems. The night-nurses allowed me to work in bed until midnight so long as I shaded my light-bulb with its green silk shade.

I foresaw, but was not daunted by, the hostility that publication would excite among such English and Americans as were too well indoctrinated in Edward Fitzgerald's mid-Victorian *Rubaiyyat* not to make a sacred cow of it. I use this metaphor without disrespect for Hindus, but in the sense that sacred cows, which yield no milk and may never be slaughtered for beef, often invade Indian country market-places and greedily browse on the fruit and vegetables which poor peasants have brought for sale. Though

Hindu stall-holders dare not take offence, trouble arises when sacred cattle make free with Moslem produce. In such cases I incline to the Moslem side, being also descended, like many other Britons, including Her Majesty the Queen, from the Prophet Mohammed. Edward Fitzgerald, I feel, has also browsed and pillaged without moral right in Moslem territory. Omar Khayaam is revered as a religious teacher by some fifty million Sufis throughout the East, and especially honoured in Persia, where a national Omar Khayaam Trust has been set up to preserve his memory. He is read not so much for the felicity of his language as for the concentrated power of his thought, and for his rejection of formal dogma in favour of divine grace. Yet by an outrageous freak of fortune this blameless Moslem celebrant of mystical love has come to be elected patron saint of fifty million hearty boozers throughout the Christian West.

I had been asked to present Omar Khayaam as clearly as possible and without, if possible, making the customary genuflexions to Fitzgerald's memory; which I was glad to do, on the ground that sacred cows should be confined to their own temple paddocks and tended by their private priests. My occasional intuitions of his hidden meanings were prompted less by former contrastive studies of Hebrew and Gnostic mysticism than by a sense of kinship which I felt with mediaeval Irish poets who (as scholars now recognize) came under strong Sufic influence as early as the eighth and ninth centuries.

When our book was published in London, the first scholarly attack came from Major J. C. E. Bowen, who had been nettled by our publisher's announcement that this was the first modern re-translation of the *Rubaiyyat*. Major Bowen had himself, in 1952, versified a manuscript dated from the early thirteenth century, at the instance of its discoverer, Professor Arberry, who formerly held the Chair of Persian at London University and now holds that of Arabic at Cambridge. Major Bowen's review in *The Times* focused on our opening quatrain with comments that conveniently illustrated the textual difference between his manuscript and ours, as also the deformatory process of Fitzgerald's *Rubaiyyat*, and the unscholarly habits of his successors:

'The Persian text is exactly the same as that of quatrain No. 134 in the Calcutta manuscript sent to FitzGerald from India by Professor Cowell, except that where the Graves–Shah manuscript has *badeh* (wine) the Calcutta manuscript has *mohreh* (pebble or bead); so the opening lines of the Calcutta quatrain, used by FitzGerald, run literally:

> The sun has flung the noose of dawn upon the roof.
> The Kaikhosru of day has flung the pebble into
> the bowl (of departure).

'These lines were translated, with reasonable accuracy, by FitzGerald as:

> Awake! for Morning in the Bowl of Night
> Has flung the Stone that puts the Stars to
> Flight:
> And lo! the Hunter of the East has caught
> The Sultan's Turret in a Noose of light.

'Mr. Graves, handicapped by the (probably corrupt) reading of 'wine' for 'pebble', has translated the quatrain as:

> While Dawn, Day's herald straddling the whole
> sky,
> Offers the drowsy world a toast 'To Wine',
> The Sun spills early gold on city roofs—
> Day's regal Host, replenishing his jug.

'Did Mr. Graves (one is tempted to wonder) relinquish Omar's splendid metaphor of the Noose of Light merely in order to differ from FitzGerald? Or did Ali-Shah not explain to him the line's significance?

'Doubt as to whether Mr. Graves has fully understood the complexity of the task he has undertaken is roused by two references in his introduction to Omar's *Rubaiyat* as 'a poem', which of course, they—for *rubaiyat* is merely the plural of the Persian word *ruba'i* (quatrain)—are not. It is well known that every *Diwan*, or collection of Persian poetry, is arranged so that each poem is grouped with others having the same letter-ending in the first line. This arrangement by letters rules out the possibility of any significance being attached to the sequence. FitzGerald, on the other hand, made what he called a *tesselation* of the quatrains he paraphrased, to form one long English poem, leading from Dawn to Dusk—and the down-turned glass. . . .

'Nor is the quality of Mr. Graves's verse impressive. It rarely rises above the humdrum level of his opening stanza, quoted above, in which the ugly and inappropriate word 'straddling' is used.'

Perhaps Major Bowen cast doubt on the authenticity of the Jan Fishan Khan manuscript because the Arberry manuscript from which he worked had been omitted by Omar Ali-Shah from our list of *Khayaamiana* as suspect. And Major Bowen is certainly mistaken in suggesting that Fitzgerald had imposed a decent order on the original. On the contrary, our text offers a more exact temporal sequence; Fitzgerald deliberately broke it in several places, and omitted the splendid closing stanzas.

Omar Ali-Shah replied to Major Bowen:

'. . . Concerning the suggestion of the lack of authenticity of our verse, I must point out that very serious doubts have been cast upon the authenticity of the A.D. 1259 Chester Beatty MS. from which the reviewer himself worked. Serious students of oriental literature are referred to the article by Professor Minovi, the distinguished Persian authority, in *Rahnemayi Ketab*, organ of the Book Society of Persia (April 1963), and the recent book on Omar Khayaam by Professor Jelaluddin Homayi published jointly by the Society of National Monuments and the Custodians of the Omar Khayaam Trust of Iran.

'Anyone who takes the trouble to aquaint himself with the findings of these academicians will understand why I have not been able to include these in my bibliography of MSS.'

These scholars have, in fact, condemned as blatant forgeries the two Khayaam manuscripts identified and authenticated by Professor Arberry, and cite verses contained in them now known to have been composed by Persian poets who lived far later than the dates given. One of these manuscripts was sold to Cambridge University; the other is in the Chester Beatty Collection.

Omar Ali-Shah continues:

'The reviewer further states that the Jan Fishan MS. Verse One is almost exactly similar to verse 134 of the Calcutta MS. which is one of those said to have been used by Edward Fitzgerald. He adds, however, that it differs in the "probably corrupt reading of 'wine' for 'pebble' ". Yet may I point out that the Rosen MS., the Saida Nafisi MS. and a twelfth century

MS. owned by Professor Minovi, also read "wine"? This is moreover considered a more valid metaphor.

'I am additionally taken to task . . . for not having explained to Robert "Omar's splendid metaphor of the Noose of Light" and allowed him to stumble on and produce a "humdrum stanza" lacking the all-important Noose. Yet how can one "noose" the flat roofs of Nishapur with never a minaret in sight (at least in the original)? "*Kamand*" in Persia certainly means "noose" but in poetic usage also means "shaft, ray or effusion". Hence our version. Mr. J. C. E. Bowen (enriching the original in his translation) makes the "Hunter of the Dark" throw a noose "across the world" though neither phrase exists even in the "A.D. 1259" MS. which he uses.

'Omar Khayaam's *Rubaiyyat* (from the Arabic word *Ruba'i*) *is* a poem and not a collection (*diwan*) . . .

'I cannot concur that Robert's use of the good English word "straddling" is "ugly" or "inappropriate" . . .'

Later a Mr. Leaper took up the cudgels in the same columns:

'Mr Ali-Shah's letter today invites a number of comments more concerned with poetry than with scholarship: the authenticity of the manuscripts is a question which cannot concern those to whom the *Rubaiyat* is a poem rather than a study.

'Mr. Ali-Shah does not seem to recognize that the word *straddling* is appropriate (as a word) only in a suitable context, and in this particular context most readers would find it ugly. His preference for standards and criteria other than poetic is also shown by his comment about the noose and the lack of minarets around which to fling the light. The idea and metaphor are, however, quite beautiful.'

In my rendering of the original I had agreed with Omar Ali-Shah to omit the name of the early mediaeval potentate Kai Khosru to whom the rising sun is here likened when he replenishes his immortal pitcher with wine. Since this mention would have called for a footnote and distracted the reader's attention, I merely called him a 'regal host'. To have made 'Kai Khosru' intelligible to the English reader by turning him into 'King Arthur'—as Fitzgerald introduces 'buried Caesars' into his version—would have been historically false. 'Poetry' as Robert Frost said 'is what gets lost in translation'; but in mistranslation it gets positively benighted. Since the original quatrain referred to the spread of dawn from east to west I made the host 'straddle the whole sky'. 'Straddle' is a reputable Elizabethan word poetically applied by Shakespeare's noble contemporary Michael Drayton to the North Wind's mighty reach from coast to coast. I had indeed been assured by Omar Ali-Shah that no turret occurs in the original verse, and that a simple shaft or dazzle of light was thrown on the flat roofs; but in any case I should have suspected the 'noose of light' metaphor as unauthentic. Early sunlight flashed on a turret does not 'noose' it; the western part must remain relatively unilluminated. For a poet of Khayaam's calibre no such faulty metaphor would have seemed 'quite beautiful'.

As for the word *mohreh* (pebble) which has been substituted in later manuscripts for *badeh* (wine) and is glossed by Major Bowen (following Fitzgerald's often ignorant mentor, Professor Cowell) to mean a pebble thrown into a drinking cup as a signal for 'Strike Camp!', I am assured by Omar Ali-Shah that this is a historical error. The signal given was not the clink of a pebble in a bowl but the boom of a huge stone flung into the camp cauldron where a communal stew had boiled the previous evening. And even 'stone in the Cauldron of Night' would have been a curiously inappropriate metaphor for sunrise: the Sun may perhaps resemble a fiery stone thrown by Morning, but since it soars up from the cauldron of Night rather than being flung into it, Khayaam, whose metaphors were always clear and logical, could never have used it.

The same Mr. Leaper held that 'the authenticity of a manuscript cannot concern readers of poetry'. Not even if it misrepresents and deforms a classic? A reviewer from the B.B.C. journal, *The Listener*, commended Fitzgerald for having accomplished 'an incredible literary feat, giving us a close equivalent in English of Omar's languorous music'. Yet the original verse, which the reviewer had not read, is not in the least languorous. Elsewhere another reviewer asked:

'Does it matter that [Fitzgerald] travestied the original? Or that he turned an Oriental mystic into a toping Victorian sceptic? Only, I think, if the original is at least of equal quality. Graves does not convince here. He has produced a prosy New English Bible sort of Khayaam, whose cloudy mysticism raises more

questions about evil than it answers. At the very least, Fitzgerald found a decent form for his poem, a stanza in which
"the penultimate line seems to lift and suspend the wave that
falls over in the last". Graves produces ripples in a sea of sludge:

> Let me speak out, unallegorically:
> We are mere puppets of our Master, toys
> On the Table of Existence, one by one
> Flung back into the toy box of Non-Existence.

'Surely no one in his right mind could prefer this to Fitzgerald's fine carelessness:

> 'Tis all a Chequerboard of Nights and Days
> Where Destiny with Man for Pieces plays:
>   Hither and thither moves, and mates and slays
> And one by one back in the Closet lays.'

The fact is that here Fitzgerald's 'fine carelessness' had interrupted
the sequence of Omar Khayaam's thought by breaking off short
the shadow-show metaphor and interpolating an unnecessary
game of chess. The original reads:

> This vault, underneath which we lie bemused
> Is, so to speak, God's magic shadow-show:
> With sun for lamp, the world as a wide screen
> For countless lie-rehearsing silhouettes.

> Let me speak out, unallegorically:
> We are mere puppets of our Master, toys
> On the Table of Existence, one by one
> Flung back in [not 'into'] the toy box of
>   Non-existence.

Fitzgerald had said: 'At all costs a Thing must Live—with a
Transfusion of one's own worse Life if he can't retain the Original's
better. Better a live Sparrow than a stuffed Eagle.' He based this
remark on the scornful old proverb: 'Better a live dog than a
dead lion'—a coward's excuse for avoiding the defence of his
country in battle. So here, for once, Fitzgerald honestly confesses
that his own crude versifying is at odds with Omar's poetic genius.
Elsewhere, however, he pretends that the Persians were so deficient
in poetry that their ghosts could surely not grudge the extravagant
licence he so often took while embellishing their works with a

little art! At all events, he translated Khayaam's thirteenth stanza as:

> 'How sweet is Mortal Sovranty!' think some,
> Others—'How blest the Paradise to come!'
> Ah, take the Cash in hand and waive the rest;
> Oh, the brave Music of a *distant* Drum!

though the original contains references neither to ambition for mortal sovereignty nor to any hopes for an orthodox Islamic Paradise. It runs:

> They say that Eden is bejewelled with houris.
> I answer that grape-nectar has no price—
> So laugh at long-term credit, stick to coin,
> Though distant drums beguile your greedy ear.

Fitzgerald has missed the satiric sense. Khayaam is referring to a wholly unKoranic Paradise promised by Arab chieftains as a spur to simple soldiers: if they should die in battle they will visit a glorious Palace stocked with expensive houris to indulge their carnal appetites. But, just as any honest soldier would prefer a good drinking bout before battle to vague promises of a superlative Rest and Recreation Camp after the campaign had ended, so here Khayaam prefers a Sufi life, in which sufficient spiritual joy and beauty can daily be found, to any gloomy Puritanical one preached by orthodox mullahs with promises of a glorious world to come.

A Scottish reviewer from Glasgow, where a popular students' drinking resort is named 'The Bowl of Night', writes:

> 'The trouble with FitzGerald, apparently, was that he was ill-acquainted with Sufic symbolism and Sufic metaphor. And our own critical deficiency is, of course, that we are no more interested in the authentic thoughts and philosophies of the real Omar than we are in the true history and accurate biography of Robin Hood. . . . Sufic thought is for scholars; Omar is for less cultivated ears and lips and for artless intellects that do not find it an evil paradox that an old Persian mystical poem should be accepted as "a drunkard's rambling profession of a hedonist creed".

'Indeed Khayaam himself has been past caring these 800 years, and so, let the orientalists make of the original what they like, we prefer our old hackneyed and well-rounded Moving Finger that writes, and the Piety and Wit that cannot lure it back to cancel half a line, far above the workaday statement of Robert Graves that:

> What we shall be is written, and we are so.
> Heedless of God or Evil, pen, write on!
> By the first day all futures were decided;
> Which gives our griefs and pains irrelevancy.'

Khayaam the Sufi, whose spirit is very far from dead, did not make a profession of doubt, but pointed out that one logical result of the belief in God, as an All-Father and Supreme Judge who made man in His image, must be to accuse Him of human frailties. God, for Omar, was the spirit of creative love which animates all noble spirits. He admits the occasional onset of doubt, which, however, he regards as necessary to a better understanding of the human condition, writing:

> One breath parts infidelity from faith,
> Another breath parts certitude from doubt.
> Yet cherish breath, never make light of it—
> Is not such breath the harvest of our being?

> My heart complained: 'I long for inspiration,
> I long for wisdom, to be taught and learn.'
> I breathed the letter A. My heart replied:
> 'A is enough to occupy this house.'

For Khayaam, as for Jesus who, in the *Gospel of Thomas*, asked his school teacher Zacchaeus: 'If thou knowest not Alpha according to its nature, how canst thou teach others the Beta?', the letter A (*Alpha* or *Alif*) took precedence over all other letters because it was the first letter of God's name, in Hebrew as in Arabic. Fitzgerald has once more missed the point by converting Khayaam's inspiriting view into a pessimistic suggestion that only by the remotest guess can man find the truth.

> Would you that spangle of Existence spend
> About the Secret—quick about it, Friend!
>   A Hair, they say, divides the false and true
> And upon what, prithee, does Life depend?

> A hair, they say, divides the false and true
> Yes; and a single *Alif* were the clue,
>   Could you but find it, to the Treasure-house
> And peradventure to the Master too.

Omar despised intellectuality, as he had a right to do after achieving international fame as a philosopher and mathematician. His thirtieth stanza was:

> Man's brain has never solved the eternal why
> Nor foraged past the frontier set for thought.
> All intellect, be sure, proves nugatory,
> However hard we either teach or learn.

He goes even further:

> Misguided foes call me philosopher—
> God knows that this is the one thing I am not.
> I am even less: in such a nest of sorrows
> I cannot tell you even who I am.

And he addresses God, this same bright element of Truth and Love:

> Hidden you live, inscrutable as ever;
> A person sometimes, but sometimes a place,
> Showing this costly spectacle to no one
> You the sole audience and the actor too.

Persian and English poems, in careful translation from each other, work out at about the same verse-length, and if one preserves only Khayaam's quatrain form, not his metrical measure or his rhyming scheme, there is no need either to cut or expand the sense. Nevertheless, the concentration of meaning in some of Khayaam's lines is intense. For example:

> The Moon, by her own nature prone to change,
> Varies from animal form to vegetable:
> Destroy her form, you have destroyed nothing,
> For what she seems survives her not yet being.

Which, expanded to prose would read, I think, something like this:

> Woman, man's complementary sex, resembles the Moon, if only because her menstrual course corresponds closely with the Moon's mensual one. Like the Moon, whose first appearance suggests the bright horn of an animal, and whose bulk when at the full resembles a ripe melon soon to be eaten away, woman varies, as she grows older, from either reckless or shy animality to lazy, plump domesticity. Though you may expose the physical phases of a woman's life by such a comparison, you will not have accounted for the magical hold that she may exercise even on a reasonable man. For he cannot honestly deny her power over his heart; and a wise man knows that one day when women are no longer mere chattels bought and sold for male diversion, but recognized as having minds, such a hold will be amply justified as it cannot yet be.

Fitzgerald usually took the easy and even banal way out in translation: he writes in his seventeenth quatrain (second edition):

> The Worldly Hope men set their Hearts upon
> Turns ashes—or it prospers; and anon,
>   Like Snow upon the Desert's dusty Face
> Lighting a little Hour or two—is gone.

This is the same morose 'Ashes to ashes and dust to dust' sentiment that one finds cut on eighteenth century tombstones. What Khayaam wrote (stanza 16) was altogether different. He advised his friends to accept the world as it was and make the very best of their sojourn in it, though recognizing that this could not last more than a couple of generations, or three at the outside. Our translation runs:

> Think of this world as modelled to your whim.
> Perfectly trimmed for you from east to west;
> Yet know yourself a snowdrift on the sand
> Heaped for two days or three, then thawed and
>   gone.

Fitzgerald has composed another truistic quatrain on the theme that nobody has ever returned from the dead to describe his experiences:

> Strange, is it not? that of the myriads who
> Before us pass'd the Door of Darkness through,
>   Not one returns to tell us of the Road
> Which to discover we must travel too.

Khayaam, however, was here, stanza 68, commenting, rather, on the extraordinary variety of experience that life offers, and on every life's uniqueness:

> My wandering feet have led me through far plains
> And valleys: I have strayed this way and that
> Yet nowhere found a traveller who could boast
> That he had ever trod the same road twice.

Again, Khayaam in his satiric portrayal of the anthropomorphic God (stanza 83), writes with Sufic humour:

> That sin is irresistible He knows:
> Yet He commands us to abstain from sin.
> Thus irresistibility confounds us
> With prohibition: 'Lean, but never fall!'

Fitzgerald found it necessary to present this as simple Victorian agnosticism, and characteristically translated it into terms of money; which resulted in the following confused stanza:

> What! from his helpless Creature be repaid
> Pure gold for what he lent us dross-allay'd
>   Sue for a Debt we never did contract
> And cannot answer—Oh, the sorry trade!

a purposeful contradiction of the familiar hymn:

> O Lord since all I give to Thee
> Repaid a thousand-fold shall be
> Therefore I offer willingly
> My soul to be Thy trust.

And every true poet would prefer Khayaam's simple antithetical
quatrain (stanza 50):

> This world must long survive our poor departure,
> Persisting without name or note of us.
> Before we came, it never grudged our absence;
> When we have gone, how can it feel regret?

to Fitzgerald's artistic and over-metaphorical:

> When you and I behind the Veil are past
> Oh, but the long, long while the World shall last,
>   Which of our Coming and Departure heeds
> As much as Ocean of a pebble cast.

Khayaam used the same economical style in addressing (stanza
67) his Orthodox colleagues who, because arrack (date liquor) had
been forbidden them in the *Koran* extended the Prophet's ban to
wine, which the Hebrew mystics, Khayaam's predecessors, had
likewise used as a symbol of divine joy:

> They say: 'Be sober, lest you die of drink
> And earn Hell-fire on God's last Judgement Day.'
> Nevertheless my blaze of drunkenness
> Outshines both worlds: your Now and your Hereafter.

Fitzgerald has converted this into a mere preference of a good
vintage claret to an orgy of metaphysical argument:

> Waste not your Hour, nor in the vain pursuit
> Of this and that endeavour and dispute.
>   Better be merry with the fruitful grape
> Than sadden after none, or bitter, fruit.

Here, as often, his search for a suitable rhyme has made him do
violence to the English language. One can write 'Sadden after
bitter fruit or none', but 'none or bitter fruit'—one cannot
'sadden after none fruit'—is listed by the *Oxford English Dictionary*
as a novel usage.

Near the beginning of this transmogrified *Rubaiyyat* Fitzgerald has printed his version of the awesome stanza which concludes the true one. He writes:

> The Palace that to Heav'n his pillars threw
> And Kings the forehead on his threshold drew—
>   I saw the solitary Ringdove there,
> And 'Coo, coo, coo,' she cried; and 'Coo, coo, coo.'

The use of *his* for *its* is misleading, since it seems a reference to Bahram the Great hunter in the preceding verse, and what does 'Kings drew the forehead on his threshold' mean, unless that they chalked a drawing of Bahram's forehead on the threshold of his former palace? We have translated the original in its quiet simplicity:

> The palace with huge walls soaring to Heaven
> Where prostrate Kings did reverence at the gate:
> A ring-dove perches on its battlements:—
> 'Where, where?' it coos, 'where, where?'

This is the visionary palace gate which dying men or takers of hallucinatory drugs frequently see opening for them: the Portals of Death. The ring-dove cries '*ku-ku*' in Persian, meaning 'where, where?' exactly as the cuckoo does in Wales where the word *ku* has the same meaning. The cuckoo is known there as the 'sorrowful bird', because it returns in the spring from the South and asks what has happened to so many neighbours who have disappeared during its absence. Similarly the Persian ring-dove does not coo lovingly as in England; but mourns the death of kings.

*   *   *   *   *

Any attempt at improving or altering Khayaam's poetic intentions would have seemed shocking to me when I was working on the Rubaiyyat at St. Thomas's Hospital. The thought was hard, clear and closely woven; and it is only now, a year later, that I can view the poem as a whole and follow its kaleidoscopic changes. These vary from spiritual autobiography to straight-faced satire and to sudden simple statements of his faith in love, seen as the perpetual miracle that dissipates all mental and moral confusion. What I have written, under Omar Ali-Shah's surveillance, may seem to inebriated members of the Fitz-Omar cult prosaic ripples on a sea of sludge, but may also one day prove useful to students who find that they think as Omar thought and decide to read the *Rubaiyyat* in the original Persian. My twin principles were: 'Stick as strictly to the script as you can' and 'Respect the tradition of English verse as first confirmed by the better Tudor poets: which is to be as explicit as possible on every occasion and never play down to ignorance.'

28

An absolute criminal

I have never before in all my long life been confronted with absolute crime. So it came as a great shock when gentle Stephanie Sweet, an Honours graduate at St. Anne's, Oxford, who had often spent summer holidays with us here in Majorca as my daughter Lucia's close friend, was publicly branded as an absolute criminal.

In law an absolute crime is one that can be awarded summary punishment, whatever the degree of criminal intent. It does not, in fact, matter whether the criminal knew that his offence, either of commission or omission, was a crime. He remains unalterably due for punishment. The absolute crime in the *Sweet* v. *Parsley* case consisted of 'managing' premises in which an offence had been committed even though admittedly without her knowledge or consent. The offence was the smoking of 'pot' by a group of sub-tenants, and the police approach seems to have been modelled on the habitual rough-arm procedure used when charging landlords with allowing their premises to be used as houses of prostitution.

It all began with a Morris car, licence number YMM 664 which my son William used while at London University for geological trips all over Europe. First nicknamed 'Young Man's Machine' it was passed on to Lucia and renamed 'Young Maiden's Misery' because of its frequent mechanical failures. Lucia gave it to Stephanie and it finally broke down with a complete confusion of gears and engine. Stephanie, having rented a farmhouse at Water Eaton, far along the Woodstock Road, could no longer, without YMM 664, travel to and from work in the city. So she sublet the farm to a group of easy-going students whom she had casually met and who did not need to be in Oxford every morning at 8.45.

From her new rooms in Oxford, she paid occasional visits to the farm to see her cat, collect the rent and any letters that might have come in for her; but she never became a personal friend of the tenants.

One evening in June last year Stephanie turned up at the farm but found it empty, with the door open. In the hall was a note saying 'Please get in touch at once with the Woodstock Police'. She rang them up and they arrived half an hour later headed by a bucolic-looking policeman named Sergeant Parsley. He warned her that he had a search warrant for the farmhouse, on which he had acted, and as a result must ask her to come to the police station with him. Here she was informed that she was under arrest, drugs having been found at the farmhouse, to wit cannabis and L.S.D.

After keeping her waiting for three-quarters of an hour—she supposes to create the necessary suspense before forcing a confession—they subjected her to the customary indignities. A tough-looking policewoman marched in, made her strip to the skin, searched her for drugs or needle marks, all the while whistling through her teeth the same line of 'Westminster Sunset'. Later followed a search of her handbag—she was relieved to find afterwards that no 'pot' had been planted on her clothes—and then her cross-examination began. The police had also found a coffee-machine full of flower petals, apparently buttercups, the use of which neither they nor she could explain, and a toy hookah which they asked her to identify. Stephanie agreed that the hookah was hers: a Christmas present from a Pakistani undergraduate, which she had hung up as an ornament. But the police insisted that it had been used for smoking hashish—as indeed was later proved by chemical analysis. They also showed her small torn pieces of white wrapping-paper and asked her if she knew what they were. She answered they seemed to be torn pieces of white wrapping-paper. 'Don't you know that hashish comes wrapped up in this?' No, she did not. Confronted with a bottle of nose-drops she still showed no sign of guilt, although Sergeant Parsley menacingly informed her that it was L.S.D. The whole business lasted for about four hours. She was offered no refreshment but asked for and was given a glass of water. By this time it was past midnight. She had missed her supper and had to go to work early next morning.

Stephanie had no lawyer, and unluckily approached one whose firm was later briefed for the prosecution. So she had to find a replacement. The new lawyer, after talking things over with her, warned her that the magistrates all over England were being urged to convict anyone who had come under the remotest suspicion of drug offences. He also told her that the farmhouse had made a very bad impression on the austere Sergeant Parsley because of the brass-knobbed double-beds with which she had furnished it. This had seemed evidence of the premises having been used as a house of prostitution. The truth was that, the farmhouse being unfurnished when she rented it from one Farmer Cook, who in turn had rented it from Exeter College, Stephanie furnished it herself from a junk yard near Wantage for less than ten pounds. The furniture included four big brass double-beds at a pound a-piece; and the same number of single beds, which she would have had to buy new at a furniture store, would have cost her fifty or sixty pounds.

The case came before the Woodstock Magistrates. Although the prosecuting counsel admitted that Stephanie had had no knowledge that the premises were being used for drug-taking and though the tenant charged, who pleaded guilty, supported this evidence when questioned, the charge of 'managing' was pressed. Stephanie was found guilty and fined twenty-five pounds.

'What a waste,' she told us afterwards, 'My lawyer advised me to look as unhippy as possible when I appeared before the magistrates. So since, like everyone else, I had only miniskirts in my wardrobe I fitted myself out at a chain-store with a respectable knee-length black and white dress—the sort worn by middle-aged Oxford landladies. I even put my hair up, but it didn't work.'

We advised her to appeal; which she did. Meanwhile a letter had arrived from the Department of Education and Science to the effect that her conviction had proved that she was no longer a fit person to teach children, and that if she wished to protest this decision she must visit a psychiatrist and submit his report as well as providing the most solid references from her university superiors. Would Exeter College, the landlords, be similarly warned?

Six months later she lost the appeal because 'management', though hitherto arguable, has now become an absolute crime, this seeming to the judges of the Queen's Bench Division the only possible means of stamping out drug addiction. It has even been suggested that merely by being the landlord of premises one becomes responsible at law for all sorts of offences that might be committed, however gross. Also that, since 'managing' is an absolute crime, it would not have helped Stephanie had she denounced her tenants to the Woodstock police. She would still have been absolutely responsible for their offences, even if, as a judge of the Divisional Court suggested, she had bound them by a clause in the contract not to take 'pot' or other drugs on the premises.

The Divisional Court has not only rejected her appeal, but— strange as it may seem—refused to certify that her case is of general public importance, and so denied her the right of appeal to the House of Lords. She can do no more, it seems, except try to make the Home Secretary recommend her for the Queen's pardon. Meanwhile, Stephanie remains an absolute criminal.

This legal return to the ancient concept of absolute crime is of great interest to anthropologists. In primitive communities if a man, hunting in the forest, should have the bad luck to see his mother-in-law bathing naked in a lonely pool, this may well be a mortal sin without either excuse or escape. He must die. As a rule he prefers to starve himself to death in his hut or commit suicide by jumping head first from the top of a lofty tree. The classical Greek case was Oedipus's murder of his father and marriage to his mother while still ignorant about his parentage. The penalty was banishment and universal abhorrence. Nowadays, I suppose, if the case came up in court, he would be refused all gainful employment in the United Kingdom and sentenced to twenty-five years on the Freudian couch.

* * * * *

Sweet v. Parsley

Whatever Sweet might do was wrong
   Even if she did not do it:
Absolute crime is far too strong
   For felons not to rue it.
So Parsley, armed with the Law's might,
Proves abso-bally-lutely right:
Her case is closed in Hell's despite—
   No counsel can pursue it.*

* *Postscript.* Nevertheless, the case was reopened with the help of public-spirited friends from both Houses of Parliament and the Law Society, and has now made legal history in the House of Lords.